AF645986

The Future of Tourism

The Future of Tourism

Rakesh Kumar Sah

RANDOM

RANDOM PUBLICATIONS

NEW DELHI (INDIA)

The Future of Tourism

ISBN 978-93-5111-331-7

© Reserved

All Rights Reserved. No Part of this book may be reproduced in any manner without written permission.

Published in 2014 in India by

RANDOM PUBLICATIONS

4376-A/4B, Gali Murari Lal, Ansari Road
New Delhi-110 002
Phone : +91-11-43580356, +91-11-23289044
e-mail: randomexports@gmail.com, sales@randompublications.com, info@randompublications.com

Reprinted 2026

Type Setting by : Keystoneprintads, Delhi-110051

Preface

The building up of tourist infrastructure is aimed at extending inter-regional economic ties which promote and accelerate the formation of domestic market, expansion of transport system which increases the ties of the country-side with the tourist resort and promotes the integration of natural economy. India faces a lot of problems in building the necessary tourist infrastructure which plays crucial role in accelerating economic development. The development of tourism requires financial resources and technical personnel for a large scale exploration and evaluation of the tourist areas which determines the potential of modern tourism.

This work is an attempt in the collection of first hand information from various areas of tourism industry, draw from wide range of sources, both Indian and foreign, as a highly useful study material, to provide the students of travel and tourism courses all over the country as a broad band insight into the basic forms and contents of tourism industry and the travel philosophy. This will be a very useful reference literature in area of tourism industry.

I would like to thank my team for standing beside me throughout my career and writing this book. My special thanks go to "Random Publications" who have published the book.

– Rakesh Kumar Sah

Contents

1

Advertising Strategies and Future of Tourism

INTRODUCTION

Advertising is not modern in origin. It undoubtedly began at the earliest time when competition caused each man to make efforts to gain prominence—a process of human nature which has gone on ever since. Competition naturally arose at the earliest time of civilization when communities were brought together and each individual followed the urge to better himself. In present context, without advertising a business cannot run successfully. Before going in depth of what advertising industry is, lets have a brief view of what a hotel normally provide and how it functions.

A comfortable room, good food, and a helpful staff can make being away from home an enjoyable experience for both vacationing families and business travellers. While most lodging managers work in traditional hotels and motels, some work in other lodging establishments, such as camps, inns, boardinghouses, dude ranches, and recreational resorts. In full-service hotels, lodging managers help their guests have a pleasant stay by providing many of the comforts of home, including cable television, fitness equipment, and voice mail, as well as specialized services such as health spas. For business travellers, lodging managers often schedule available meeting rooms and electronic equipment, including slide projectors and fax machines.

Lodging managers are responsible for keeping their establishments efficient and profitable. In a small establishment with a limited staff, the manager may oversee all aspects of operations. However, large hotels may employ hundreds of workers, and the general manager usually is aided by a number of assistant managers assigned to the various departments of the operation. In hotels of every size, managerial duties vary significantly by job title.

General managers have overall responsibility for the operation of the hotel. Within guidelines established by the owners of the hotel or executives of the hotel chain, the general manager sets room rates, allocates funds to departments, approves expenditures, and ensures expected standards for guest service, decor, housekeeping, food quality, and banquet operations. Managers who work for chains also may organize and staff a newly built hotel, refurbish an older hotel, or reorganize a hotel or motel that is not operating successfully. In order to fill entry-level service and clerical jobs in hotels, some managers attend career fairs.

Resident or hotel managers are responsible for the day-to-day operations of the property. In larger properties, more than one of these managers may assist the general manager, frequently dividing responsibilities between the food and beverage operations and the rooms or lodging services. At least one manager, either the general manager or a hotel manager, is on call 24 hours a day to resolve problems or emergencies. Assistant managers help run the day-to-day operations of the hotel. In large hotels, they may be responsible for activities such as personnel, accounting, office administration, marketing and sales, purchasing, security, maintenance, and pool, spa, or recreational facilities. In smaller hotels, these duties may be combined into one position. Assistant managers may adjust charges on a hotel guest's bill when a manager is unavailable.

An Executive Committee made up of a hotel's senior managers advises the general manager, assists in setting hotel policy, coordinates services that cross departmental boundaries, and collaborates on efforts to ensure consistent and efficient guest services throughout the hotel. The Committee may be comprised of the department heads for housekeeping, front office, food and beverage, security, sales and public relations, meetings and conventions, engineering and building maintenance, and human resources. Executive committee members bring a different perspective of guest service to the total management objective reflecting the unique expertise and training of their positions.

Executive housekeepers ensure that guest rooms, meeting and banquet rooms, and public areas are clean, orderly, and well maintained. They also train, schedule, and supervise the work of housekeepers, inspect rooms, and order cleaning supplies.

Front office managers coordinate reservations and room assignments, as well as train and direct the hotel's front desk staff. They ensure that guests are treated courteously, complaints and problems are resolved, and requests for special services are carried out. Front office managers may adjust charges posted on a customer's bill.

Convention services managers coordinate the activities of various departments in larger hotels to accommodate meetings, conventions, and special events. They meet with representatives of groups or organizations to plan the number of rooms to reserve, the desired configuration of the meeting space, and banquet services. During the meeting or event, they resolve unexpected problems and monitor activities to ensure that hotel operations conform to the expectations of the group.

Food and beverage managers oversee all food service operations maintained by the hotel. They coordinate menus with the Executive Chef for the hotel's restaurants, lounges, and room service operations. They supervise the ordering of food and supplies, direct service and maintenance contracts within the kitchens and dining areas, and manage food service budgets. Catering managers arrange for food service in a hotel's meeting and convention rooms. They coordinate menus and costs for banquets, parties, and events with meeting and convention planners or individual clients. They coordinate staffing needs and arrange schedules with kitchen personnel to ensure appropriate food service.

Sales or marketing directors and public relations directors oversee the advertising and promotion of hotel operations and functions, including lodging and dining specials and special events, such as holiday or seasonal specials. They direct the efforts of their staff to purchase advertising and market their property to organizations or groups seeking a venue for conferences, conventions, business meetings, trade shows, and special events. They also coordinate media relations and answer questions from the press.

Human resources directors manage the personnel functions of a hotel, ensuring that all accounting, payroll, and employee relations matters are handled in compliance with hotel policy and applicable laws. They also oversee hiring practices and standards and ensure that training and promotion programs reflect appropriate employee development guidelines. Finance (or revenue) directors monitor room sales and reservations. In addition to overseeing accounting and cash-flow matters at the hotel, they also project occupancy levels, decide which rooms to discount and when to offer rate specials.

Computers are used extensively by lodging managers and their assistants to keep track of guests' bills, reservations, room assignments, meetings, and special events. In addition, computers are used to order food, beverages, and supplies, as well as to prepare reports for hotel owners and top-level managers. Managers work with computer specialists to ensure that the hotel's computer system functions properly. Should the hotel's computer system fail, managers must continue to meet the needs of hotel guests and staff.

THE BEGINNINGS OF ADVERTISING

Advertising, then, is nearly as old as civilization. There are records more than three thousand years old of announcements advertising for runaway slaves, written on papyri and exhumed from the ruins of Thebes. The Greek and Roman advertisements of gladiatorial exhibitions are reminiscent of the modern "billing" of circuses.

There is linguistic proof of the existence of the town crier in early Hebrew civilization, and of hawkers of retail wares in Roman times. The excavations of Pompeii have revealed various "bills"—tablets attached to pillars—on the walls of that ancient city, and there are records in literature of signs over shops and stalls in Rome advertising crafts and merchandise.

As early as the late seventeenth century, advertising was already a source of profits for the first newspapers. From the first daily published in England in Queen Anne's time until the nineteenth century, newspaper advertising was limited to announcements identifying craftsmen, merchandise and services for sale.

Even in the early nineteenth century, the newspaper was a local venture usually religious or political in nature. Few had large circulations. If a company wished to advertise, it dealt 6 directly with the paper. There was no particular skill involved in newspaper advertising in the early stages. A simple announcement served both the advertiser and the public.

After the phase of Great Expansion—industrial, geographical and modern mass production methods—production facilities were greatly in excess of natural demand. This brought about the necessity of the persuasive sales appeal—the need to create new markets and new customers. The businessman began to feel the need to *persuade* prospective customers. The businessman *and* the periodicals felt the need to cover wider geographic areas in a more persuasive manner. The problems and profits inherent in this situation were the foundations of the modern advertising agency.

The Rise of the Agency

The first advertising agent was a middleman or jobber in advertising space. He contracted space from publishers, which in turn he retailed to advertisers at a profit.

In 1820 there were about 360 newspapers published in the United States. In 1830 there were over one thousand. In 1841 there is the first definite record of the advertising agent, who, according to Rowell, was Volney B. Palmer. Palmer set himself up in Philadelphia as an agent for country newspapers, obtaining orders for advertising, forwarding the copy to the paper and collecting payment.

Palmer was closely followed by others and before long there were a number of agents in the business. Only a few years passed before the jobbers changed their methods of operation. They soon began to act as space brokers. They made contracts for space on their own accounts and resold the space to advertisers.

The early days of the agency business occupy a unique position in business history in that the affairs were conducted in confused state. The early agents were at once agents for the advertiser and for the publication, and space brokers on their own behalf, while some dealt also in printers' materials; and, finally, a few published their own periodicals, selling advertising in these periodicals to the same newspaper for which they acted as agent and whose space they brokered. It was indeed a catch-as-catch-can business, with payments sometimes being made in "supplies" and with great "flexibility" of rates, etc. Yet since about Palmer's time, for over a hundred years, the agency has been the nerve-center of the advertising business. But it is only today that the advertising agent has achieved the stature of a professional man.

The last lap in the progress of the agency began about 1930. It was a fork in the road for the agency: Either fold-up or gear-up. Business couldn't depend on old-fashioned methods to help push it out of the red. The agency had to devise new ways to serve. That agency which was able to gear-up to the new demands of the early '30'$ was the agency which was successful. It is that agency which represents what is typical in the new attitude of the agency business which has made a simple sales job into a complex professional service.

THE EVOLUTION OF ADVERTISING

In the nineteenth century a substantial part of advertising consisted of what would now be termed announcements and of items we now find in the classified advertising section of newspapers. In addition to these, however, the advertising agencies sold a quantity of space to the "patent medicine" business. During the period around 1870, modern medicine was in its infancy. As a result there was a considerable field for the sale of all sorts of remedies. These accounts, which almost any agency would frown on today, were perhaps the backbone of the early agency business.

Those were the days of rugged individualism, not of professional ethics. It was the pioneering period. There was no social legislation and, looking backward, it appears that there was little conscience or application of a moral standard in most business. Thus it was natural that the advertising agency seldom investigated the merits of the product it advertised. Actually, it can scarcely be said that the agency was responsible for the advertising that it sold and placed. In most cases, the advertiser and not the agency prepared the copy for the advertisement. All the agent did was to sell the space, forward the advertising copy and instructions to the publisher, and collect for the advertisement.

In addition to the classified and patent medicine advertising, the early agency placed what we today might consider legitimate advertising, including local notices and the advertising of farm implements and a few other products. Mail-order houses and manufacturers of farm products, books and machinery were some of the first industries to use advertising as a sales tool. The 1870 advertisement is a far cry from the elaborately designed advertisement for the same store today; while the 1911 advertisement for the Buick Motor Company shows that the trend was beginning to change into what is used in present-day styles of advertising.

The nature of the advertising agency business, as it was first constituted, was bound to cause trouble. Nearly all agencies were committed for large amounts of space in the publications which they represented. Consequently, it was profitable for them to urge their clients to use those particular papers. This, of course, was not economically sound. In addition, if the advertiser wanted to use space in periodicals that the agency did not have direct representation for, it was necessary for the agent to try some makeshift negotiations for the space. Agencies were in constant competition with each other in an effort to secure the space that an advertiser wanted. At the best, the agencies' basis of operations was not conducive to creating confidence between the advertiser and the agent since it was never clear to whom the agency was responsible.

This confused state of affairs finally stimulated a clarification of the business, and toward the close of the nineteenth century the agencies began to give up the position of space jobber by instituting what was called the open contract.

The Open Contract

Under the open contract plan, the agency became the representative of the advertiser. The open contract provided that the advertiser have free access to all of the information available to the agency. The agency promised to buy the space needed by the advertiser at the lowest possible rates, and in return charge a commission for its services. The agency began to promise the advertiser unbiased recommendations concerning circulation, population, general reputation of the paper, etc.

The open contract clearly was the beginning of the system existing today for remunerating advertising agencies through a commission paid by the publication.

In 1891, George Batten opened an agency in New York City. From the very beginning, he adhered to the new principle of buying space for the advertiser at the lowest possible cost. To this cost he added fifteen percent for his services.

In contrast to the questionable speculative profit that agencies had received when they jobbed space, this new basis provided a reasonable profit margin. It placed the agency in a more secure position and enabled it to develop services for the advertiser.

As agencies throughout the country began to adhere more and more to the open contract system, two important developments occurred:

1. They had made their decision to work for the advertisers' interests exclusively.
2. In addition to buying space for the advertiser at the lowest possible cost, they began to provide additional services and to be known as service organizations.

It is during this period that we first hear of "copywriters." Simultaneously with this development in the advertising agency business, publishers began to stabilize their rates so that those agencies which still acted as space brokers had difficulty in buying space below the market. By about 1890, many newspapers had arranged to pay advertising agencies a commission of fifteen percent on the space placed.

National magazines at that time were paying agencies a commission of ten percent. During the period from 1890 to about 1930 when agencies were making the transition from space brokers to service organizations, there were many agencies and advertisers who still were wedded to the old idea of buying space below the market.

This brought about the vicious practice of price cutting, which the agencies accomplished by rebating a part of their commissions to the advertisers. In 1910, out of twenty-five reasonably large advertising agencies doing business with the Curtis Publishing Company, ten were suspected of rebating commissions. In 1920, six of these ten price-cutting agencies were still in business, but by 1930 only one of them remained.

During the period from 1890 to 1930, publishers began to see that the advertising agency was a valuable tool for legitimately creating advertising business. There was a real incentive for them to protect the agency from price cutting and unsound competition, for the publisher wanted the advertiser to get his money's worth. Since the publishers were not in a position to conceive the advertising campaign, select the media, prepare the copy and visualize the art work, the advertising agency was the perfect answer to their problem.

In 1893, the American Newspaper Publishers' Association adopted a resolution which provided that agencies' commissions be paid only to advertising agencies and that no similar price reduction be allowed to advertisers. The Curtis Publishing Company in 1901 put into effect a new contract arrangement with advertising agencies. This new contract provided for a commission of ten percent to approve advertising agencies. To be approved the agencies agreed to charge advertisers the full card rate, less only the cash discount for prompt payment.

The agreement provided that in the event an agency quoted space in the Curtis publications for less than the published rate, such a quotation would be considered a violation of the contract. The contract provided that upon a second violation, the agent would be dropped from the approved list of advertising agencies.

Gradually, all publishers and other media fell in line with the commission system which stabilized advertising rates and the income of the advertising agencies. Magazine publishers increased the commission basis first from ten to thirteen percent. In 1918, the American Association of Advertising Agencies sought to increase the commission basis of magazines from thirteen to fifteen percent, with an additional two percent cash discount for prompt payment. Today, the fifteen percent agency commission is standard with only inconsequential exceptions.

On various occasions from 1890 to the present time, publishers and advertisers have questioned both the commission system itself and the rate of commission paid; but since 1925, it has been more or less standard practice for the advertising agencies to receive a fifteen percent commission allowed by the publishers and other advertising media.

THE DEVELOPMENT OF THE MODERN AGENCY

The Space Buyer

The first service performed by the twentieth-century advertising agency was that of selecting the publications for the advertiser. Before the days of the open contract, there was considerable doubt whether this job was done to the best advantage of the advertiser; but certainly after the introduction of the open contract basis, it proved to be a valuable service to advertisers. The selection of advertising media, still a difficult job, was much more difficult around 1900. Before relatively recent times, there was not the information available concerning circulation, type of readers and geographical distribution which is published now.

In addition to the difficulty in selecting media, the early advertising agencies were faced with the question of the "best buy." Today, rates for advertising space are standardized and published. With the exception of a few small weekly papers and highly specialized publications, such as yearbooks and religious papers, the advertiser must pay the quoted price. There is no bargaining.

The prices of printed advertising media today are based chiefly on the circulation of the media, so that in determining the best buy, the agency is mainly concerned with the type of readers as it relates to the advertisers' products. Even as late as the 1920, the space buyer was a key man in nearly every advertising agency. If he was a sharp buyer he secured some space at bargain prices.

He studied markets and types of circulation. He had an intimate acquaintance with many of the publications and he could point out the advantages and disadvantages of most of them. Space buying, then, was a legitimate and important element of service in the early advertising agency, and still is, for proper selection can save substantial sums for the advertiser.

The Copywriter

Long before 1900, advertising agencies began to feel the need for the proper preparation and wording of advertisements. So long as advertising was confined to local announcements and classified ads, there was little importance attached to the preparation of advertising copy. It was not long before the agencies began to find that the advertising message could be something more than an announcement. Agencies recognized the importance of selling copy. About 1880, a few agencies announced that they would prepare advertisements for their clients. The preparation of copy began merely as an added service.

Not much importance was placed on it at the start. But with the rapid expansion of industry, manufacturers began to feel the need for wider distribution of their products, and advertising became an important tool for such added distribution. Advertising agencies quickly expanded and found themselves serving all sorts of businesses. Advertising copy took on great importance and the work of the copywriter soon began to vie with that of the space buyer in the importance of the services rendered by the agency to its clients.

As an example of this, as early as 1905, Albert D. Lasker of Lord & Thomas employed John E. Kennedy as a copywriter, paying him $28,000 a year, and publicized this fact.

The Art Director

Art work played some part in ancient as well as in early modern advertising. The Roman signs we have mentioned often contained pictures. The tavern, for example, was represented by a suspended shield, indeed, the rate of literacy was then so low that the picture communicated more readily than the word.

Care in lay-out, too, appeared in the earliest modern advertisements. One published in 1878 advertises compound oxygen as a new treatment for the cure of chronic diseases by the true process of revitalization. In this advertisement, Drs. Starkee and Palen claim that this treatment cures consumption, asthma, catarrh, bronchitis, dyspepsia, headache, rheumatism, neuralgia, etc. There was no picture in the advertisement of this elixir, but it did contain bold headlines and subheads.

In 1888, in an advertisement published by Ferris Bros., a number of drawings appear illustrating the use of corded corset waists. It was common in these early days of advertising to publish a picture of the founder of or some important personality in the business. An examination of these early lay-outs causes one to doubt whether the illustrations could really be called art work.

However, the Uneeda Biscuit advertisement, published by the National Biscuit Company in 1899, clearly illustrates the function of planned art work in a printed advertising message. As the use of art work became more extensive in advertising, agencies developed certain methods and techniques to coordinate art work and advertising copy. Many advertising agencies in the early 1900's set up art departments or at least employed one or more persons whose job was to secure or produce the needed art work for the advertisements placed by the agency.

It was soon determined that no one agency could contain among its personnel a sufficient number of artists to produce the varied types of art work required in the advertisements produced for the different clients of the agency. For that reason, it has become more or less general practice for the agency itself to make the lay-out for the advertisement and perhaps to produce a very rough sketch of the art work required. After this has been done, the art director of the agency selects the artist who he feels can do the best job in producing the type of art work required. The art work is then purchased on the outside.

In certain specialized types of advertising agencies, it was necessary to expand the art service rendered; for this reason, some agencies actually employed artists to prepare the finished drawing or painting. Because it became a generally accepted fact that the illustration in an advertisement may be equally as important as the printed message, the art department of an advertising agency has become one of the important parts of the organization.

Research

In the very early days of the advertising agency, perhaps even before 1880, some agencies realized the importance of research. In the days before the open contract, when agencies were most interested in selling the space in the papers they represented, it became important to convince an advertiser that certain advertising media had greater value than others. For this reason, it was necessary to determine such things as circulation figures and the type of persons who read particular publications.

In an effort to sell the space they had available, some of the agencies actually studied these things so as to convince the advertiser that he should place his advertisements in certain media. With the advent of modern types of outdoor advertising and car card advertising, it became necessary to determine the value of these new advertising media. This required statistics, which in turn required research.

Consequently, many studies were made by newspapers, magazines and outdoor plants. While some research work was attempted by agencies before this century, it is doubtful if much really extensive research work, such as market analysis as we understand it today, was performed by agencies until about 1930.

By that time advertising had become recognized as a powerful and essential tool to modern business. Nearly every large manufacturer realized the need of distributing his products over a wide area. Millions of dollars were being spent to acquaint the public with the products available and the relative merits of each. The Federal Food, Drug and Cosmetic Act had done much to clean up the fantastic claims made by manufacturers of patent medicines.

As the science of marketing and merchandising developed, many questions presented themselves to advertisers, such as: What size package will sell best? Will the consumer prefer a liquid or a powder? What type of retail outlet can best distribute a certain product? Should a manufacturer push a low-priced, middle-priced or high-priced product? What is the best geographical area for the distribution of certain products?

Many advertisers came to their agents for the answers to these questions. It was logical, then, that the advertising agency began to feel the need to conduct studies in an effort to find the answers to the questions posed by the advertisers. Some agencies employed one or more persons to spend their full time conducting research studies for their clients.

Others believed that they should consider their clients' problems and secure specialists on the outside to study the questions and resolve the answers. The quantity and quality of research work has varied, and still varies, between one agency and another.

Another Measurement of Growth

It is not practicable to discuss the history of each of the other departments of an agency at this point. One additional subject however is interesting and indicative of the quick growth of the agency. How has the volume of the advertising agency business grown? Unfortunately, there is no reliable source from which to secure accurate figures to indicate the volume of advertising in the early years of the business.

There are statistics which tend to indicate that the largest of the very early agencies prior to 1875 conducted a volume of business of from $5,000 to approximately $100,000 a year. By 1890 some of these agencies were doing a volume of nearly $1,000,000 a year and by 1900 a few were doing as much as double this.

After the first World War the largest were doing a volume of about $10,000,000 a year. Today, there are two or three agencies that transact a business having an annual volume in excess of $50,000,000. Like any personal service business, most of the agencies deliver such a highly personalized service that their size is restricted. Out of about two thousand agencies today, approximately fifteen hundred handle a yearly volume of less than $500,000 each.

RECAPITULATION

We have found that although advertising is as old as civilization, the advertising agency is a product of modern times.

It has gone through four stages:

1. Infancy: Before 1900, there were few in the business who even knew how they wanted to conduct the business, or whether they represented the advertiser or the publisher. Late in the nineteenth century, most agencies were space brokers, who bought space at wholesale and sold it at retail.

2. Adolescence: From 1900 to 1918 agencies were developing their organizations to become a positive force in business. A standard commission from publications was received by all recognized agencies, and the development of service departments was beginning. The techniques of media selection, copywriting and art work were being refined.
3. Early maturity: There was still considerable mystery in the business before 1930; thereafter the business settled down. Most of the functions to be performed by the advertising agency had been determined and competition between one agency and another was purely on the basis of who could best serve the client. The agency in its mature form has become, in some aspects, a profession.
4. Professional concept: The professional elements of the agency business are those related to the personal service offered to clients by the agency in connection with idea development, product analysis, the development of marketing techniques, the personal attention to writing, lay-out, art work, etc. In addition, there are the commercial elements of the business, those related to the purchase of advertising space and materials, the use of capital and routine functions such as checking copy, measuring ads, buying printing, billing, paying and accounting.

FUNCTIONS OF THE AGENCY AND PLANNING THE CAMPAIGN

The advertising agency business, having passed the period of adolescence, is now mature and in certain aspects it is achieving a professional level. In the earlier stages of agency development, the functions performed and the services rendered varied widely between one agency and another.

Now, most agencies offer many of the same types of service. The modern agency, of course, still buys and sells advertising media as did the early agencies, but in addition it offers professional services in planning, developing and executing advertising campaigns.

General Outline of Functions

The following outline of some of the principal functions of the modern agency indicates both the maturity of the business and its claim to professional status.

Campaigns

It plans the actual advertising campaigns, and outlines many related activities to be carried on both within the agency and in the company whose product or service it is advertising, carefully integrating both.

Copy Preparation

It studies the product and the need for the product, and then determines selling points and makes the appeal.

Copy Testing

It endeavours to determine in advance, in so far as possible, how well comparative appeals will pull.

Space or Time Buying

It selects various advertising media and analyzes media according to coverage, costs and effectiveness. It orders, specifies and buys the advertising space or time planned for the campaign. It checks advertising as it appears, then audits quantity and quality and handles claims for shortages and substandard quality.

Research and Counsel

It conducts research regarding markets, copy, products, appeals, uses, etc.

Radio

It may have an entire department devoted to radio advertising, including programs and research.

Production

It specifies and purchases the production materials required for the campaign.

Publicity

It occasionally conducts or directs publicity campaigns in behalf of its client.

Dealer Helps

It may plan dealer helps, including displays.

Sales Helps

It prepares sales portfolios and manuals.

Design

It prepares packages and labels.

Retail Promotion

It plans retail promotion, including sales helps for retail clerks, local advertising tie-ins, etc.

Miscellaneous

It performs numerous services of a miscellaneous nature related to the following:

- Sales and consumer films.
- Direct mail
- Contests
- Sales training
- Exhibits
- Premiums
- Instruction and recipe books
- Catalog planning
- House organ planning
- Planning sales policies
- Product design
- Sales meetings
- New product development
- Public relations
- Distribution channels
- Annual reports
- Working with salesmen in the field.

Billing

It bills advertising space and materials, and radio time, talent and mechanics, and furnishes the advertiser with statistics in relation to these.

In order to understand each of these functions, it is necessary to go into some detail to define what the usual practice and procedures are.

PLANNING THE CAMPAIGN

This is one of the creative services performed by advertising agencies. It includes such activities as:

Product

Selecting the products to be advertised.

Markets

Determining where the advertising should appear.

Media

Deciding what general class of media should be used.

Copy

Conceiving and developing the "copy idea."

Visualization

Visualizing the advertising.

Imtegration

Cooperating with the manufacturer's advertising department on such matters as follow-through, dealer helps and the like.

It is not the purpose of this book to describe how an advertising campaign is conceived and developed. These services, which are acknowledged to be highly important in the agency business, are not directly connected with the subject of financial management except as the cost of performing these services affects finances. Usually owners of smaller agencies, and contact men in larger agencies, perform the important functions included in conceiving and developing the advertising campaign. In the larger agency, certain separate elements of work are delegated to departments or individuals within the agency. These would embrace copywriting and art work, including visualization.

It is customary for the contact men in the larger agency or the owner in the smaller agency to develop the advertising campaign and discuss it rather extensively with the advertiser.

Much of this work is called "client contact," and the contact man in an agency for this reason is an important factor in the success or failure of an advertising campaign. The contact man, therefore, has a great effect on the cost of performing all of the work for advertisers. If the contact man understands his job and issues careful instructions and orders to agency employees based on the actual needs of the advertiser, considerable waste will be eliminated.

It is also important that a contact man have the courage of his convictions so that if a piece of work is completed satisfactorily he will avoid continual changes which are unnecessary and costly. Many books have been written on the subject of copywriting and others on the subject of advertising art. As stated previously, it is not the purpose of this volume to discuss the creative elements of the agency business.

RESEARCH

The research activities of the agency are currently the subject of much controversy and questioning. The main stream of belief is that where large sums of money are expended for advertising it pays handsome dividends to know as much about the product, the market and competition as it is possible to learn. This indicates rather extensive research activities. The question is whether the agency or the advertiser should initiate the research and, if the agency does, whether it should receive a special fee.

Few agencies are equipped to conduct extensive research operations, consequently there is considerable merit to the position that outside specialists should conduct them. However, at the outset it is necessary for the agency to know a good deal about the product it is going to advertise and the market in which the product is to be advertised. The implication is that in any event the agency must perform a certain amount of research.

When an agency first secures an account, it is standard practice to study the products to be advertised, the market for the products, and the competition, including advertising campaigns conducted in connection with the distribution and sale of competing products. Upon receiving a new account, the agency will often find that it has employees who have had experience with products similar to that of their new client. If not, provided that the size of the account warrants it, the agency often employs a person or persons with previous experience in advertising similar products.

Research by Agencies

It is difficult to generalize on the subject of research activities that are conducted as a preliminary to advertising, because the type and extent of research activities are largely dependent on the particular product to be advertised.

Market and product analyses are specialties which would require a substantial number of highly trained and experienced persons in order to answer the questions that arise from time to time concerning the varied products with which an average agency is involved.

The research activities generally conducted by an agency at its own expense are confined to a superficial analysis of:

1. The product to be advertised.
2. The market for the product.
3. The competition with other products.

Research by Outside Organizations

Often an agency recommends market analyses and other research activities. In such cases, the agency may suggest the research organization that is best equipped to make the studies. In all cases, the agency certainly should be furnished with a copy of any market studies or product analyses that are available.

The U. S. Department of Commerce publishes numerous analytical reports that furnish considerable revealing information on products and markets. These statistics are available to the public and they are generally used by advertising agencies in planning advertising campaigns. In addition, the various advertising media have made intensive market studies which are made available to advertising agencies. These reports are constantly referred to by agencies in their study and preparation for advertising campaigns.

Certain organizations have specialized in rating the effectiveness of advertising messages. Advertising agencies frequently contract for the services of these organizations to determine the effectiveness of their campaigns and of the campaigns conducted by other agencies for clients in competition with theirs. Research work as it affects advertising and regardless of who does it may be broadly divided into two classifications: product analysis and market analysis.

Product Analysis

Product analysis can involve many different subjects. Among these the most significant are:

1. Investigation of the company, including its capacity for production and for growth, and its sales set-up.
2. Engineering analysis to determine the quality of the product and its merit in relation to competing products.
3. Study to determine the kind of product needed in relation to its usefulness and some existing or potential need.

   This must be generally correlated to engineering analysis and market analysis.
4. Research to determine price and production scale. This too should be correlated with market analysis.
5. Analysis to determine methods of packaging, selling and distributing.

Generally, the product analyses are undertaken by advertisers rather than by advertising agencies. Of course, this type of research can have an important bearing on the effectiveness of the advertising campaign. Consequently the agency is always interested in these analyses and should always be consulted about them. Often the agency itself suggests a product analysis. This type of research is usually paid for by the advertiser. If the study is initiated by the agency, then the agency arranges for a fee on a cost plus basis or on a flat fee basis. Rarely does the agency undertake a product analysis without securing a special fee for the work.

Market Analysis

Market analysis may be undertaken to determine:

1. Size of the market or quantity of goods that the market can be expected to absorb.
2. Geographic location of the market.
3. Type of individual or company that is the logical prospective buyer of the product.
4. Seasonable factors which affect the sale of the goods.
5. Price level at which the product can be sold most effectively to produce a profitable result.
6. Most efficient methods of distribution.

Market analyses, like product analyses, vary considerably. Some analyses can be made through questionnaires sent to dealers or distributors to determine the best policies for the marketing of a product. Often the agencies themselves undertake this kind of study. In such cases, it is usual for the agency to charge a fee for conducting the study.

Dealer and Consumer Surveys

Occasionally an agency undertakes to make a dealer survey at its own expense but this is the exception rather than the rule. Consumer surveys are usually more costly than dealer surveys because to conduct a study among customers it is necessary to reach a large number of people.

Consumer surveys are made in four principal ways:

1. Personal interviews.
2. Questionnaires mailed or otherwise distributed.
3. Telephone interviews.
4. Consumer panels.

Before making a consumer survey, it is necessary to determine what information is needed and how it can be used. When this has been established, if the survey is to be made by method "1," "2," or "3," a questionnaire is generally prepared so that simple yes or no answers can be secured to a question or series of questions.

The answers to the questions are secured and the results are tabulated. After interpreting these results, the advertiser or agency draws conclusions upon which future policies are based.

Consumer Panels

This fourth type of consumer research is an intricate procedure which may operate after the following pattern:

1. A number of typical consumers are selected in the geographical areas from which information is required.
2. These persons are furnished with daily, weekly or monthly questionnaires which when answered will indicate:
   a. Each of the items that the consumer purchased during a period of time.
   b. Who in the family made the purchase.
   c. What influenced the purchase.

The questionnaires used are often lengthy and sometimes require detailed answers to one hundred or more questions. Through a tabulation of the answers, the research organization can determine just what each person or family has purchased during the entire period covered. Several research companies operate research panels and at least one large advertising agency operates a panel. The tabulations made as a result of the questionnaires furnish statistics on many different articles and in many different geographic and economic areas. This has a much broader use than the tabulations made from a survey which is conducted for one specific purpose.

Since the consumer study is far more costly than the distributor or dealer study, it is rare for an agency to undertake a consumer research study at its own cost.

Often consumer research is conducted by the advertiser himself or through a research organization employed by the advertiser. As consumer research studies can have an important bearing on the advertising campaign, agencies prefer to have at least a part in supervising the studies.

Who Pays The Bills?

If any generalization can be made as to whether the agency or the advertiser pays the cost of research activities, it is this: Where the study is performed specifically in connection with the development of an advertising campaign, the cost is paid by the agency. Where the study is made for the general benefit of the advertiser, the cost is paid by the advertiser.

It is impossible to make satisfactory generalizations as to what research activities the advertiser should expect to receive from the agency. The advertising agency should not be expected to conduct market analyses and product research; rather, it should avail itself of existing information that will assist it in the preparation of the advertising campaign.

The agency executives, in addition, should help determine what additional facts are needed to develop the most effective advertising campaign. They should recommend that the advertiser secure that information by employing outside specialists to make the studies required, and should point out that where the agency directs the research activities, it is necessary for the agency to charge a special fee to cover the cost of such direction.

Certainly research studies, including product and market analyses, can be extremely important factors in the development of an advertising campaign. Such research activities are not an integral part of an advertising campaign any more than product engineering (which has an important bearing on salts) is a direct or integral part of an advertising campaign.

For this reason, the agency can be expected only to express its opinion concerning the need for research; this in contrast to the job of actually performing the study.

Distribution and Sales

Since an advertising message is generally intended to reach the ultimate purchaser of a product, it is wasteful to advertise to persons who are not prospective customers; that is, to persons who cannot conveniently purchase the advertised article. A businessman would not advertise coal in an area which he did not serve; rather, he would concentrate his advertising in the area in which he distributed his product. The manner of distribution or type of retail outlet also becomes an important element to be considered in connection with the development of an advertising campaign. Often the manufacturer has a choice of the type of outlet through which he can distribute his product.

For example, some manufacturers of phonograph records distribute records through jobbers, each jobber having the exclusive rights in a specific geographical area. Other manufacturers of phonograph records distribute their products directly to the retail stores.

The advertising agency should be in a position to advise the advertiser concerning the various available methods of distribution. One method of distribution may provide a much greater rate of gross profit than another. Obviously, where the profit margin is larger, there are more funds available for advertising.

On the other hand, it can be assumed that a method of distribution which provides a smaller profit rate presupposes the need for less sales expense and probably smaller advertising appropriations. The advertising agency can be expected to be of valuable assistance in determining the most efficient method of distribution, but it cannot be expected to be of actual assistance in distributing the goods. This is a job for the advertiser and his salesmen.

In any event, the method of distribution must be determined before the advertising campaign can be successfully planned. The agency should be taken into the advertiser's confidence and should be fully informed of the distribution methods used by the advertiser and of any contemplated changes in the methods. The agency should be informed of the current sales rate in each territory and through each type of distributor, dealer or jobber. Such facts are helpful to the agency and will indicate where the advertising is successful and where it is not.

MEDIA SELECTION

It is pointed out that how the early advertising agencies performed the single function of buying advertising space and selling it to the advertiser. This phase of the agency business has continued to be one of its important functions, and this chapter, therefore deals with the problems and methods of selecting advertising media. This is a complex process which calls for wide knowledge and acute judgment.'

Types of Media

The types of media from which selection must be made according to their appropriateness for advertising a particular product are:

1. Daily newspapers; Sunday newspapers; weekly newspapers; farm papers; national magazines; trade papers and magazines; and various specialized or restricted publications.

2. Radio and television, including sponsored programmes or spot announcements, either local or network.
3. Outdoor advertising, including posted outdoor displays, painted outdoor display signs and spectaculars, and car cards as they appear in streetcars, busses, subways, elevated trains and other forms of commuter transportation.
4. Direct-mail materials, dealer displays, catalogs, etc.
5. Special advertising, including commercial moving picture productions, sky-writing, sales-convention materials, etc.

Procedure Followed

The agency executive in meetings with the advertiser develops a general plan for the campaign. When the plan has developed to a point that will permit a determination of the kinds of advertising media to be used, it is necessary to determine which publications, which radio stations and what outdoor locations or car cards are to be used.

The space buyer in an advertising agency and the space-buying department until recent years specialized in analyzing, selecting and buying printed media, i.e., newspaper and magazine space. With the advent and popularity of radio advertising, it became necessary for the agencies to provide a means of analyzing the effectiveness of the various radio networks and independent stations in order to determine which stations and chains were best suited for each advertising problem. Today the selection of printed media is quite separate and apart from the selection of radio advertising media.

The selection of outdoor advertising space is a relatively simple matter; consequently an established media department is usually assigned the task of selecting this medium.

The National Outdoor Advertising Bureau compiles statistics relative to the effectiveness of various outdoor advertising locations. In addition, each outdoor advertising plant has many available statistics showing the effectiveness of each of its various locations. When the agency and the client have tentatively determined the types of media to be used and the approximate advertising budget for each type, the problem of actual selection of the specific media is at hand.

The Contact Man

Usually, the contact man or account executive has a general idea of the type of coverage that would serve the advertiser best. He may suggest, for example, that morning newspapers be used in preference to evening papers, or that Sunday editions be used exclusively. He may suggest that the product be advertised only in cities having a population in excess of a certain minimum; or, conversely, that the product be advertised only in small weekly papers.

If the problem concerns magazine choice, he may recommend those magazines appealing to the quality buyer; or, conversely, those appealing to the larger group of popular-price brand buyers. The contact man may have a well-defined opinion concerning the type of radio network or independent station that should be used, or he may suggest at what time of day the programme would be most effective.

(In any case, the contact man, with or without the media-selection department, will develop a general idea of the time or space to be used. The media-selection department will then analyze the available publications, radio stations, outdoor locations, etc. This analysis will consist of a detailed study of population, "circulation, type of circulation, comparative costs of equal quantities of space and comparative" costs of getting the advertising message before each reader or listener.

For example, one radio station may charge one hundred dollars for a two-minute announcement; another may charge only fifty dollars. However, the importance is not only in the length of time the message is on the air; it includes also the number of people who will hear the message. But the question is further complicated: It is also necessary to determine how many actual prospects may listen to the message.

If an advertiser is selling dog food, it is important to know how many listeners own dogs and therefore would be prospective purchasers of dog food. A similar type of analysis is necessary in connection with printed advertising appearing in magazines, newspapers, yearbooks, theater programmes, classified telephone directories, etc. it is necessary for the media-selection department to determine the cost per unit of space, the comparative cost of reaching each reader, and the comparative cost of reaching each prospective buyer.

Where to Get the Facts

Nearly every newspaper, magazine, radio station and outdoor plant has compiled statistics from which the media-selection department can secure many facts to assist in the selection of the proper media for each campaign. In addition, there are other sources for obtaining statistical information, such as Standard Rate & Data, a service of directories which lists each advertising medium with its advertising rates, circulation, population and like data. Ayer's Directory of Newspapers and Periodicals, published annually, furnishes considerable information on nearly every publication in the United States.

This book, along with Standard Rate k Data, will be found in every agency's media department.

The Media Recommendation

Upon completing the study to determine where the advertiser's product can be advertised most effectively, a media recommendation is prepared which consists of the following:

1. List of various advertising media to be used.
2. Dates and quantities of space to be used on each date.
3. Total quantity of space to be used during the advertising period.
4. Cost of each advertisement.
5. Total cost of the advertising in each medium.

The media recommendation is discussed in detail with the contact man, who may suggest revisions. When the recommendation is in its final form, the contact man presents it to the advertiser and discusses the merits of the recommendation in whatever detail is pertinent.

It should be noted that the entire advertising appropriation cannot be spent for advertising space, since a substantial sum must be reserved for the cost of the various advertising materials required to produce the advertising. This refers mainly to print advertising in newspapers and magazines. Here art work in the form of lay-outs and finished art, engravings, typesetting, electros, mats, Photostats, etc., are required. In an advertising campaign running in newspapers or magazines, from eight to fifteen percent of the total advertising budget may be spent for advertising materials.)

The selection of radio advertising presents problems different from those connected with printed advertising. In radio advertising, it is necessary not only to select the network station and the time of day for the advertising, but it is also imperative that the type of show or announcement fit the product. Obviously, the soap operas which are currently popular would not be in keeping for an advertisement of Cadillac cars or Steinway pianos. Conversely, a symphony orchestra programme would not be suitable for advertising, say, bubble gum. In radio advertising, the selection of one station over another or one network over another is often not so important as the selection of the programme or type of programme.

The spot announcement or chain break is a form of advertisement that has paid nice dividends. This presents an additional problem for the agency. It is necessary to determine if the programme is to take the form of spot announcements and chain breaks or if it is to be a sponsored programme. After this determination has been made, if the decision is for the spot announcement or chain break, the procedure follows a pattern similar to that of printed advertising. A radio media recommendation would contain a list of the stations to be used, the hours during each date on which the programme would be broadcast, the cost of each broadcast, and the total cost of advertising on each station.

When the sponsored programme is decided upon, the agency encounters a more difficult job. Here it is necessary to determine first what type of programme is to be used; second, what kind of talent is available; and third, what radio time is available on each station or network. Sometimes the agency can buy a "package show," which means that one lump sum is paid for the talent and the radio time. In other cases, the agency secures the talent, which is paid for separately from the radio time.

The sponsored-programme form of radio advertising usually involves substantial expenditures. Generally, not only the media-selection department, but also the executives of the agency will give serious consideration to all of the elements involved in selecting a sponsored programme for an advertiser, in presenting its recommendation to the advertiser, the agency will submit statistics showing the approximate audience for each programme suggested. There are various independent organizations which rate radio shows and indicate the approximate number of listeners.

The services of these organizations are often purchased by agencies in an effort to determine the effectiveness and circulation of the programme. (Kledia selection, whether it is in connection with printed advertising, radio advertising or outdoor advertising, is an established service of the advertising agency.

The function of media selection never ceases; and even though an advertising campaign has been completely decided upon, the agency continually reviews the various media being used by a client in order to determine the comparative effectiveness of the advertising. This is a service which the advertising agency renders to its clients in consideration of the commissions received from the newspapers, magazines, radio stations, etc. No additional charge is customary for media-selection service.

SPACE BUYING

After the media recommendation has been approved, it is necessary to make arrangements for purchasing the publication space, radio time or outdoor displays. In small agencies, it is not practicable to have a separate department to carry out this function, in which case the space is purchased by one of the principals of the firm. In larger agencies, the space-buying job is assigned to a department consisting of one or more space buyers and the necessary assistants. Prior to the actual purchasing of space, a media recommendation may have been made as described in the preceding chapter.

Where no formal media recommendation has been prepared in advance of the space-buying operation, there is always at least an informal media recommendation.

Space in newspapers and magazines is generally contracted for in advance for a period of a year. The contracts with newspapers sometimes call for "space as required."

Radio time is purchased in terms of weeks of broadcasting, thirteen weeks generally being the minimum contract period. Frequently, radio time is contracted for longer periods, contracts being commonly issued for twenty-six, thirty-nine, or fifty-two weeks.

The Space Buyer

With the media recommendation at hand, the space buyer refers to various statistical records such as Standard Rate & Data to secure the terms and conditions for purchasing space from each source. Sometimes when it is not possible to secure sufficient information from the published data, the buyer must contact representatives of the radio station, periodical or outdoor plant.

Most of the printed advertising media (newspapers and magazines) have either their own direct salesmen or a special representative located in each of the principal cities of the country. The appointed representatives are usually companies that make a business of representing newspapers or magazines. They are commonly called "space reps."

The function of the space representative is much the same as was that of the advertising agency itself in the early days of the business. The space representative has a contract with each of a number of newspapers or other publications. He solicits business from the agencies and acts very much like a direct salesman for the paper. Often the space representative forwards the copy to the paper and collects from the advertising agency, in which case he furnishes bills for the space and proof of its insertion.

Contracts and Rates

After the space buyer has secured the necessary facts regarding the advertising media, he prepares and issues contracts. Each contract covers the space to be used by one client only. Although the advertising agency may use space in the same periodical or radio station for many clients, the space is contracted for each client separately.

It may be that the rate charged for the advertising space varies from one client to another. Such rate differences occur because of different total quantities of space contracted for and different times of placing contracts. It is important to note here that newspapers, magazines and radio stations offer different rates for advertising space depending on the conditions under which they serve the advertiser. The rate for a black-and-white advertisement is usually less than for a two-colour one; likewise, a two-colour advertisement is cheaper than a four-colour one.

Special positions take special charges; for example, an advertisement on the financial page or on the sports page will take a higher rate than one which can be inserted anywhere in the paper; likewise, magazines charge more for the inside front or back cover than for space elsewhere in the publication. In addition to these variances in rate, many newspapers offer combination rates for combination advertisements that are run both evening and morning, or that are run both daily and on Sunday. As a general rule, all newspapers charge higher rates for space in Sunday editions than in daily editions. Some newspapers offer "sliding-scale" rates; that is, the rate per line is set on a minimum amount of space, and if the advertiser uses more space, the rate is reduced. For example, a paper might offer a rate of thirty cents a line for the first two thousand lines, after which the rate is reduced to twenty-five cents a line until the total amount of space during the year has equalled five thousand lines, at which time the rate will be reduced to perhaps twenty cents. Often these rate reductions of sliding-scale papers are retroactive to the beginning of the contract year.

There are many small weekly newspapers published throughout the country. These weekly newspapers are excellent advertising media for certain advertisers, but buying space in these papers is more difficult than carrying on business with the larger daily papers.

For this reason, several associations have been formed to represent groups of weekly papers. These associations offer space in a large number of weekly papers. Space contracts sometimes can be let for a group of papers through such associations. The associations then assume the responsibility for billing and for furnishing copies of the papers in which the advertising appears.

Contracts for advertising space in newspapers, whether small or large, and for all kinds of magazines will ordinarily include the following information:

1. The name of the advertising agency contracting for space.
2. The name of the client on whose account space is purchased.
3. The product to be advertised.
4. The kind of space purchased—whether daily, Sunday, combination daily and Sunday, combination morning and evening, etc.
5. The rates at which space is purchased.
6. The frequency of insertions (in reference to magazines).
7. The position requested (run-of-paper, back cover, front cover, financial page, etc.).
8. The period covered by the contract (this is usually one year).

The above list includes the major items; however, the contract often includes further specifications, such as to whom tear pages or proofs of insertion are to be sent, where bills for advertising are to be sent, how many copies of such bills are required, and the general terms and conditions of the contract.

STANDARD CONTRACTS

Standard conditions governing advertising contracts and orders were adopted in 1920 and revised in 1933 by the American Newspaper Publishers Association, Periodical Publishers Association, Agricultural Publishers Association, and the Associated Business Papers, in cooperation with the American Association of Advertising Agencies. Agencies that are members of the American Association of Advertising Agencies or that are "recognized" by one of the publishers' associations listed, usually print these terms and conditions on the reverse side of each contract. If the standard conditions are changed in any way, there is a possibility that such a change could affect the liability of the agency and any change in these conditions could result in confusion and delay.

Contracts for radio time and outdoor advertising usually take a form that is different from contracts for newspaper and magazine space. When network radio shows are purchased, special contracts are drawn up to cover each situation. Spot radio broadcast contracts are much simpler in form and follow a pattern similar to the contract for printed advertising space in newspapers and magazines.

Terms of Payment

(a) The Agency agrees to pay and the publisher agrees to hold the agency solely liable for payment for the advertising covered by this contract.

The agency personally agrees to pay for advertising covered by this contract at the office of the publisher or his authorized representative on or before the last day of the month following that in which the advertising is published unless otherwise stipulated on publisher's rate card on which this contract was based, or when cash discount is deducted but payment date not specified on the publisher's rate card, on the 15th of the month following.

Bills must be rendered not less often than monthly but failure to do so shall not constitute breach of contract.

(b) The agency agrees to pay in the manner specified in paragraph (a) for all drawings, composition, cuts or mats if furnished by the publisher at the request of the agency provided it is the practice of the publisher to charge for such service.

(c) Cuts and mats shall be sent to the publisher prepaid. If they are not, the publisher may accept them, and pay transportation and import charges and the agency shall promptly reimburse the publisher.

(d) If at the end of the advertising period named in the contract or upon prior termination of the contract for any cause, the agency has not used the full amount of advertising contracted for, the agency shall pay to the publisher such additional sum on all advertising so published as shall be equal to the difference, if any, between the amount due at the rate named in the contract and the amount due at the rate applicable to the quantity of space used, according to that schedule of advertising rates of the publisher on which the contract was based, and upon such expiration or termination said additional sum shall become immediately due and payable. Short rate bills must be rendered within sixty days after the expiration of the contract period, otherwise the publisher agrees to a settlement at the rate named in the original contract. Unless otherwise expressed on the face hereof, this contract may be cancelled by the agency, or less space used, in accordance with the provisions of this paragraph.

(e) Any bill rendered to the agency by the publisher shall be conclusive as to the correctness of the items therein set forth and shall constitute an account stated unless written objection is made thereto by the publisher or the agency within sixty days from the rendering thereof.

(f) The publisher reserves the right to cancel the contract at any time upon default by the agency in the payment of bills, or other breach, or in the event of any material violation on the part of the agency of any of the conditions herein named; and upon such cancellation all advertising done hereunder, including short rates or other charges under this contract, and unpaid, shall become immediately due and payable. In case of delinquency in payment or impaired credit of the agency the publisher shall have the right at any time to change the requirements as to the terms of payment for further advertising under this contract as he may see fit.

(g) In all cases where date of payment is material, unless otherwise stipulated the postmark date on the envelope properly addressed to the publisher or to his representative shall be considered the date when payment was made.

Rates

(a) All rates shall be published. There shall be no secret rates, rebates, or agreements affecting rates. All rates shall be furnished agencies if requested.

(b) "Publisher's rate card" shall be understood to mean that" schedule of advertising rates of the publisher upon which this contract is based.

(c) The rate stated in the contract is the minimum rate at which an equal or less amount of space, for the same class of advertising, to be published in a like position, under the same conditions, within the same period of time, can be secured.

(d) If additional space is used within the period covered by the contract where the publisher has a schedule of graduated rates, any lower rate shall be given if earned, according to the publisher's rate card on which this contract is based.

Advertising Material

(a) The subject matter, form, size, wording, illustration and typography of the advertising shall be subject to the approval of the publisher but unless otherwise authorized in advance no change shall be made without the consent of the agency.

(b) If the publisher is unable to set any advertisement in the type or style requested, he may set such advertisement in such other type or style as in his opinion most nearly corresponds thereto, and the advertisement may be inserted without submission of proof unless proof before insertion is requested on the face of the order.

(c) Where cuts, electrotypes, or material furnished by the agency occupy more space than specified in the contract or insertion order, publisher should immediately communicate with the agency for definite instructions. If the publisher is unable to secure definite instructions from the agency, the advertising shall be omitted.

(d) If agency has contracted for a series of insertions in a publication, and before closing date insertion order and copy for next issue have not been received by publisher, publisher shall notify agency and follow agency's instructions.

(e) Advertisements ordered set in "space as required" shall be measured from office ad. rule to office ad. rule.

Proof of Insertion

(a) The page containing the advertising or, at the request of the agency a copy of each issue in which the advertising appears, shall be mailed or otherwise supplied to the agency, which shall be deemed to have received such copy or page unless the publisher is notified in writing of the non-receipt thereof within thirty days after the date of publication. The publisher may mail or otherwise supply an affidavit of publication in lieu of a second copy or page containing the advertisement. Failure to forward or furnish such copy, page or affidavit shall not constitute a breach of the contract.

Circulation

(a) Unless the publisher is a member of the Audit Bureau of Circulations, the agency shall be entitled, upon request, to a statement of net paid circulation verified by a certified public accountant, or in lieu thereof to the right to examine the publisher's circulation books.

Omission of Adverting

(a) Failure by the publisher to insert in any particular issue or issues invalidates the order for insertion in the missed issue but shall not constitute a breach of contract.

In newspapers the advertising must appear in all regular editions issued on the date for which the advertising is ordered. Advertisements omitted from any particular edition or editions must be reported to the agency and if received in time and omitted through fault of publisher must be made up or adjusted unless otherwise instructed.

Unless otherwise stipulated, the publisher shall have the right to omit any advertisement when the space allotted to advertising in the issue for which such advertisement is ordered has all been taken, and also to limit the amount of space an advertiser may use in any one issue.

General

(a) The agency agrees that it will not rebate to its client any part of the commission allowed by the publisher.

(b) In dealing with agencies, the publisher shall follow a uniform policy to avoid discrimination.

(c) Unless later date is specified in publisher's rate card, advertising in newspapers shall begin within thirty days from the date of this contract, or contract becomes null and void.

(d) A waiver by the publisher of any default or breach by the agency shall not be considered as a waiver of any subsequent default or breach of the same or any other provisions hereof.

Insertion Orders

After the space contracts have been issued and prior to the insertion of each advertisement in the printed media, it is necessary to issue what is commonly called an insertion order. The space contract has simply reserved the space and established the terms and conditions under which the purchase is to be made. The insertion order is a detailed description of the space to be used for each advertisement. When the agency has prepared an advertisement, the insertion order is issued by the space-buying department. The insertion order is often sent with copy instructions, mats, plates, etc.

The insertion order should contain the following:

1. The name of the advertising agency.
2. The name of the advertiser.
3. The name of the product to be advertised.
4. The date for the insertion of the advertising. (This includes the edition, or editions if the publication has more than one edition.)
5. The amount of space to be occupied by the advertisement.
6. The position requested in the publication.
7. The number of colors to be used in printing the advertisement.

In addition, the agency often includes other information on the insertion order, such as to whom tear pages or copies of the publication are to be sent as proof of insertion; the number of copies of invoices requested and to whom they are to be sent; and special instructions regarding the printing of the advertisement. This usually refers to position and may include a statement that the advertisement is not to be printed next to competing copy, etc.

After the space-buying department has issued the insertion order, it has completed its function in connection with space buying with only one exception. It is the responsibility of the space-buying department to see that the agency fulfils its contract requirements with each vendor of advertising media. It is important to note that an advertising agency ordinarily does not act as an agent in the accepted legal sense. The advertising agency is itself financially responsible for carrying out its commitments. It is financially liable to pay for the space it buys. Whether or not the client pays is of no legal importance in the transaction between the agency and the publisher, radio station, etc.

Many newspapers, magazines, radio stations and outdoor advertising plants offer cash discounts in consideration of prompt payment of invoices. To secure this additional revenue, the agency must pay its bills in accordance with the vendors' terms.

Therefore, it becomes important to set up a means by which the agency can collect from the advertiser before the cash discount payment date offered by the vendor. This subject will be discussed in a later chapter, but it should be emphasized here that the term "advertising agency" is misleading. The advertising agency, in the legal sense, is not an agent. It is responsible for whatever commitments for advertising space it makes.

CHECKING ADVERTISING

The purchaser of an article wants to be sure he receives it and wants to verify the quantity and quality before he pays for it. Printed advertising is purchased in accordance with definite terms and conditions as to quantity, quality and time of publication.

Before the agency makes payment to the publisher, it is desirable to check the advertising to determine whether it meets the specifications in accordance with the contract and order. In most agencies one or more persons are assigned the job of checking the advertising. This is a routine job and usually follows a more or less standard pattern.

News Papers

A copy of each newspaper insertion order is sent to the checking department. Newspaper orders are filed by state and city in which the paper is published. Upon receipt of publications, agencies usually sort them in the same manner in which insertion orders are filed. Then, by referring to the insertion order bearing the same name as the publication, the checker is able to determine what advertising to look for. For example, if the checking department receives a copy of the Chicago *Sun,* the checker then looks in the file under "Illinois, Chicago, *Sun*" A copy of the insertion order covering the advertising should be filed there. If the title discloses an insertion order for "Illinois, Chicago, *Sun*" covering an insertion in a particular edition on a specified date, the checker then looks at the order further to find the name of the advertiser and the product, after which he runs through the paper to locate the advertisement.

When this is located, the checker examines it for quality and correctness. Assuming that the correct advertisement has been published and that the quality of printing is acceptable, the checker then measures the advertisement to determine the amount of space occupied by it.

Newspaper space is usually sold in lines or inches. Daily papers usually sell space by lines; the small papers and weekly papers usually sell it by inches. An inch represents fourteen lines of "agate" type. The insertion order indicates whether the space is purchased by lines or inches. The checker is furnished with a rule calibrated in both.

A line of space is the depth measure, a column is the width measure. In other words, if an advertisement occupies three columns in width and ten lines in depth, the space measurement would be thirty lines. The same rule holds true when the unit is inches instead of lines; that is, if an advertisement is three columns wide and three inches deep, the measurement would be nine inches.

Some agencies have established the practice of rating the various positions in which advertising appears in newspapers. The purpose of such a rating system is to determine whether or not a particular newspaper is giving the advertiser reasonably good positions in the paper.

Generally, advertising which appears on the first few pages of a newspaper is considered to be more effective than that appearing far back in the paper. Advertising appearing in the upper right-hand corner of a page generally may be considered more effective than advertising appearing on the left bottom corner, etc.

After advertisement positions are rated, position reports are prepared to show the number of advertisements that secured the best position, the number that secured the second best position, etc. With these reports, the space buyer is in a position to determine which papers have been giving the advertiser reasonably good advertising positions and which have not.

He can then call the representative of the paper that is not giving the advertiser reasonably good advertising positions and can demand greater consideration in the future.

Where the agency rates the positions of advertising, the key or code for such positions is noted on the insertion order at the time the checker examines and measures the advertisement. The position indication would be as follows: Date of Insertion Ad Number Space Ordered Space Used Position.

Magazines and Trade Papers

Checking magazine and trade-paper space is considerably simpler than checking newspaper space. Space in magazines is usually purchased in units of pages or fractions thereof, although occasionally magazines arid trade papers sell space by columns or inches. The usual magazine advertisement occupying a page, half-page, quarter-page, etc. is not subject to shrinkage. This is because electrotypes and half-tones are used instead of mats. These are built to occupy the exact amount of space ordered. The checker, then, needs to inspect a magazine advertisement only for quality of print and position.

Some agencies, in addition to checking the appearance of advertising for quality and quantity, wish to determine the position secured in either a paper or a magazine.

There are different methods of rating the comparative position of advertisements, but among the most important factors to be considered are:

1. The page number on which the advertisement appears.
2. The section in which the advertisement appears (such as buyer's guide, society section, financial section, etc.).
3. The position on the page.
4. Whether or not the advertisement appears adjacent to competitive copy.

Where the agency is interested in rating the position of the advertising, the checker usually is furnished with a code for this purpose. The code is entered on an accounting record from which the agency can prepare a report showing the various positions secured from the different publications.

Radio

The checking of radio advertising is, obviously, a different matter from checking printed advertising. Usually the broadcasting station sends the agency an affidavit certifying the fact that each message or programme was actually broadcast. Such affidavits are required by agencies before bills for broadcasting are paid. At times, advertising agencies have attempted to listen to each broadcast to check the message or programme, but this practice was never general. Most agencies rely on the honesty of the broadcasting stations and on other reports secured from the advertiser or his distributors in each town where a programme is broadcast. These distributors, of course, are acquainted with the facts concerning the advertiser's programme. Since the advertising is important to the distributor, it may be expected that the distributor would report any omissions or other defects in the radio advertising campaign.

In addition, there is a radio checking service available on both the East and West Coasts. Clients are furnished with actual recordings of what is said on the air waves on a particular programme, product or topic, or, occasionally, with programme scripts. There is available, also, a spot-checking service, with listeners or monitors in several hundred cities. Agencies and advertisers are advised whether the spots were actually used at the time they were scheduled; what the adjacencies were; the caliber of the presentation; and other pertinent data bearing on the effectiveness of the spot message.

Other Media

It is not a general practice for agencies to check the appearance of outdoor advertising and car cards. Lithographs or other material are sent to the outdoor advertising plants, which certify the actual placing and appearance of the advertising. It would be extremely difficult for an agency to check the posting date and the quality of the posting of each outdoor sign. The cost of such checking would not be warranted. For this reason, agencies do little or no checking of outdoor advertising space.

The National Outdoor Advertising Bureau does render a valuable service in this regard. In addition to checking the appearance of outdoor advertising, the Bureau furnishes other services.

One agency checked every outdoor location to determine the date on which each billboard was posted and the quality of the posting. In addition, for several years, this agency made intensive studies to determine the comparative value of the locations used. This practice was discontinued by the agency after a few years when it was found that the outdoor plants billed correctly for the space used and that the statistics furnished by the plant owners were reliable.

This, they concluded, made independent checking and study of little value. Checking the appearance of advertising in the manner discussed is a service that the agency renders to the advertiser in consideration of the commissions received from the advertising media. No special or extra charge is made for such service.

Advertising Materials, Publicity and Miscellaneous

Certain materials are necessary to produce a printed advertisement. These are called mechanical production or advertising materials. They include art work, photography, typography, engravings, half-tones, electrotypes, mats, stereos, Photostats, etc.

WHY AGENCY SHOULD SPECIFY, ADVERTISING MATERIALS

It is highly desirable and almost essential for the agency to specify and purchase these materials, for only in this way can it control the final result or appearance of the advertising. Production work starts almost as soon as the contact man and the client have agreed on an advertising campaign, at which time it becomes necessary to visualize, at least roughly, the various advertisements as they are to appear. To do this, the agency prepares rough sketches of each advertisement. Sometimes these sketches merely take the form of rough lay-outs that are quickly penciled up by the agency's art department. In other cases, the visuals become more comprehensive and include an explanation of the final art work and a paste-up of the whole advertisement including the type, etc.

In any event, when the kind of advertisement has finally been approved by the client, the agency sets about procuring the necessary materials for printing it.

The agency at the outset prepares a timetable showing on what dates each item of material is required, because it is necessary to secure the art work before plates can be made, etc., and all materials, including the final mats or half-tones, must be complete in time to send them to the publisher for printing the advertisement.

Production Orders

Orders are issued in the production department of an advertising agency for each of the materials as it is required; and, as the materials are received with bills from suppliers, all of the production elements for the advertisement are gathered together until the final piece of material is received.

The engraving, electrotype, mat or stereo is forwarded to the publication and the cost of all of the items is invoiced to the client. In some agencies, the art work required for the production of advertising is segregated from the other materials. In such cases, the securing of the needed art work becomes the function of the art director or art department and the securing of the other materials is delegated to the production manager or production department.

There is no standard of procedure in the operation of production and art departments of advertising agencies but there is some uniformity of operation among agencies in regard to certain parts of the art and production work. Most agencies prepare rough lay-outs and nearly all agencies undertake to secure the final art work required, either by creating the art work in their own department or by purchasing it on the outside. Nearly all agencies undertake to secure the other materials required, such as type, electros, half-tones and mats. The difference in the operation of production departments among agencies comes in the charges made for performing the functions. This subject will be discussed in the chapter "Basis of the Agency's Compensation."

Some agencies operate production departments in which the entire responsibility for securing all required mechanical elements rests within the department. This includes the scheduling of materials so that they are received when they are required. It also includes the responsibility of getting the final plates or mats to the publisher before a closing date. In other agencies, the production department is charged merely with the responsibility of purchasing the advertising materials required; the scheduling and expediting duties are delegated to a separate traffic department.

Publicity

Publicity, in the sense it is used here, may be defined as the dissemination of information regarding products or industries without the overt purpose of selling. It takes the form of news stories and feature articles in the press, in national magazines, in trade papers and in farm papers. Some publicity is also accomplished through the radio in connection with news and other programs.

There is a growing feeling among agencies that publicity campaigns can be best conducted by publicity or public relations firms which specialize in this work. This feeling is emphasized by the attitude among publishers that advertising agencies, in attempting to secure publicity, are actually endeavouring to divert what should be paid advertising into free publicity.

Nevertheless there are a number of agencies that have completely organized publicity departments. These agencies plan, create, develop and place publicity as an extra service to certain clients.

Unless the advertiser's account is very large and highly profitable, the agency cannot afford to provide a publicity service without arranging for a special fee to cover the cost of the work. On the other hand, most agencies do counsel and advise with their clients concerning publicity. They further assist the clients by cooperating with the publicity firms which handle that phase of service for the client.

Miscellaneous Functions

In addition to the principal services which have been discussed, agencies perform many diverse and incidental services, dependent on the need of the advertiser and the skill and elasticity of the agency.

Some of these miscellaneous services are:

1. Making a study of competitive advertising.
2. Assisting the client in his own sales work in order to insure the greatest effectiveness from the advertising.

(This type of service often includes the attendance at sales conventions, and the preparation of material to be used for dealers' and distributors' conventions.)

3. Testing copy—an innovation in the agency service.
4. Preparing house organs, catalogs, and the like.
5. Testing recipes for making food products.
6. Securing personnel for the client's advertising department.
7. Preparing booklets to be distributed to dealers and jobbers.

8. Preparing sales manuals, etc.
9. Preparing exhibits for conventions and industry shows.
10. Supervising the production of commercial films.

Usually all of these special services involve expenditures on the part of the agency; therefore, since the average advertising account does not provide a sufficient margin of profit to allow for such expenditures, the agency usually arranges for a special fee for doing such work. These fees are generally on a cost-plus basis, but such jobs are sometimes undertaken on a flat fee basis as well.

2

Looking into the Future of Ecotourism and Sustainable Tourism

INTRODUCTION

As one of the world's largest industries, tourism is associated with many of the prime sectors of the world's economy. Any such phenomenon that is intricately interwoven into the fabric of life—economically, socio-culturally, and environmentally—and relies on primary, secondary, and tertiary levels of production and service, is difficult to define in simple terms. This difficulty is mirrored in a 1991 issue of *The Economist:*

There is no accepted definition of what constitutes the [tourism] industry; any definition runs the risk of either overestimating or underestimating economic activity. At its simplest, the industry is one that gets people from their home to somewhere else (and back), and which provides lodging and food for them while they are away. But that does not get you far. For example, if all the sales of restaurants were counted as travel and tourism, the figure would be artificially inflated by sales to locals. But to exclude all restaurant sales would be just as misleading.

It is this complex integration within our socio-economic system (a critical absence of focus), according to Clawson and Knetsch and Mitchell, that complicates efforts to define tourism. Tourism studies are often placed poles apart in terms of philosophical approach, methodological orientation, or intent of the investigation.

A variety of tourism definitions each with disciplinary attributes that reflect research initiatives corresponding to various fields. For example, tourism shares strong fundamental characteristics and theoretical foundations with the recreation and leisure studies field.

According to Jansen-Verbeke and Dietvorst the terms leisure, recreation, and tourism represent a type of loose, harmonious unity which focuses on the experiential and activity-based features that typify these terms. On the other hand, economic and technical/statistical definitions generally ignore the human experiential elements of the concept in favour of an approach based on the movement of people over political borders and the amount of money generated from this movement.

It is this relationship with other disciplines, e.g. psychology, sociology, anthropology, geography, economics, which seems to have defined the complexion of tourism. However, despite its strong reliance on such disciplines, some, including Leiper, have advocated a move away in favour of a distinct tourism discipline. To Leiper the way in which we need to approach the tourism discipline should be built around the structure of the industry, which he considers as an open system of five elements interacting with broader environments:

- A dynamic human element,
- A generating region,
- A transit region,
- A destination region, and
- The tourist industry.

This definition is similar to one established by Mathieson and Wall (1982), who see tourism as comprising three basic elements:

- A dynamic element, which involves travel to a selected destination;
- A static element, which involves a stay at the destination; and
- A consequential element, resulting from the above two, which is concerned with the effects on the economic, social, and physical subsystems with which the tourist is directly or indirectly in contact.

Others, including Mill and Morrison, define tourism as a system of interrelated parts. The system is 'like a spider's web—touch one part of it and reverberations will be felt throughout'.

Included in their tourism system are four component parts, including Market (reaching the marketplace), Travel (the purchase of travel products), Destination (the shape of travel demand), and Marketing (the selling of travel).

In recognition of the difficulty in defining tourism, Smith feels that it is more realistic to accept the existence of a number of different definitions, each designed to serve different purposes. This may in fact prove to be the most practical of approaches to follow.

In this book, tourism is defined as the interrelated system that includes tourists and the associated services that are provided and utilised (facilities, attractions, transportation, and accommodation) to aid in their movement, while a tourist, as established by the World Tourism Organization, is defined as a person travelling for pleasure for a period of at least one night, but not more than one year for international tourists and six months for persons travelling in their own countries, with the main purpose of the visit being other than to engage in activities for remuneration in the place(s) visited.

TOURISM ATTRACTIONS

The tourism industry includes a number of key elements that tourists rely upon to achieve their general and specific goals and needs within a destination. Broadly categorised, they include facilities, accommodation, transportation, and attractions.

Although an in-depth discussion of each is beyond the scope of this book, there is merit in elaborating upon the importance of tourism attractions as a fundamental element of the tourist experience. Past tourism research has tended to rely more on the understanding of attractions, and how they affect tourists, than of other components of the industry. As Gunn has suggested, 'they [attractions] represent the most important reasons for travel to destinations' (1972:24).

MacCannell described tourism attractions as 'empirical relationships between a tourist, a site and a marker' (1989:41). The tourist represents the human component, the site includes the actual destination or physical entity, and the marker represents some form of information that the tourist uses to identify and give meaning to a particular attraction.

Lew (1987), however, took a different view, arguing that under the conditions of tourist-site-marker, virtually anything could become an attraction, including services and facilities.

Lew chose to emphasise the objective and subjective characteristics of attractions by suggesting that researchers ought to be concerned with three main areas of the attraction:

- *Ideographic*: Describes the concrete uniqueness of a site. Sites are individually identified by name and usually associated with small regions. This is the most frequent form of attraction studied in tourism research.
- *Organisational*: The focus is not on the attractions themselves, but rather on their spatial, capacity, and temporal nature. Scale continua are based on the size of the area which the attraction encompasses.
- *Cognitive*: A place that fosters the feeling of being a tourist. Attractions are places that elicit feelings related to what Relph (1976) termed 'insider' 'outsider', and the authenticity of MacCannell's (1989) front and back regions.

Leiper (1990:381) further added to the debate by adapting MacCannell's model into a systems definition. He wrote that:

A tourist attraction is a systematic arrangement of three elements: a person with touristic needs, a nucleus (any feature or characteristic of a place they might visit) and at least one marker (information about the nucleus).

The type of approach established by Leiper is also reflected in the efforts of Gunn (1972), who has written at length on the importance of attractions in tourism research. Gunn produced a model of tourist attractions that contained three separate zones, including:

- The nuclei, or core of the attraction;
- The inviolate belt, which is the space needed to set the nuclei in a context; and
- The zone of closure, which includes desirable tourism infrastructure such as toilets and information. Gunn argued that an attraction missing one of these zones will be incomplete and difficult to manage.

Some authors, including Pearce (1982), Gunn (1988), and Leiper (1990), have made reference to the fact that attractions occur on various hierarchies of scale, from very specific and small objects within a site, to entire countries and continents. This scale variability further complicates the analysis of attractions as both sites and regions. Consequently, there exists a series of attraction cores and attraction peripheries, within different regions, between regions, and from the perspective of the types of tourists who visit them. Spatially, and with the influence of time, the number and type of attractions visited by tourists and tourist groups may create a niche; a role certain types of tourists occupy within a vacation destination.

Through an analysis of space, time, and other behavioural factors, tourists can be fitted into a typology based on their utilisation and travel between selected attractions. One could make the assumption that tourist groups differ on the basis of the type of attractions they choose to visit, and according to how much time they spend at them. The implications for the tourism industry are that often it must provide a broad range of experiences for tourists interested in different aspects of a region.

A specific destination region, for example, may recognise the importance of providing a mix of touristic opportunities, from the very specific, to more general interest experiences for the tourists in search of cultural and natural experiences, in urban, rural, and back-country settings. Attractions have also been referred to in past research as sedentary, physical entities of a cultural or natural form. Although Gunn acknowledges wildlife as a *foundation* for attractions, it has been clear that wildlife is not simply the foundation of attractions, but an attraction in and of itself.

To a birder, for example, individual species become attractions of the most specific and most sought-after kind. A case in point is the annual return of a single albatross at the Hermaness National Nature Reserve in Unst, Shetland, Scotland. The arrival of this species prompts birdwatching tourists immediately to change their plans in an effort to travel to Hermaness. The albatross has become a major attraction for birder-tourists, while Hermaness, in a broader context, acts as a medium (attraction cluster) by which to present the attraction (bird). Natural attractions can be transitory in space and time, and this time may be measured for particular species in seconds, hours, days, weeks, months, seasons, or years. For tourists who travel with the prime reason to experience these transitory attractions, their movement is a source of both challenge and frustration.

MASS AND ALTERNATIVE TOURISM

Tourism has been both lauded and denounced for its ability to develop and therefore transform regions into completely different settings. In the former case, tourism is seen to have provided the impetus for appropriate long-term development; in the latter the ecological and sociological disturbance to transformed regions can be overwhelming. While most of the documented cases of the negative impacts of tourism are in the developing world, the developed world is certainly not an exception.

Young (1983), for example, documented the transformation of a small fishing-farming community in Malta by graphically illustrating the extent to which tourism development—through an increasingly complex system of transportation, resort development, and social behaviour—overwhelms such areas over time.

These days we are more prone to vilify or characterise conventional mass tourism as a beast; a monstrosity which has few redeeming qualities for the destination region, their people and their natural resource base. Consequently, mass tourism has been criticised for the fact that it dominates tourism within a region owing to its non-local orientation, and the fact that very little money spent within the destination actually stays and generates more income.

It is quite often the hotel or mega-resort that is the symbol of mass tourism's domination of a region, are often created using non-local products, having little requirement for local food products, and owned by metropolitan interests.

Hotel marketing occurs on the basis of high volume, attracting as many people as possible, often over seasonal periods of time. The implications of this seasonality are such that local people are at times moved in and out of paid positions that are based solely on this volume of touristic traffic.

Development exists as a means by which to concentrate people in very high densities, displacing local people from traditional subsistence-style livelihoods (as outlined by Young 1983) to ones that are subservience based. Finally, the attractions that lie in and around these massive developments are created and transformed to meet the expectations and demands of visitors.

Emphasis is often on commercialisation of natural and cultural resources, and the result is a contrived and inauthentic representation of, for example, a cultural theme or event that has been eroded into a distant memory. Admittedly the picture of mass tourism painted above is outlined to illustrate the point that the tourism industry has not always operated with the interests of local people and the resource base in mind. This was most emphatically articulated through much of the tourism research that emerged in the 1980s, which argued for a new, more socially and ecologically benign alternative to mass tourism development. According to Krippendorf (1982), the philosophy behind alternative tourism (AT)—forms of tourism that advocate an approach opposite to mass conventional tourism—was to ensure that tourism policies should no longer concentrate on economic and technical necessities alone, but rather emphasise the demand for an unspoiled environment and consideration of the needs of local people.

This 'softer' approach places the natural and cultural resources at the forefront of planning and development, instead of as an afterthought.

Also, as an inherent function, alternative forms of tourism provide the means for countries to eliminate outside influences, and to sanction projects themselves and to participate in their development—in essence, to win back the decision-making power in essential matters rather than conceding to outside people and institutions.

AT is a generic term that encompasses a whole range of tourism strategies (e.g. 'appropriate', 'eco-', 'soft', 'responsible', 'people to people', 'controlled', 'small-scale', 'cottage', and 'green' tourism), all of which purport to offer a more benign alternative to conventional mass tourism in certain types of destinations (Conference Report 1990, cited in Weaver 1991).

Dernoi (1981) illustrates that the advantages of AT will be felt in five ways:

- There will be benefits for the individual or family: accommodation based in local homes will channel revenue directly to families. Also families will acquire managerial skills.
- The local community will benefit: AT will generate direct revenue for community members, in addition to upgrading housing standards while avoiding huge public infrastructure expenses.
- For the host country, AT will help avoid the leakage of tourism revenue outside the country. AT will also help prevent social tensions and may preserve local traditions.
- For those in the industrialised generating country, AT is ideal for cost-conscious travellers or for people who prefer close contacts with locals.
- There will be benefits for international relations: AT may promote international-interregional-intercultural understanding.

More specifically, Weaver (1993) has analysed the potential benefits of an AT design from the perspective of accommodation, attractions, market, economic impact, and regulation. This more sensitive approach to tourism development strives to satisfy the needs of local people, tourists, and the resource base in a complementary rather than a competitive manner.

Some researchers, however, are quick to point out that as an option to mass tourism, full-fledged alternative tourism cannot replace conventional tourism simply because of mass tourism's varied and many-sided associated phenomena. Instead, it is more realistic to concentrate efforts in attempts to reform the worst prevailing situations, not the development of alternatives.

Butler (1990) feels that mass tourism has not been rejected outright for two main reasons. The first is economic, in that it provides a significant amount of foreign exchange for countries; the second is socio-psychological and relates to the fact that many people seem to enjoy being a mass tourist. They actually like not having to make their own travel arrangements, not having to find accommodation when they arrive at a destination, being able to obtain goods and services without learning a foreign language, being able to stay in reasonable, in some cases considerable comfort, being able to eat reasonably familiar food, and not having to spend vast amounts of money or time to achieve these goals.

SUSTAINABLE DEVELOPMENT AND TOURISM

The measurement of development (i.e. a nation's stage of socio-economic advancement) has conventionally been accomplished through the implementation of a number of key economic indicators. Among others, these include variables such as protein intake, access to potable water, air quality, fuel, health care, education, employment, GDP, and GNP.

The so-called 'developed' world (countries like Australia, the USA, Canada, and those of Western Europe) therefore is defined by the existence of these socio-economic conditions, whereby those with more are considered more highly developed.

Furthermore, one's level of development, either objectively or subjectively, is often equated or synonymous with one's perceived stage of 'civilisation', whereby progress (usually economic) is a key to the relationship between who is civilised and who is not. The *Oxford English Dictionary* defines civilisation as an 'advanced stage of social development', and civilise as 'bring out of barbarism, enlighten'.

The point to be made is that perhaps our perception of what is developed and what isn't, what is civilised and what isn't, is a matter of debate and one that our more recent approaches to development need to better address. For example, it has been noted that the most developed 20 per cent of the world's population (those in the 'West') are thought to use some 80 per cent of the world's resources with which to achieve development. If it is our goal to have the entire world 'developed' according to this Western paradigm, the planet will be in serious jeopardy. Perhaps in a hundred or two hundred years *Homo sapiens* will look back at Western civilisation as the most barbaric time period in recorded history.

Deming (1996) shares the view that humanity needs to take a good long look at civilisation. She writes that people have an insatiable hunger to see more and more of the planet, and to get closer and closer to its natural attractions. This behaviour surfaces continually in tourism as the tentacles of the tourist seek to push the fine line that exists between acceptable and unacceptable human-wildlife interactions. For example, animal harassment regularly occurs in Point Pelee National Park in Ontario, Canada, as thousands of birders converge on the spring migration of birds in the park. Despite posted warnings, tourists continue to venture off the designated paths in identifying and photographing species.

Potential benefits derived from an alternative tourism strategy:

Accommodation:

- Does not overwhelm the community.
- Benefits (jobs, expenditures) are more evenly distributed.
- Less competition with homes and businesses for the use of infrastructure.
- A larger percentage of revenues accrue to local areas.
- Greater opportunity for local entrepreneurs to participate in the tourism sector.

Attractions:

- Authenticity and uniqueness of community is promoted and enhanced.
- Attractions are educational and promote self-fulfilment.
- Locals can benefit from existence of the attractions even if tourists are not present.

Market:

- Tourists do not overwhelm locals in numbers; stress is avoided.
- 'Drought/deluge' cycles are avoided, and equilibrium is fostered.
- A more desirable visitor type.
- Less vulnerability to disruption within a single major market.

Economic impact:

- Economic diversity is promoted to avoid single-sector dependence.
- Sectors interact and reinforce each other.
- Net revenues are proportionally higher; money circulates within the community.
- More jobs and economic activity are generated.

Regulation:

- Community makes the critical development/strategy decisions.
- Planning to meet ecological, social, and economic carrying capacities.
- Holistic approach stresses integration and well-being of community interests.
- Long-term approach takes into account the welfare of future generations.
- Integrity of foundation assets is protected.
- Possibility of irreversibilities is reduced.

Deming asks: in the face of global warming, diminishing habitat, and massive extinctions, what can it mean to be civilised? Her response is a plead for limits, both social and ecological, in facing the enemy within:

As Pogo said during the Vietnam War, 'We've seen the enemy and it is us.' Suddenly we are both the invading barbarians and the only ones around to protect the city. Each one of us is at the centre of the civilized world and on its edge.

Milgrath (1989) talked of values as fundamental to everything we do. He argues that humans have as a central value their personal desire to preserve their lives.

This naturally evolves into a concern and value for other people—a social value. Milgrath suggests that it is inappropriate to elevate the preservation of each human life to a central concern because every person dies and this social preservation can never be realised. He feels instead that we should value the preservation of our ecosystems over society. Beyond the socially oriented values of society, Milgrath says we have given top priority to economic development, the result being that society will not be able to sustain itself over the long term.

Sustainable development has been proposed as a model that can have utility in creating the impetus for structural change within society, one that ventures away from a strictly socio-economic focus to one where development 'meets the goals of the present without compromising the ability of future generations to meet their own needs' (World Commission on Environment and Development 1987:43).

As such, the principles of ecology are essential to the process of economic development, with the aim of increasing the material standards of people living in the world who are impoverished. Even more fundamentally, though, it would seem more inspiring to hope that sustainable development would increase the moral standards of people living everywhere, which might naturally spill over into the realm of economics, which we know is critical to our viability. Tourism's international importance as an engine for economic growth, as well as its potential for growth, makes it particularly relevant to sustainable development. Consequently there is a wealth of literature emerging that is directly related to the sustainability of tourism, however broadly defined.

One of the first action strategies on tourism and sustainability emerged from the Globe '90 conference in British Columbia, Canada. Here, representatives from the tourism industry, government, non-governmental organisations (NGOs), and academia discussed the importance of the environment in sustaining the tourism industry, and how poorly planned tourism developments often erode the very qualities of the natural and human environment that attract visitors.

The conference delegates suggested that the goals of sustainable tourism are:

- To develop greater awareness and understanding of the significant contributions that tourism can make to environment and the economy;

- To promote equity and development;
- To improve the quality of life of the host community;
- To provide a high quality of experience for the visitor; and
- To maintain the quality of the environment on which the foregoing objectives depend.

Although their definition of sustainable tourism development was somewhat non-committal (i.e. 'meeting the needs of present tourist and host region while protecting and enhancing opportunity for the future'), a number of good recommendations were developed for policy, government, NGOs, the tourism industry, tourists, and international organisations.

For example, the policy section contains 15 recommendations related to how tourism should be promoted, developed, defined, in addition to a series of regional, interregional, and spatial and temporal implications. One of the policy recommendations states that 'sustainable tourism requires the placing of guidelines for levels and types of acceptable growth but does not preclude new facilities and experiences'.

From the perspective of financial prosperity and growth, there is an economic rationale for sustainability; as McCool (1995:3) asserts, 'once communities lose the character that makes them distinctive and attractive to nonresidents, they have lost their ability to vie for tourist-based income in an increasingly global and competitive marketplace'. In addition, McCool quotes Fallon in suggesting that sustainability is all about the pursuit of goals and measuring progress towards them.

No longer is it appropriate to gauge appropriate development by physical output or economic bottom lines; these must also be consideration of social order and justice.

McCool feels, therefore, that in order for sustainable tourism to be successful, humans must consider the following:

- How tourists value and use natural environments;
- How communities are enhanced through tourism;
- Identification of tourism's social and ecological impacts; and
- Management of these impacts.

Accordingly, many researchers and associations have initiated the process of determining and measuring impacts. As outlined above, Globe '90 was one of the initial and integral forces in linking tourism with sustainable development.

This was followed by Globe '92 and the move from principles to practice in implementing measures of sustainability in tourism. Even so, it was recognised in this conference that there was much work to be done in implementing sustainable principles in tourism, as emphasised by Roy:

Sustainable tourism is an extension of the new emphasis on sustainable development. Both remain concepts. I have not found a single example of either in India. The closest for tourism is in Bhutan. Very severe control of visitors—2000 per year—conserves the environment and the country's unique socio-cultural identity. Even there, trekking in the high altitudes, I find the routes littered with the garbage of civilization.

Although many examples exist in the literature on tourism and sustainable development, few sustainable tourism projects have withstood the test of time. An initiative that has received some exposure in the literature is the Bali Sustainable Development Project, coordinated through the University of Waterloo, Canada, and Gadjahmada University in Indonesia. This is a project that has been applied at a multisectoral level. Tourism, then, is one of many sectors, albeit a prime one, that drives the Balinese economy. Wall (1993) suggests that some of the main conclusions from his work on the project are as follows:

- Be as culturally sensitive as possible in developing a sustainable development strategy.
- Work within existing institutional frameworks as opposed to creating new ones.
- Multi-sectoral planning is critical to a sustainable development strategy and means must be created to allow all affected stakeholders to participate in decision-making.

The integration of tourism with other land uses in a region has also been addressed by Butler (1993:221), who sees integration as 'the incorporation of an activity into an area on a basis acceptable to other activities and the environment within the general goal of sustainable or long-term development'. Butler identified complementarity, compatibility, and competitiveness as variables that could be used as a first step in prioritising land uses, where complementarity leads to a higher degree of integration and competitiveness leads to segregation of the activity relative to other land uses. Other models have been more unisectoral in their approach to the place of tourism within a destination region. These have tended to identify a range of indicators that identify a sustainable approach or unsustainable approach to the delivery of tourism.

Examples include Canova's (1994) illustration of how tourists can be responsible towards the environment and local populations; Forsyth's (1995) overview of sustainable tourism and self-regulation; Moscardo *et al.'s* (1996) look at ecologically sustainable forms of tourism accommodation; and Consulting and Audit Canada's (1995) guide to the development of core and site-specific sustainable tourism indicators. These core indicators (e.g. site protection, stress, use intensity, waste management, and so on) must, according to the report, be used in concert with specific site or destination indicators.

This report identifies two categories of this latter group of indicators:

- Supplementary ecosystem-specific indicators (applied to specific biophysical land and water regions), and
- Site-specific indicators, which are developed for a particular site.

Table. Core Indicators of Sustainable Tourism.

Indicator	Specific measures
Site protection	Category of site protection according to IUCN index
Stress	Tourist numbers visiting site (per annum/peak month)
Use intensity	Intensity of use in peak period (persons/hectare)
Social impact	Ratio of tourists to locals (peak period and over time)
Development	Existence of environmental review procedure or control formal controls over development of site and use densities
Waste	Percentage of sewage from site receiving management treatment (additional indicators may include structural limits of other infrastructural capacity on site, such as water supply)
Planning	Existence of organised regional plan for tourist process destination region (including tourism component)
Critical ecosystems	Number of rare or endangered species
Consumer satisfaction	Level of satisfaction by visitors (survey-based)
Local satisfaction	Level of satisfaction by visitors (survey-based)
Tourism contribution to local economy	Proportion of total economic activity generated by tourism
Composite indices	
Carrying	Composite early warning measure of key factors capacity affecting the ability of the site to support different levels of tourism
Site stress	Composite measure of levels of impact on the site (its natural/ cultural attributes due to tourism and other sector cumulative stress)
Attractivity	Qualitative measure of those site attributes that make it attractive to tourism and can change over time

Table. Ecosystem-specific Indicators.

Ecosystem	Sample indicators[a]
Coastal zones	Degradation (percentage of beach degraded, eroded)
	Use intensity (persons per metre of accessible beach)
	Water quality (faecal coliform and heavy metals counts)
Mountain regions	Erosion (percentage of surface area eroded)
	Biodiversity (key species counts)
	Access to key sites (hours' wait)

Managed wildlife	Species health (reproductive success, species parks diversity) Use intensity (ratio of visitors to game) Encroachment (percentage of park affected by unauthorised activity)
Ecologically unique	Ecosystem degradation (number and mix of sites species, percentage area with change in cover) Stress on site (number of operators using site) Number of tourist sitings of key species (percentage success)
Urban environments	Safety (crime numbers) Waste counts (amounts of rubbish, costs) Pollution (air pollution counts)
Cultural sites (built)	Site degradation (restoration/repair costs) Structure degradation (precipitation acidity, air pollution counts) Safety (crime levels)
Cultural sites	Potential social stress (ratio average income (traditional) of tourists/locals) In season sites (percentage of vendors open year round) Antagonism (reported incidents between locals and tourists)
Small islands	Currency leakage (percentage of loss from total tourism revenues) Ownership (percentage foreign ownership of tourism establishments) Water availability (costs, remaining supply)

Some publications have discussed tourism and sustainability from the perspective of codes of ethics. While indicators are variables that are identified and used to measure and monitor tourism impacts, codes of ethics or conduct are lists designed to elicit a change in behaviour of particular stakeholder groups; a form of compliance for acceptable behaviour at a tourism setting.

The *Beyond the Green Horizon* paper on sustainable tourism is a good example of this form of education. To Tourism Concern, sustainable tourism is: tourism and associated infrastructures that, both now and in the future: operate within natural capacities for the regeneration and future productivity of natural resources; recognise the contribution that people and communities, customs and lifestyles, make to the tourism experience; accept that these people must have an equitable share in the economic benefits of tourism; are guided by the wishes of local people and communities in the host areas.

Nothing is measured but 'rules' are stated for the purpose of prompting or reinforcing this appropriate behaviour. The Tourism Industry Association of Canada (1995) joined forces with the National Round Table on the Environment and the Economy in creating a document that demonstrates commitment and responsibility to protecting the environment through cooperation with other sectors and governments at all levels.

Their sustainable tourism guidelines were developed for tourists, the tourism industry, industry associations, accommodation, food services, tour operators, and Ministries of Tourism. Each of these sections contains appropriate guidelines that deal with policy and planning; the tourism experience; the host community; development; natural, cultural, and historic resources; conservation of natural resources; environmental protection; marketing; research and education; public awareness; industry cooperation; and the global village.

A final publication that merits attention in this section is the work of the Federation of Nature and National Parks of Europe (1993). Its comprehensive look at sustainable tourism in Europe's nature and national parks provides good insight into the challenge of implementing sustainability in that part of the world.

Many of the protected areas in Europe are situated in rural working landscapes (e.g. England, Wales, Luxembourg) and must contend with different pressures as compared with some of the larger and less densely populated areas surrounding the protected areas of Australia and New Zealand, Canada, and the United States.

However, Europe also contains many large national parks and biosphere reserves that are maintained accordingly. In both cases (rural and wilderness environments) policy-makers and practitioners are charged with the task of implementing sustainable tourism in these varied settings. The European national parks document recognises that people must be able to improve the quality of their lives, maintain jobs, improve their economy, enjoy their cultures, and promote harmony between cultures.

These must be accomplished with an eye to environmental education, political support for the environment, and the protection of heritage values through restorative projects and direct practical help.

Sustainable tourism, however, is not without its critics. Hunter (1995), for example, suggests that the current approach to sustainable tourism development is one that is flawed because it condones the planning and management of tourism in a manner inconsistent with the design of sustainable development. In particular, tourism does not adequately address issues of geographical scale and intersectoral cooperation which are so important to achieving sustainable development.

Furthermore, Macbeth (1994) calls attention to the fact that sustainable tourism is more reactionary than proactive in nature. Macbeth suggests that 'the history of capitalism is full of examples of how reactionary tendencies are easily co-opted by capitalism to sustain its own existence, thus extending the status quo of exploitive relations rather than overthrowing them'. This will continue to occur, according to Macbeth, unless the present form of capitalism is overcome.

McKercher (1993a) feels that tourism is vulnerable to losing sustainability for four main reasons. First, tourism is not recognised as a natural resource-dependent industry; second, the tourism industry is invisible, especially in urban areas; third, tourism is electorally weak, with little support in government; and fourth, there is a distinct lack of leadership driving the industry, which ultimately makes tourism vulnerable to attacks from other land users. McKercher cites the example of resource use in northern Ontario as a case in point. In this region the economy has been dominated politically by the large extractive industries (forestry and mining).

The disaggregated structure of the tourism industry in Ontario's north (predominantly outfitters and lodges) prevents it from having any political decision-making influence at all.

Other critical reviews of tourism and sustainability include Goodall and Cater's (1996) belief that sustainable tourism will probably not be achieved, despite the most committed environmental performance, and Burr's (1995) work illustrating that sustainable tourism development is unlikely to occur unless the people of rural tourism communities work together to make it happen.

There appears to be certain agreement that if sustainability is to occur at all, it must be done at the local level, and perhaps shaped loosely by a broader national or international policy.

The notions of policy and local participation have been examined by Laarman and Gregersen (1994), who feel that sustainable nature tourism policy must include the following three areas: (1) national support and advanced planning; (2) appropriate pricing and revenue policies; and (3) local participation and benefits.

CASE STUDY

SUSTAINABLE TOURISM AND THE GREEN VILLAGES OF AUSTRIA

Understanding the vital link between landscape and tourism, Austria has embarked upon a policy of sustainable tourism with the aim of preservation and an overall improvement in the quality of the natural environment.

Specifically, the following measures have been proposed:

- A straightening out of the demand curve to avoid peak demands and burdens;
- Reducing the consumption of space for tourism;
- Preservation of natural landscapes;
- Cooperation with other industries, in particular agriculture and forestry;
- Professionalism within the industry; and
- A changing of the behaviour of tourists.

One of the most significant programmes in Austria is the Green Village endeavour, which is designed to allow communities to accommodate the growing demands of tourism in a sustainable way.

Towns are encouraged to incorporate solar panels in their heating, restrict building height to no more than three storeys, keep parking places a minimum of 80 metres away from buildings to eliminate noise and fumes, keep motorways at least 3 km away from Green Villages, restrict vehicular traffic through villages, designate cycle paths, recycle, restrict building to the town site only, eliminate single-crop farming in adjacent farmlands, discriminate in favour of sustainable craftsmen, build hotels using natural products, insist that farmers be able to sell their products locally, and use local, natural pharmaceuticals.

Such a philosophy, it is thought, will benefit both communities and the tourism industry.

Some authors have identified unique sustainable tourism market segments, suggesting that each uses the natural environment, has long-term economic benefits, involves continuous environmental protection, and stimulates local community development. Although each of the foregoing variables can be used to define sustainable tourism, it is important to realise that AT may be no more sustainable than Cancún and the nearby Cozumel Island if improperly managed, and there are decidedly few examples proven to be properly managed. It is therefore potentially dangerous to look at sustainable tourism as a specific market, instead of from site-specific or regional case studies.

The illustration recognises that in essence the tourism industry experiences a tremendous degree of fragmentation by virtue of the fact that consistency in sustainability is not likely to be found across all sectors. The aim, then, for sustainability is to ensure that all aspects of the industry are working in concert. In addition, the figure incorporates the notion of both human and physical elements working within each of the four sectors; that is, the fact that the people working at a physical attraction very much dictate the extent to which sustainability is achieved at the site.

CONCEPTUALISING TOURISM AND SUSTAINABILITY

In the previous discussion, mass tourism, AT, and sustainable tourism have been analysed individually. In a general sense, the illustration provides a good sense of the relative size of mass tourism and alternative tourism according to the corresponding circles in the diagram.

Although mass tourism may be said to be predominantly unsustainable, more recently new and existing developments in the industry have attempted to encourage more sustainable practice through various measures, some of which include the controlled use of electricity, a rotating laundry schedule, and the disposal of wastes (the arrow indicates that there is a move towards an increasing degree of sustainability in this sector). On the other hand, the illustration indicates that most forms of alternative tourism are sustainable in nature (in theory).

The AT sphere is shown to comprise two types of tourism, socio-cultural tourism and ecotourism. Socio-cultural AT includes, for example, rural or farm tourism, where a large portion of the touristic experience is founded upon the cultural milieu that corresponds to the environment in which farms operate. Ecotourism, however, involves a type of tourism that is less socio-cultural in its orientation, and more dependent upon nature and natural resources as the primary component or motivator of the trip, hence the division within the AT sphere. The focus of this book is on this lower half of the AT circle only, and the belief that ecotourism is distinct from mass tourism and various other forms of AT.

Given the emergent wealth of literature on tourism, AT and sustainability, one cannot help but reflect on where we have been, but also on what is missing. Researchers have written countless reports, codes of conduct, guidelines, and indicators, but few attempts and successes can be drawn upon to point the direction, as illustrated in Butler's (1991) sobering analysis of tourism, environment, and sustainable development. Perhaps it is still too early, and these anticipated successes will be the next stage of tourism's rather tenuous relationship with sustainability.

However, there is a pressing need to move beyond the rhetoric; beyond the table and into practice, for according to Leslie (1994:35), 'tourism in terms of practice in developing countries is a mirror in which we see the possible mistakes identifiable retrospectively in the development and wasteful consumerist lifestyles of the west'. One cannot discount the importance of the public in operationalising AT and sustainable tourism practices.

People have the power to demand goods and services that are developed and presented in an ecologically friendly manner. The public must demand accountability of tourism products, and tourism service providers must demonstrate an adherence to an appropriate vision in striving for meritorious achievements in the area of sustainable development. In doing so, it is those who achieve such lofty levels who may ultimately prosper financially.

ECOTOURISM AND ECOTOURISTS

Until recently, there has been some confusion surrounding the etymology or origin of the term 'ecotourism', as evident in the tremendous volume of literature on the topic. For example, Orams (1995) and Hvenegaard (1994) write that the term can be traced back only to the late 1980s, while others suggest that it can be traced to the late 1970s, through the work of Miller on ecodevelopment.

One of the consistent themes emergent in the literature supports the fact that Ceballos-Lascuráin was the first to coin the phrase in the early 1980s. He defined it as 'traveling to relatively undisturbed or uncontaminated natural areas with the specific objective of studying, admiring, and enjoying the scenery and its wild plants and animals, as well as any existing cultural manifestations (both past and present) found in these areas'. In an interview, Ceballos-Lascuráin illustrates that his initial reference to the phrase occurred in 1983, while he was in the process of developing PRONATURA, an NGO in Mexico.

Recently, however, the term has been traced further back to the work of Hetzer (1965), who used it to explain the intricate relationship between tourists and the environments and cultures in which they interact. Hetzer identified four fundamental pillars that needed to be followed for a more responsible form of tourism.

These included:

- Minimum environmental impact;
- Minimum impact on—and maximum respect for—host cultures;
- Maximum economic benefits to the host country's grassroots; and
- Maximum 'recreational' satisfaction to participating tourists.

The development of the concept of ecotourism grew, according to Hetzer (personal communication, October 1997), as a culmination of dissatisfaction with governments' and society's negative approach to development, especially from an ecological point of view.

Nelson (1994) also adopts this particular stand in illustrating that the idea of ecotourism is in fact an old one, which manifested itself during the late 1960s and early 1970s, when researchers became concerned over inappropriate use of natural resources. Nelson suggests that the term 'eco-development' was introduced as a means by which to reduce such development.

In other related research, Fennell (1998) found evidence of Canadian government 'ecotours' which were operational during the mid-1970s. These ecotours centred around the Trans-Canada Highway and were developed on the basis of different ecological zones found along the course of the highway.

The first of these encounters was developed in 1976. Based on the ecozone concept, they were felt to be rather progressive for the time despite the lack of a focused look at low impact, sustainability, community development, and the moral philosophy labels that are attached to ecotourism in the 1990s.

The ecotours were developed at a time when the Canadian government felt it important to allow Canadian and foreign travellers to appreciate the human-land relationship in Canada, through the interpretation of the natural environment. Although a set definition of ecotourism was not provided, each of the ecotour guides contains the following foreword:

Ecotours are prepared by the Canadian Forestry Service to help you, as a traveller, understand the features of the landscape you see as you cross the country. Both natural and human history are described and interpreted. The route covered by the Ecotours is divided into major landscape types, or Ecozones, and a map of each Ecozone shows the location of interesting features (identified by code numbers). While most features can be seen from your car, stops are suggested for some of them.

Distances between points of interest are given in kilometres. Where side trips are described, distances are given to the turnoff from the highway. You will derive the maximum value from this Ecotour if you keep a record of the distance travelled and read the information on each point of interest before reaching it.

Fennell goes on to suggest that ecotourism most likely has a convergent evolution, 'where many places and people independently responded to the need for more nature travel opportunities in line with society's efforts to become more ecologically minded', as also suggested by Nelson. This evidence comes at a time when researchers have been struggling to find common ground between ecotourism and its relationship to other forms of tourism, related and unrelated.

There seems to be universal acceptance of the fact that ecotourism was viable long before the 1980s in practice, if not in name. For example, Blangy and Nielson (1993) illustrate that the travel department of the American Museum of Natural History has conducted natural history tours since 1953. Probably the finest examples of the evolution of ecotourism can be found in the African wildlife-based examples of tourism developed in the early twentieth century and, to some, the nature tourism enterprises of the mid-nineteenth century. There are examples in the literature that illustrate that human beings, at least since the Romantic period, have travelled to wilderness for the intrinsic nature of the experience.

Nash writes that during the nineteenth century many people travelled both in Europe and North America for the primary purpose of enjoying the outdoors, as illustrated in the following passage:

Alexis de Tocqeville resolved to see wilderness during his 1831 trip to the United States, and in Michigan Territory in July the young Frenchman found himself at last on the fringe of civilization. But when he informed the frontiersmen of his desire to travel for pleasure into the primitive forest, they thought him mad. The Americans required considerable persuasion from Tocqueville to convince them that his interests lay in matters other than lumbering or land speculation.

Tocqueville was after something that we consider as an essential psychological factor in travel: novelty. Nash (1982) credits the intellectual revolution in the eighteenth and nineteenth centuries as the push needed to inspire the belief that unmodified nature could act as a deep spiritual and psychological tonic. It required the emergence of a group of affluent and cultured persons who largely resided in urban environments to garnish this appreciation.

For these people, Nash writes, 'wilderness could become an intriguing novelty and even a deep spiritual and psychological need'. In the United States, the sentiment at the time was not as strong as it was in Europe, where 'as late as the 1870s almost all nature tourists on the American frontier continued to be foreigners'. When Americans did start travelling to the wild parts of their country it was the privileged classes that held the exclusive rights. A trip to Yellowstone in the 1880s, according to O'Gara (1996), was about three times as expensive as travel to Europe at the time. There was no question that those from the city were especially taken with Yellowstone's majesty, but their mannerisms left much to be desired, as evident in an account of such tourists by Rudyard Kipling:

It is not the ghastly vulgarity, the oozing, rampant Bessemer steel self-sufficiency and ignorance of the men that revolts me, so much as the display of these same qualities in the womenfolk.... All the young ladies...remarked that [Old Faithful] was 'elegant' and betook themselves to writing their names in the bottoms of the shallow pools. Nature fixes the insult indelibly, and the after-years will learn that 'Hattie,' 'Sadie,' 'Mamie,' 'Sophie,' and so forth, have taken out their hairpins and scrawled in the face of Old Faithful.

CONCEPTS AND VARIABLES

Given the ambiguity associated with the historical origins of ecotourism, the purpose of the present section is to identify the key features, concepts, and principles of the term, especially the link between nature tourism (or nature-oriented tourism) and ecotourism. For example, Laarman and Durst, in their early reference to ecotourism, defined it as a nature tourism in which the 'traveller is drawn to a destination because of his or her interest in one or more features of that destination's natural history.

The visit combines education, recreation, and often adventure'. In addition, these authors were perhaps the first to make reference to nature tourism's hard and soft dimensions, based on the physical rigour of the experience and also the level of interest in natural history. Laarman and Durst suggested that scientists would in most likelihood be more dedicated than casual in their pursuit of ecotourism, and that some types of ecotourists would be more willing to endure hardships than others in order to secure their experiences.

The letter 'B' identifies a harder ecotourism experience based on a more difficult or rigorous experience, and also based on the dedication shown by the ecotourist relative to the interest in the activity. A subsequent definition by these authors identifies a conceptual difference between ecotourism and nature tourism. In recognising the difficulties in defining nature tourism, they establish both a narrow and broad scope to its definition.

Narrowly, they say, it refers to operators running nature-oriented tours; however, broadly it applies to tourism's use of natural resources including beaches and country landscapes. In their research they define nature tourism as 'tourism focused principally on natural resources such as relatively undisturbed parks and natural areas, wetlands, wildlife reserves, and other areas of protected flora, fauna, and habitats'. Given this perspective, there appears to be some consensus mounting in the literature that describes ecotourism as one part of a broader nature-based tourism. This becomes evident in the discussion by Goodwin, who wrote that *nature tourism* encompasses all forms of tourism—mass tourism, adventure tourism, low-impact tourism, ecotourism—which use natural resources in a wild or undeveloped form—including species, habitat, landscape, scenery and salt and fresh-water features. Nature tourism is travel for the purpose of enjoying undeveloped natural areas or wildlife.

And conversely, that *ecotourism* is low impact nature tourism which contributes to the maintenance of species and habitats either directly through a contribution to conservation and/or indirectly by providing revenue to the local community sufficient for local people to value, and therefore protect, their wildlife heritage area as a source of income.

Apart from the differences apparent in the work of Goodwin, some of the key variables or principles that separate ecotourism from its more broad-based nature counterpart include an educative component and a sustainability component, and the ethical nature of the experience.

In view of the relationship between the two concepts, there does seem to be some merit in linking ecotourism to nature tourism, given the tremendous variety of nature-related tourism interests. However, there is also ambiguity in separating nature tourism from other forms of tourism, all of which rely upon the use of natural resources.

Even mass, resort-based tourism relies upon undeveloped resources (i.e. beaches and the ocean) as a central component of the product and experience. An important aspect of Goodwin's discussion includes the fact that not all types of nature tourism are necessarily compatible with each other or the environment. Examples include hunting and birdwatching, which place different demands on the resource base, and users, and which have a different managerial focus (if managed at all) which is based on the consumptive nature of these activities.

The importance of management in guiding the ecotourism product was central to the work of Fennell and Eagles (1990), who included the resource tour as the principal component of the ecotourism experience; the service industry, including tour operation, government policy, resource management, and community development; and the visitor experience, based on marketing, visitor management, and visitor attitudes. In their work, Fennell and Eagles recognised the value in management from the visitors' perspective, but also from the community and resource-based perspectives.

CASE STUDY

NATURE TOURISM IN TEXAS

Ecotourism in Texas provides an excellent example of how ecotourism is subsumed by nature tourism. In Texas, nature tourism is defined as 'discretionary travel to natural areas that conserves the environmental, social and cultural values while generating an economic benefit to the local community'.

Although hunting and fishing are reported to be traditional mainstays of nature tourism in Texas, the Task Force on Nature Tourism states that non-consumptive activities such as bird and wildlife watching, nature study and photography, hiking, camping, rafting, and hiking have experienced the greatest growth over the past few years. In Texas, the task force reports that tourism is the third largest industry in Texas, generating $23 billion annually, with the potential to replace oil and gas, and manufacturing as the highest income earner by the turn of the century.

The Great Texas Coastal Birding Trail is a key ecotourism attraction in the Lone Star State. The goal of this trail is to increase the opportunities for nature tourism in the coastal communities of Texas, in addition to conveying the value of conservation to people living in the region. Although the trail was conceived by the Texas Parks and Wildlife Department, it was made possible by transportation enhancement funds and the Texas Department of Transportation.

The trail utilises existing transportation infrastructure (viewing platforms and boardwalks are being added on a continual basis) in creating recreational, economic, and educational opportunities for local people and tourists alike. Upon completion in 1998, it will comprise three main sections and span over 600 miles of coastline, incorporating some 300 birding stops in nine wildlife refuges, eleven state parks, one national seashore, and several city and county preserves.

The variability of approaches used to define ecotourism has quite naturally given way to many comprehensive approaches used to understand the term. In her approach to the concept, Ziffer (1989) acknowledges the variety of descriptive terms such as nature travel, adventure travel, and cultural travel, which are largely activity based; and also the value-laden terms such as responsible, alternative, and ethical tourism, which underscore the need to consider impacts and the consequences of travel.

Ziffer feels that nature tourism, while not necessarily ecologically sound in principle, concentrates more on the motivation and the behaviour of the individual tourist. Conversely, ecotourism is much more difficult to attain owing to its overall comprehensiveness (the need for planning and the achievement of societal goals). She defines ecotourism as follows: a form of tourism inspired primarily by the natural history of an area, including its indigenous cultures. The ecotourist visits relatively undeveloped areas in the spirit of appreciation, participation and sensitivity. The ecotourist practises a non-consumptive use of wildlife and natural resources and contributes to the visited area through labour or financial means aimed at directly benefiting the conservation of the site and the economic well-being of the local residents.

The visit should strengthen the ecotourist's appreciation and dedication to conservation issues in general, and to the specific needs of the locale. Ecotourism also implies a managed approach by the host country or region which commits itself to establishing and maintaining the sites with the participation of local residents, marketing them appropriately, enforcing regulations, and using the proceeds of the enterprise to fund the area's land management as well as community development.

Like Ziffer's, the following definition by Wallace and Pierce (1996:848) is also quite comprehensive, acknowledging the importance of a broad number of variables. To these authors, ecotourism is travel to relatively undisturbed natural areas for study, enjoyment, or volunteer assistance.

It is travel that concerns itself with the flora, fauna, geology, and ecosystems of an area, as well as the people (caretakers) who live nearby, their needs, their culture, and their relationship to the land, it *[sic]* views natural areas both as 'home to all of us' in a global sense ('eco' meaning home) but 'home to nearby residents' specifically. It is envisioned as a tool for both conservation and sustainable development—especially in areas where local people are asked to forgo the consumptive use of resources for others.

Wallace and Pierce suggest that this tourism may be said to be true ecotourism if it addresses six principles:

- It entails a type of use that minimises negative impacts to the environment and to local people.
- It increases the awareness and understanding of an area's natural and cultural systems and the subsequent involvement of visitors in issues affecting those systems.
- It contributes to the conservation and management of legally protected and other natural areas.
- It maximises the early and long-term participation of local people in the decision-making process that determines the kind and amount of tourism that should occur.
- It directs economic and other benefits to local people that complement rather than overwhelm or replace traditional practices (farming, fishing, social systems, etc.).
- It provides special opportunities for local people and nature tourism employees to utilise and visit natural areas and learn more about the wonders that other visitors come to see.

Both Ziffer and Wallace and Pierce recognise that for ecotourism to exist, it must strive to reach very lofty goals. By comparison, the Ecotourism Society advocates a much more general definition of the term, one that advocates a 'middle-of-the-road' or passive position, and one which is more easily articulated. This organisation defines ecotourism as 'responsible travel to natural areas which conserves the environment and improves the welfare of local people'. Preece *et al.* (1995) used the Australian National Ecotourism Strategy definition of ecotourism in their overview of biodiversity and ecotourism, which is also one that is quite general in nature. The strategy defines ecotourism as nature-based tourism that involves education and interpretation of the natural environment and is managed to be ecologically sustainable.

Although quite straightforward, these definitions leave much to the interpretation of the reader. Definitions of ecotourism over the years have emphasised different aspects of nature, relationships with local people, conservation and preservation, and so on. The main issue confronting researchers who are bent on structuring definitions is either to include a whole series of principles and variables related to the term, or to try to isolate specific variables which can be used to best represent the overall concept. The fact of the matter is that, either implicitly or explicitly, such variables or principles need to be more effectively used to observe, measure, and evaluate what is and what is not ecotourism.

In line with the previous discussion, Bottrill and Pearce (1995) point to the fact that the rich array of definitions of ecotourism has done little to clarify its meaning. Instead they opt for a means by which to operationalise ecotourism through the development of a set of measurable key elements for participant, operators, and managers.

In an analysis of 22 ecotourism ventures only five were classified as ecotourism using the following criteria: motivation (physical activity, education, participation), sensitive management, and protected area status. The authors submit that more work should follow to further define and modify the points and criteria raised.

Their paper quite nicely addressed the need to move beyond definition to a position where ecotourism operators should be open to ethical and operational scrutiny by the public and other concerned stakeholders. This leads to the contentions of Miller and Kaye (1993:37), who suggest that 'the merits or deficiencies of ecotourism...are not to be found in any label *per se*, but in the quality and intensity of specific environmental and social impacts of human activity in an ecological system'.

Some researchers have discussed the placing of time on determining whether tourists are ecotourists or not. For example, Ballantine and Eagles (1994) suggested that ecotourists could be defined on the basis of an intention to learn about nature, an intention to visit undisturbed areas, and a commitment of at least 33 per cent of their time to the first two criteria. Blamey (1995) sees some inherent problems with the implementation of such a measure.

The time factor advocated by Ballantine and Eagles may be applicable in the safari ecotourism settings of Africa, but could be more problematic in less structured ecotourism settings and situations.

For instance, Blamey asks if a ten-minute guided nature tour qualifies as a day ecotourism visit. Yet one can't help but grapple for acceptable definitions of ecotourism, as Ballantine and Eagles and others have done; the same has occurred with the meaning of 'tourism' in the past, and similarly for many other social science disciplines. While the tourism literature has seen fit to define 'tourism' under many different circumstances—time, space, economics, whole systems models—the same will likely occur for ecotourism. It depends on who is operationalising the concept, and for what purpose.

Given the foregoing discussion, I have elected to provide my own definition of ecotourism. In light of the review of a significant number of definitions, it is based on what is felt to be the most important aspects of the phenomenon and on the need to be concise in including such principles. It is as follows:

Ecotourism is a sustainable form of natural resource-based tourism that focuses primarily on experiencing and learning about nature, and which is ethically managed to be low-impact, non-consumptive, and locally oriented (control, benefits, and scale). It typically occurs in natural areas, and should contribute to the conservation or preservation of such areas.

Admittedly, this is more comprehensive than other definitions, but it strives to recognise that having been identified as a separate form of tourism, ecotourism must be classified and defined as such in order to maintain an element of homogeneity. This feeling is not expressed without some hesitation based on the writing of some other authors who imply that most people who demand ecotourism want a softer, easily accessible, front-country type of experience and that the 'popular' form of ecotourism demands mechanised transport, easy accessibility, and a high level of services. The relationship between this very soft form of ecotourism and other types of tourism has not been fully examined.

The belief in this book is that much more than simply demand must go into the understanding of ecotourism and ecotourists. In an attempt to stay clear of this fine line, a harder stance on ecotourism is adopted. Furthermore, a stricter definition of ecotourism begs for the employment of measurable indicators in determining what is and is not ecotourism. An early example of this type of thinking can be seen through the efforts of Shores (1992), who identified the need for higher standards in the ecotourism industry through the implementation of a scale to measure the level of achievement according to the principles of ecotourism.

The scale ranges from 0 (travellers made aware of the fragility of the environment in a general capacity) to 5 (a trip where the entire system was operating in an environmental way). The reader will most certainly recognise the absence of culture as a fundamental principle of ecotourism in the aforementioned definition. This definition views culture only inasmuch as the benefits from ecotourism accrue to local people, recognising that culture, whether exotic or not, is part of any tourism experience. If culture was a primary theme of ecotourism then it would be cultural tourism.

There is no doubt that culture can be part of the ecotourism experience; the point is, however, that it is more likely to be a secondary motivation to the overall experience, not primary as in the case of nature and natural resources. For example, in a study completed by Fennell (1990) it was found that there was no statistically significant difference between the average Canadian traveller and ecotourists as regards many cultural attractions, including museums and art galleries, local festivals and events, and local crafts.

If one is to accept the fact that there currently exists an uneven base with which conceptually and empirically to determine differences in forms or types of nature tourists, it should thus be the task of researchers to focus on the isolation of variables by which to understand better the manifest and latent traits of these groups. Past research has combined education, experience, and learning into a comprehensive model of wilderness education. In this model learning is a key feature and is a variable which may also provide a basis from which to compare the on-site characteristics of the *nature tourism experience* over other familiar variables such as management, culture, economics, and benefits.

Other important variables to be considered (besides learning) may include the employment of skills or actions in the pursuit of the primary activity; the degree to which one subscribes to a strong or weak sense of what might be considered as 'biological or preservationist affect' (the emotional tie that one has with plants, animals, or nature as a whole); and finally the degree of impact (consumptive to non-consumptive) caused by the type of tourism.

More specifically, learning relates to the need to gain knowledge on-site through interpretation and the information provided by guides and other facilitators. Further research in this area might endeavour to understand the differences or similarities between novelty and curiosity, and learning. In whalewatching, for example, many people just want to see a whale (novelty or curiosity), while conversely others want a more comprehensive learning-based whale-watching experience.

In addition, future research may wish to examine the relationship between knowledge and learning in nature tourism. Knowledge can be thought of as information one applies to a situation, whereas learning is something that results from participation.

There is little question that nature tourists learn from the experience, but it is important to view learning in terms of the primary motivation of the tourist. Second, skill may also be examined because it demonstrates that the application of skill is often employed at the expense of the environment rather than in some other benign fashion. Skill also relates to the previous discussion on primary motivation for participation in the nature tourism activity.

There can be a strong case made for the assumption that ecotourism is learning based in its orientation, while other forms of nature tourism (e.g. mountain climbing) may be more skills based in their orientation. Third, biological affect may also provide some inroads in differentiating between nature tourists because it seeks to understand the perceptual place that flora, fauna, geological features, etc. occupy in the mind of the tourist.

Consequently, the feelings of such users may dictate the forms of recreation participated in, and the effects of such activities on the natural world. This type of thinking relates to the work of Kellert (1985) on the attitudes of people towards animals on the basis of nine variables (negativistic and dominionistic as the most negative attitudes, versus naturalistic and ecologistic as the most positive).

Kellert suggests that people and the activities they choose can be correlated with these values towards wildlife.

Finally, consumptiveness of the activity (non-consumptive to consumptive) should be considered to illustrate that all forms of outdoor recreation and tourism have some type of impact—however insignificant—on the resource base, with some being less severe than others (consumptive forms of tourism include those that are said to consume resources, such as hunting and fishing).

Despite how the term *nature tourism* has evolved in the recent past, it is still difficult to equate it with activities that are more consumptive in their orientation (e.g. hunting). The activities that we now group under nature tourism, including adventure tourism, fishing, hunting, whalewatching, and ecotourism, might best be labelled *natural resource-based tourism*.

This latter categorisation implies a element of use, which we know corresponds to any form of tourism that occurs outside and which relies specifically on the natural resource base. Furthermore, it is more analogous to the continuum of conservation (saving for use) and preservation (saving from use).

Ecotourism, although it entails use, should apply more to the preservation end of this continuum, while hunting and fishing relate more to the aspect of conservation. This sentiment related to the work of Ewert (1997), who writes that 'resource-based' tourism includes a variety of tourism endeavours including ecotourism, adventure tourism, and indigenous tourism, and their various activities.

CASE STUDY

NATURE TOURISM IN THE USA

The Recreation Executive report of the US Forest Service (1994) illustrates that nature-based recreation trends as we approach the year 2000 show increases in many non-consumptive outdoor activities. Outdoor photography is up 23 per cent, wildlife watching is up 16 per cent, backpacking is up 34 per cent, and day hiking is up 34 per cent. Also, the National Survey on Recreation and the Environment, a study conducted by the US federal government, concluded that of a number of outdoor recreation activities, birding, hiking, and backpacking experienced the most significant growth in participation between 1982-83 and 1994-95.

Birdwatching increased 155 per cent, hiking increased 93 per cent, and backpacking increased 73 per cent. Conversely, hunting and fishing experienced negative growth over this period of time (-12 per cent and -9 per cent, respectively).

Further to this, the White House Conference on Tourism in October 1995 indicated the following with respect to the nonconsumptive use of birds:

Number of participants:	$25 million
Retail sales:	$5 billion
Wages and salaries:	$4 billion
Full and part-time jobs:	191,000
Tax revenues	
State sales:	$306 million
State income:	$74 million
Federal income:	$516 million
Total economic output:	$16 billion

ADVENTURE TOURISM OR ECOTOURISM

A few hours of mountain climbing turn a villain and a saint into two rather equal creatures. Exhaustion is the shortest way to equality and fraternity—and liberty is added eventually by sleep.—Nietzsche

A close cousin that has developed alongside ecotourism is adventure travel, which in some circles is felt to subsume ecotourism. For example, in suggesting that ecotourism is a branch of adventure tourism, Dyess (1997:2) admits that he did not have a full appreciation of the heated disagreement that 'exists over the semantics of the two terms, as proponents of ecotourism and adventure travel strive to define and sanctify their own approach to travel'.

In a general sense, differentiation between the two forms of travel can simply be based on the type of activity pursued (again, with respect to the primary motivation in participating in the activity).

However, in cases where activities are broadly categorised as either ecotourism or adventure tourism, there may be problems, as evident in the following example. Tourism Canada has defined adventure tourism as 'an outdoor leisure activity that takes place in an unusual, exotic, remote or wilderness destination, involves some form of unconventional means of transportation, and tends to be associated with low or high levels of activity'.

The following is a list of adventure travel activities developed by the Canadian Tourism Commission (CTC) under this definition:

- Nature observation;
- Wildlife viewing (e.g. birding, whalewatching);
- Water adventure products (e.g. canoeing, kayaking);
- Land adventure products (e.g. hiking, climbing);
- Winter adventure products (e.g. dog sledding, cross-country skiing); and
- Air adventure products, including hot air ballooning, hang-gliding, air safaris, bungee jumping, and parachuting.

The point to be made from this example is that both ecotourism and adventure tourism products may adhere to the CTC's definition, despite the fact that to many there is a clear distinction between nature observation (ecotourism) and kayaking (adventure tourism). Clearly, further analysis of these activities is required in order to detect similarities and differences.

However, while activity is important (an outdoor pursuit) to identifying adventure activities, Priest (1990) writes that there must be an element of uncertainty associated with the event.

The answer to the question of how adventure and non-adventure tourism experiences like ecotourism differ may lie in the realm of social psychology, which examines why participation occurs from a cognitive and behavioural standpoint (instead of some arbitrary basis established on the basis of setting and other such variables). Both Ewert (1985) and Hall (1992) write that it is risk that plays a primary role in the decision to engage in adventurous activities. In addition, Hall suggests that it is the activity more than the setting that provides the dominant attraction for pursuit of adventure recreation and tourism.

Two other factors in analysing one's motivation to engage in risk-related activities include challenge and skill, the fundamental variables behind Csikszentmihalyi's (1990) model of flow. Individuals who are said to have reached a state of flow have matched their personal skills with the challenges of a particular activity. Flow includes a number of main elements as defined by Csikszentmihalyi.

These include:

- *Total immersion into the activity*: This relates to the elimination of distractions that enable the person to lose touch with his or her surroundings.
- *Enhanced concentration*: A result of the previous factor that allows the participant to forget about the unpleasant tasks that may be associated with the activity.
- *Actions directed at fulfilling the goal*: The goals and objectives of the

event are clearly understood by the participant, who knows how best to approach the situation.

- *The activity requires skill and challenge*: The relationship between these two variables is important in that if skill far exceeds challenge, boredom will result, whereas if challenge far exceeds skill, anxiety will result.
- *Flow involves control*: The participant exercises control over his or her movements and the situation, with a degree of anticipation of the events which will unfold.
- *A sense of transcendentalism*: Here the participant has the experience of transcending his or her physical being, as rooted on the face of the earth, to reach some higher level of understanding or being. A sense of oneness with the surroundings or objects involved in the experience is felt.
- *The loss of time*: Frequently participants feel as though they have been involved for a short period of time (e.g. one hour), when in fact they have been involved for a long periods of time (e.g. four hours).

Csikszentmihalyi (1990) suggests that flow is not necessarily restricted to those who engage in adventurous activities, but also includes those, for example, playing chess or physicians engaged in surgery. According to Hall, then, it may be the desire or the enhanced desire to experience the state of flow that moves individuals to participate in risk or adventure-related activities.

To Quinn (1990), adventure lies deep within the spiritual, emotional, intellectual, and objective spheres of humanity; and is the eternal seduction of the hidden. More specifically, Quinn argues that adventure is a desire for a condition that is absent within the individual. Under rather tenuous conditions, the individual must harbour doubt as to the adequacy of his or her ability. The further one attempts to go beyond one's perceived personal talents, the more intense the adventurous situation becomes. It is this element of unknown that led Einstein to suggest that 'the most beautiful and deepest experience a man can have is the sense of the mysterious'. The adventure experience therefore is one that is not discrete but rather one that varies in intensity.

The result is that in today's marketplace, tourists are able to select from a broad range of hard and soft adventure experiences, offering associated degrees of risk and uncertainty.

According to Christiansen (1990), it is the task of the adventure tour operator to provide the client with an adequate perception of risk, while ensuring a high level of safety and security. This is accomplished through an accident-free history, good planning, and the maintenance of the highest level of leadership, skills, and experience.

Christiansen provides a good understanding of the difference between soft- and hard-core adventure experiences. The soft adventure activities in the figure are pursued by those interested in a perceived risk and adventure with little actual risk, whereas the hard adventure examples included are known by both the participant and the service provider to have a high level of risk (if, indeed a service provider is involved in the experience).

In related research the link between motivation and level of experience in mountain climbers was analysed by Ewert, who based his research on the premise that the perception of danger is important in the experience of the risk recreation participant. From a survey of climbers at Mount Ranier National Park, Washington, he found that inexperienced climbers participated for recognition, escape, and social reasons. Conversely, the experienced climbers were motivated by more intrinsic reasons including exhilaration, challenge, personal testing, decision-making, and locus of control.

The implications of the research are such that over time, climbers who continue with a risk recreation activity such as scuba-diving, mountain climbing, and spelunking (cave exploration) may require conditions that are less crowded, more rugged, and less controlled than their novice counterparts.

Fennell and Eagles focused on the element of risk in examining potential differences between adventure travel, ecotourism, and mass tourism in the framework. Here it is implied that preparation and training, known/unknown results and risks, and certainty and safety are all variables that may be used to differentiate between these forms of tourism. The figure demonstrates that the three kinds of activity are not mutually exclusive; ecotourism may share some elements of the other two experiences, while still remaining distinct from mass tourism and adventure tourism.

As suggested earlier, the overlap between these three appears to have become stronger over the past few years, to the point where many studies, usually government or marketing ones, have considered them as almost completely synonymous.

Depending on the setting and situation, ACE either expands or contracts to represent different concentrations of adventure, culture, and ecotourism, either in name alone or in product content. Those situations that are classed solely as ecotourism avoid the inclusion of conditions that relate to culture tourism or adventure tourism (or both).

At the same time, there is the recognition that a continuum exists between hard- and soft-path ecotourism experiences. This figure (and the book) attempts to demonstrate that ecotourism should be considered as unique according to its function and role within the tourism marketplace, a stance which is based on the facts that (1) there is little empirical evidence demonstrating homogeneity between adventure tourism, culture tourism, and ecotourism, and (2) there may be an associated dilution factor or effect on ecotourism if these three types of tourism merge into a combined form.

TOURIST TYPOLOGIES

THE GENERAL LITERATURE

Perhaps as a function of the tremendous demand for different types of travel experiences tourism has blossomed with a rich array of terms describing different types of vacation experiences in different settings, with virtually no research available to describe these various 'types' systematically. Historically, tourism research has tended to concentrate not on tourism types, but rather on tourist types and the various individual traits, characteristics, motivations, needs, and so on of travellers.

This has ultimately enabled both researchers and practitioners to better understand tourists on the basis of the types of experiences they seek, as individuals and groups. The following section briefly examines a number of pertinent motivational/behavioural and social/cultural typologies, as a basis for understanding ecotourists.

Christaller quite effectively grasped the notion that, over time, a destination will play host to a rich variety of different types of travellers. He wrote:

The typical course of development has the following pattern. Painters search out untouched unusual places to paint. Step by step the place develops as a so-called artist colony. Soon a cluster of poets follows, kindred to the painters; then cinema people, gourmets, and the *jeunesse dorée*. The place becomes fashionable and the entrepreneur takes note. The fisherman's cottage, the shelter huts become converted into boarding houses and hotels come on the scene.... Only the painters with a commercial inclination who like to do well in business remain; they capitalize on the good name of this former painter's corner and on the gullibility of tourists.

More and more townsmen choose this place, now *en vogue* and advertised in the newspapers.... At last the tourist agencies come with their package rate travelling parties; now, the indulged public avoids such places. At the same time, in other places the cycle occurs again; more and more places come into fashion, change their type, turn into everybody's tourist haunt.

While tourist destinations were seen to be transformed under the influence of tourism, so did the type of traveller, either as a result of these changes or as responsible for initiating the changes within the region. Cohen (1972:172) commented, echoing Christaller, that 'Attractions and facilities which were previously frequented by the local population are gradually abandoned. As Greenwich Village became a tourist attraction, many of the original bohemians moved to the east Village.' Cohen used this as an analogy to demonstrate that travellers were inherently different on the basis of their relationship to both the tourist business establishment and host country.

Accordingly, he grouped tourists into four categories, including organised mass tourists, individual mass tourists, explorers, and drifters. This typology reflected a continuum such that the organised mass tourist is seen as the least adventuresome with little motivation to leave the confines of his or her home environmental bubble. The drifter, in contrast, shunned the tourist establishment, searching for the most authentic travel experiences available.

Motivation, or the drive to satisfy inner physiological and psychological needs, has been fundamental to tourism researchers interested in the 'why' of tourist travel. To Pearce (1982), there needs to exist a stronger emphasis in linking roles and motivations with social and environmental preferences of tourists, in order that destinations could be better matched with markets, travel expectations, and accommodation.

Iso-Ahola (1982) suggested that travel motivation is purely psychological and not sociological in nature.

He argued that people travel for basically two reasons:

- To seek intrinsic rewards (novelty), and
- To escape their everyday environments (escape).

These two motivations may be either of a personal nature (personal troubles or failures) or interpersonal (related to co-workers, family, or neighbours).

The amalgam of these elements is a four-cell matrix, where a single tourist could theoretically go through one or all aspects during the course of one trip. MacCannell (1989) also considered the fundamental differences between traveller types in examining the social structure of tourist space based on 'front' and 'back' regions.

Front regions are those readily experienced by tourists and places where hosts and guests regularly interact. Conversely, back regions are the preserve of the host and are essentially non-tourism oriented in their function. Tourists in search of authenticity penetrate back regions in the hope of acquiring real day-to-day mannerisms of residents.

To what degree tourists are willing or able to penetrate back regions—in identified access zones of tourism areas—may be important to their achieving their overall purpose. Although these 'places' are actual locations in the conventional economic/geographical context, in the mind of the tourist or tourist group they hold special value in defining the travel experience. In general, these back regions are sociological.

PROFILING THE ECOTOURIST

Some of the earliest studies on ecotourism attempted to classify ecotourists on the basis of setting, experience, and group dynamics.

For example, Kusler (1991) typified ecotourists as belonging to three main groups, including:

- *Do-it-yourself ecotourists*: Despite their relative anonymity, this group comprise the largest percentage of all ecotourists. These individuals stay in a variety of different types of accommodations, and have the mobility to visit any number of settings. Their experience, therefore, is marked by a high degree of flexibility.

- *Ecotourists on tours*: This group expects a high degree of organisation within their tour, and travel to exotic destinations (e.g. Antarctica).
- *School groups or scientific groups*: This group often become involved in scientific research of an organisation or individual, often stays in the same region for extensive periods of time, and is willing to endure harsher site conditions than other ecotourists.

Conversely, Lindberg (1991:3) emphasises the importance of dedication and time as a function of defining different types of ecotourists, including what tourists wish to experience from ecotourism, where they wish to travel, and how they wish to travel.

Lindberg identified four basic types:

- *Hard-core nature tourists*: scientific researchers or members of tours specifically designed for education, removal of litter, or similar purposes;
- *Dedicated nature tourists*: people who take trips specifically to see protected areas and who want to understand local natural and cultural history;
- *Mainstream nature tourists*: people who visit the Amazon, the Rwandan gorilla park, or other destinations primarily to take an unusual trip; and
- *Casual nature tourists*: People who experience nature incidentally as part of a broader trip.

Consistent with the increase in ecotourism opportunities, and the associated typologies of tourists travelling on such trips, has been an increase in the volume of literature available on the ecotourist, with much of it focusing on presenting a profile of this tourist type. Initial studies decidedly pointed to the fact that the ecotourist was predominantly male, well educated, wealthy, and long-staying. For example, Wilson (1987:21) reported the following in researching 62 tourists visiting Ecuador:

The male/female ratio was 52% to 48%, and the mean average age was 42.... Twenty-seven per cent earned a family income between US $30,000 to $60,000, before taxes annually. Approximately one-quarter earned more than $90,000 per year. About 30% had bachelors degrees, and a little over 10% had doctoral degrees.

Both Fennell and Smale (1992) and Reingold (1993) report similar results in their work on Canadian ecotourists. On average, the Canadian ecotourists in the Fennell and Smale study were 54 years of age, with the majority in the 60-69 age cohort.

The sample was predominantly male (55 per cent), earned on average about CDN$60,000, with almost one-third and two-thirds having undergraduate and graduate degrees, respectively. According to these authors, this education is well above the national average of about 19 per cent and 4 per cent of Canadians having a bachelor's degree and graduate training, respectively.

In Reingold's work, 24 per cent of Canadian ecotourists were 55 to 64 years of age, 36 per cent had annual incomes over $70,000, 65 per cent had a university degree; however, 64 per cent of the respondents of this study were female. This latter statistic goes against much of the previous research suggesting that males are slightly more representative of this group.

The general outdoor recreation literature supports the fact that most participants—two-thirds or even three-quarters—are of the male gender.

The studies involving ecotourists have been found to mirror related research on birdwatchers. For example, Applegate and Clark (1987) report that more men than women birdwatch and that they have strikingly high levels of affluence and education. More than 50 per cent of the respondents of their study had completed four years of college and had annual family incomes in excess of US$20,000. The findings of Kellert (1985) indicate that committed birders were 73 per cent male with an average age of 42.

Committed birders were also far better educated (nearly two-thirds had college and/or graduate school education) and had higher incomes than respondents who did not birdwatch. As more studies of this nature surface in the future it will be interesting to see how the profile of the ecotourist changes (or stays the same) as a function of many variables, including the types of experiences and products offered to ecotourists, and the maturity of the industry.

Beyond an analysis of socio-demographics, Fennell and Smale (1992) directly compared the average Canadian tourist against a sample of ecotourists (based on the work of Fennell 1990). These researchers used the results of a 1983 Canadian study (Tourism Attitude and Motivation Study (CTAMS)) that analysed the general attitudes and benefits sought by a sample of 11,501 Canadian tourists.

The questions used in the CTAMS were study duplicated and applied to a sample of ecotourists who had recently returned from a Costa Rican ecotourism trip between 1988 and 1989. Of 98 surveys mailed to the ecotourists (tourists were contacted by obtaining mailing lists of Canadian ecotour operators offering programmes in Costa Rica), 77 were returned and usable.

In general, the findings illustrate that the benefits sought by ecotourists may be found in new, active, and adventuresome activities and involvements; while the Canadian population benefits were more strongly related to sedentary activity and family-related endeavours. Ecotourists were found to pursue attractions related to the outdoors (wilderness areas, parks and protected areas, and rural areas); while attractions related to cities and resorts were more important to the average Canadian traveller.

The implications of the research are such that they empirically demonstrate that there is indeed a difference between ecotourists and general travellers in terms of their trip-related needs and focus. Kretchman and Eagles (1990) and Williacy and Eagles (1990) followed the initial survey design of Fennell (1990) in comparing ecotourists in a variety of different settings. These studies were combined by Eagles (1992) in a comprehensive overview of the travel motivations of Canadian ecotourists. His results generally substantiate the results of Fennell and Smale (1992), above, in suggesting that ecotourists are fundamentally different, in their travel motivations, from the average traveller.

As suggested earlier, an effective way in which to differentiate between types of tourists visiting particular regions is through an examination of various personal characteristics such as primary motives, benefits sought, and so on. Turnbull (1981), however, provides an interesting argument against such an approach. He suggests that although on the surface nature tourists travelling to Africa state that it is primarily the animals that bring them to the game parks of East Africa, on the basis of his observations he feels that the reasons for visiting Africa run much deeper.

As an anthropologist, Turnbull believes that perhaps latently it is also the 'Africa' and the 'Kilimanjaro' that bring such tourists to this setting.

In essence, he believes that people want to tap into their distant past when humans had a much stronger relationship with animals, seeing them as something more than just prey to be hunted, and it is to experience something of this relationship that is really desired by present-day tourists. He states that the tourists expect an indivisible, natural whole made up of both human and animal components. But unless they are unusually lucky this is not what tourists find on the organised safari.

All that is observed is man-made: game parks devoid of the herders and hunters who used to live there as an indispensable part of the ecosystem.

This theory gives us another means by which to further examine the intergroup differences that exist between various forms of tourism (i.e. ecotourists and non-ecotourists), but also the intragroup differences (i.e. soft-path ecotourists and hard-path ecotourists) as well. We cannot blindly accept the notion that ecotourists are one homogeneous group; instead, as outlined above, they may be differentiated on the basis of many variables.

Despite the volume of literature that has emerged on the topic of ecotourism, it is clearly at an early stage of development, as is our understanding of how ecotourism differs from other types of tourism. More research is needed to help formulate definitions acceptable to those working in the field, to help overcome this critical absence of focus.

The literature points to the fact that ecotourism is one aspect of nature-oriented tourism, which includes many other types of tourism and outdoor recreation, both consumptive and non-consumptive. Ecotourism is said to relate to adventure travel only inasmuch as it shares similar environmental settings. Differentiation between these two forms of tourism must be done on the basis of social psychology. Finally, more studies are needed to further our understanding of who the ecotourist is, especially in relation to other types of tourists.

ECOTOURISM DEVELOPMENT

Development theory explores the economic and psychological link that exists between rich and poor countries. The relationship continues to be one that often contrasts meaning and value with respect to the use of natural resources and capital. Tourism is a sector of the world's economy that has tended to underscore and exacerbate the inequalities that exist between core metropolitan nations and peripheral, marginalised economies, and in doing so perpetuates the division between those who have access to resources and those who do not.

To Vogeler and DeSouza (1980), this division has conjured up images of distorted human beings and grotesque folklorism, where the underdeveloped are like children unable to fend for themselves and with little capacity to make decisions.

Dependent countries were not considered economic entities until the late 1890s, when a new, 'lofty' responsibility regarding dependent peoples emerged (British Africa encouraged participation in the cash economy).

This lofty purpose was coupled with a crude, hypocritical view of natives and administration, with the recognition that external power had a responsibility to develop the resources of dependent countries for the benefit of the whole world. Some saw the acquisition of overseas dominions as motivated by strategic reasons, while others sought only economic incentives.

In measuring development, past research has used a variety of means to define it, including number of hospital beds, daily intake of calories, daily intake of animal protein, percentage of population in agriculture, food as a percentage of total imports, export economy, infant mortality, death rate, and aid per capita. Many of these have been criticised owing to the fact that the sociocultural, environment, and economic landscapes of each country are different.

For example, food requirements are a cultural phenomenon, where countless generations have formed the habits of food intake seen today. Comparing the daily intake of calories between North Americans and Southeast Asians is pointless. Their physiological requirements are quite different.

Resources have also been used to gauge the development status of nations, where an abundance of resources is thought to be an indicator of development. However, Mountjoy points out that even though Brazil has an abundance of resources and Denmark few, Denmark is considerably the more developed.

Thus, development should be based not upon potential, but on existing levels of material welfare. Switzerland is a further case in point, where capital is a substitute for natural resource endowment.

The progression of development, according to Brookfield (1975), occurred as a result of capitalist countries broadening or diversifying production into new sectors. This was to be achieved internationally through a widening of resource exploitation of less developed countries (LDCs). Brookfield maintains that the most aggressive industrial and trading nations (e.g. Britain) benefited most. They put pressure on other countries to open their trade. Adam Smith's *laissez-faire* philosophy was the true avenue of growth unfettered; it would work towards optimal production.

In recent years there has occurred a major paradigmatic revision in development thinking that is presenting a fundamental challenge to the conventional consensus on economic development. This new approach emphasises the basic needs of the poor, and advocates a sensitivity for development at the ground level. Real improvement cannot, therefore, occur in LDCs unless the strategies that are being formulated and implemented are environmentally sustainable (Barbier 1987). Brookfield (1975) emphasises support of this contention: the study of development joins directly with the study of all change in human use of the environment, and provides elements of empirical evidence for infusion with other theories in the task of generating a dynamic human-environment paradigm.

Mountjoy stipulates that the most important factors in gauging development are people; their number, age, enterprise, initiative, inventiveness, knowledge, and willingness to sacrifice.

It is not the responses themselves (which are passive), but the way in which they are to be utilised that is deterministic of development. The Western nations' concern for invention is not shared by all societies. Technologically inferior societies exploit single landscapes, within the framework of their social structures, while the Westerner is said to exploit all environments.

This is most clearly emphasised by the recent international debates on the implications of global warming for the future viability of the planet. LDCs make a strong case against the more industrialised developed nations for their role in the creation of the pollution (e.g. nitrogen oxide and sulphur dioxide emissions) that has contributed to global warming and ozone depletion.

TOURISM IN THE UNDERDEVELOPED WORLD

LDCs suffer from a history of colonial domination and what has been referred to as dependent development. A review of tourism literature reinforces the notion that there is a set evolutionary pattern of multinational interests in the tourism sector of the underdeveloped. Dependency, therefore, can be conceptualised as a process of historical conditioning which alters the internal functioning of economic and social subsystems within a less developed country. This dependency occurs not from processes within the LDC's economy, but rather from demand from overseas tourists and new foreign company investment in the LDC. For example, after a potential tourist destination has been identified (on the basis of unique biophysical or cultural conditions), the involvement of the multinationals increases. Foreign companies greatly influence the image of a destination country through development and promotion. Such efforts lead tourists to perceive the host country in terms of this image and the nature of hotel accommodation, attractions, and other tourist services as publicised.

Domination of the tourism sector in an LDC is most outwardly represented by the foreign ownership of airlines and hotels. However, the grip on the destination region often goes much deeper.

Because of the inability of agricultural and manufacturing producers in most underdeveloped economies to guarantee a good-quality supply of goods and services for international luxury-standard tourist facilities, there is a strong reliance on imported supplies for both the construction and the operation of tourist facilities.

Also, as Winpenny (1982) writes, middle and senior management levels of tourism developments in underdeveloped countries are often occupied by expatriates. The following scenario of metropolitan dominance serves as an example:

On arrival in a Caribbean island between plane and hotel, the tourists could well have passed through a terminal building presented by the people of Canada and have been driven along a road either built or improved 'thanks' to Canadian aid, on behalf of the expected Canadian tourists of course. At the hotel you will likely be greeted with rum punches the first of the few local products to be encompassed by the package.

At your first meal, a menu, perhaps designed in Toronto, Chicago or Miami will provide you with a selection of food imported for the greater part from North America—good familiar, homogenized, taste-free food, dressed up with a touch of local colour.

The question therefore is as follows: who owns and controls the various components of a holiday package? It has been found (Economic and Social Commission for Asia and the Pacific 1978:40) that where tour packages consist of a foreign air carrier, but include local hotel and other group services, destination countries receive on average only 40-45 per cent of the inclusive tour retail prices paid by the tourists in their home country. If both the airline and hotels are owned by foreign companies, a mere 22-25 per cent of the retail tour price stays in the destination country.

While Rajotte (1980) feels that tourism is less environmentally destructive than other forms of development that exist in tropical islands, there are still many significant effects that may be attributed to tourism. Many of these impacts are universal, but their intensity and severity are more noticeable in island environments (much of the past research on dependency and development has been linked to island environments).

Important is the notion that often with size comes ecological diversity. Nation states of the Caribbean, because of their small size, have tenuous floral and faunal vitality. Tourism can stress these systems through yearly visitation levels that exceed the local population of an island; for example, Hayward *et al.* write that in 1979, more than 600,000 tourists visited Bermuda, some ten times the population of the island.

A key area of research for the future is the need to document whether or not developing countries such as Brazil, Costa Rica, Dominica, the countries of Eastern Africa, and Ecuador undergo the same social, ecological, and economic dysfunctions from ecotourism as outlined above from the perspective of mass tourism.

For example, Kusler (1991) writes that ecotourism in the LDCs is marked by limited dollars, government-directed financing, foreign visitation, foreign ownership of hotels and other facilities, and non-existent land use planning. In this sense, ecotourism as an intervention may or may not improve the socio-economic conditions of a country from the example of mass tourism outlined above. It is important to realise, as outlined by Kusler, that the LDCs and their developed-country counterparts are separated by a number of key structural differences. These include finances, the political climate of a country, accessibility to opportunities, discretionary income, and resources for the acquisition and planning of land.

CORE-PERIPHERY CONCEPT

One of the main theoretical approaches used to explain development is the concept of core and periphery, which Freidmann and Alonso (1974) describe as characterised by a dynamic, growing central region, and a slower-growing or stagnating periphery. The core is marked by high-growth potential whereas peripheral areas are often marked by declining rural economies with low agricultural production (loss of primary resource).

Shields refers to peripheralised regions as marginal places, regions that 'are not necessarily on geographical peripheries but, first and foremost, they have been placed on the periphery of cultural systems of space in which places are ranked relative to each other'.

Important in his discussion is the fact that margins, from social, political, economic, and perceptual perspectives, are systems of centres and peripheries and are, therefore, locationally oriented.

These spatial systems are established in a series of binary relationships (economic, society, and so on) of centre and periphery, so that margins signify everything that the centre denies or represses.

Our socio-economic paradigm is constantly exercising this binary relationship, and it reaches to the furthest outposts of physical space and humanity. In a touristic sense, a classic example of the core-periphery idea can be found in Christaller's (1963) analysis of tourism location in Europe. Christaller wrote that tourism avoids central places and is drawn to the periphery, reaching the natural resource base not found in cities.

This idea has been further developed by a number of authors. In particular, Battisti (1982) reflected on the principles established by Christaller on tourist space organisation, noting that tourism is part of the continual process carried out by humankind in order to specialise and to diversify the exploitation of the soil. Battisti made reference to the distinction between peripheral regions and peripheral places. The first represents a wide range of possibilities in choosing a recreational place.

The second indicates real destinations of tourist flows, where the 'fruition of space for recreational purposes is accomplished'. The core-periphery concept has also been applied more recently to the analysis of adventure travel regions from a spatial context. Zurick (1992) suggested that the movement of adventure travellers in Nepal takes place through a complicated hierarchy of gateways.

Tourists from the core move through an international gateway (semi-periphery), to a national gateway (periphery), and further to a regional gateway (periphery frontier), said to be the adventure region. In this latter region there is often a clash between traditional interests and national development goals. As frontier regions succumb to further intrusions, the uniqueness of these areas diminishes, as does the potential for travel to untouched areas in the future as these areas become fewer in number.

One of the key defining elements of travellers to outward peripheries is the need to experience something different in a remote setting. Along with this, perhaps, is the need to escape the mainstream of tourism, which can only be achieved by taking the road less travelled.

Although there are few data at hand to support this idea, the traveller's mind-set may alter upon reaching successive outward peripheries of a destination.

Fennell (1996) thought that the following factors contributed to this feeling:

- *Familiarity with the destination*: A lack of knowledge or familiarity with a region's environment/culture may add to the uniqueness of such an area and therefore represent a perceived periphery.
- *Unscheduled change*: Movement that occurs spontaneously or that is not pre-planned (e.g. from a core region to a peripheral region).
- *Psychological and/or physiological change*: Personal adaptations that have to be made in order to feel comfortable or maximise feelings of satisfaction/pleasure, including culture, language, personal hygiene, food, and shelter.
- *Distance from amenities*: This factor reinforces the notion that a

particular peripheral region does not, cannot, or will not offer goods and services that can be found at regions closer to the core.

- *Adaptation*: As tourists move out to a new periphery, the accompanying shortage of goods and services such as shops and facilities—found at regions closer to the core—becomes more accepted. The state of the infrastructure, therefore, plays less of a role in satisfying the tourist. Poor weather may also not pose a problem because a more 'frontier-like' attitude is adopted.
- *Population density*: Regions with a lower tourist and local population density may provide an indication that the periphery has been, or is being, reached.
- *Authenticity*. As population density decreases, the authenticity and/ or incidence of natural and cultural attractions may increase in relation to the characteristics of the region. The character of the region is important, as Costa Rica may have a higher species diversity in urban areas than Shetland has at the periphery.
- *Symbolism*: The periphery may be represented by experiential, environmental, or cultural phenomena (symbols). Such phenomena may include lochs, mountains, wind, solitude, barrenness, a rainforest, or lack of banking machines. Consequently, the more these symbols are experienced, the greater might be the feeling of reaching the perimeter. Fear may also act as a symbol, as may the realisation that there is a lack of knowledge of a region and its charact-eristics.

Fear or anxiety of the unknown is an important feature of adventure tourism (characteristics that Csikszentmihalyi (1990) has reported on regarding risk-taking in rock climbers).

- *Scale of attraction*: It is the region itself that may take on characteristics of 'attraction' in the outer periphery. For example, while cities have many attractions and goods and services to offer tourists and locals alike, small, peripheral islands may have comparatively few or no structural attractions, and because of this the nature of the island's limited infrastructure, small size, and distance from the mainland may be the attraction itself.
- *Distance from home*: This factor occurs in combination with other factors. For example, travel to Sydney, Australia, from rural Canada represents a large distance, but may not necessarily represent a mental change from core to periphery.

Thus the relationship between core and periphery has not only a psychological component but, as discussed earlier, a spatial one. This spatial component occurs at a variety of scales. Examples include small islands of the South controlled by the North, and huge territories of the North controlled politically, economically, and socially by decision-makers of the core. The

Northwest Territories of Canada has been identified by Keller (1987) as an example of a peripheral region caught in transition regarding the development of its tourism industry.

To Keller, differing authorities in control of development in this region become important actors in both decision-making and implementation of a viable tourist industry. These hierarchies of control occur at local, regional, national, and international levels. As the sphere of tourism development becomes international, Keller suggests, the more the periphery has become 'a playground for exogenous investors, and the peripheral government an observer of its own fate'.

It is stated by Keller that to avoid a transgression of the above scenario, the periphery (Northwest Territories) must act to control the decision-making in the development of a tourist industry, and limit the development to a scale of growth in tune with the resources, capital, manpower, and culture within the periphery.

The implications of the core-periphery concept to ecotourism are that, often, remote travel regions are dependent on national and international markets, inbound and outbound tour operators, as well as externally based transport modes and schedules. With the inability and lack of resources fully to plan and implement ecotourism on their own, the cycle of tourism dependency continues for peripheral regions.

This lack of an ability to link directly with the market in the developed world is one of the main reasons why the benefits of ecotourism do not percolate down to the community level; and it is precisely why those who are able to coordinate ecotourism activities—whether they be expatriates or local—between the LDCs and the developed world stand greatly to gain economically.

In such a case the power to make ecotourism happen in a developing country lies in the hands of a few, and perpetuates the phenomenon of a typical LDC economic situation, with much of the money and resources lying in the hands of a few, and the majority of the population, in the absence of a prominent middle class, living in impoverished conditions.

While the preceding discussion has emphasised the significance and impact of externally based control in the development of tourism and ecotourism enterprises at a macro level, the discussion of community development to follow offers an alternative to many of the tourism development concerns outlined above. Community development, then, may be considered as a viable means by which to offset the conventional tourism development models of the past and redistribute control and decision-making among the individuals within the community, not to those from outside.

COMMUNITY DEVELOPMENT

Community development, as described by Smith (1990a), originated in the self-help programmes that were developed during the depression years in Canada, the United States, and the United Kingdom. A defining characteristic of community development is that it is based on local initiatives, in that it advocates a site-specific approach to finding solutions to community problems using community members and community resources. Bujold (1995:5) defines it as 'the process by which the efforts of the people themselves are united with those of governmental authorities to improve economic, social, and cultural conditions of communities'.

Typical community development encompasses all aspects of the community and focuses on the best quality of life possible for its members, and may involve creating new business and employment, increasing cultural awareness, or providing a range of opportunities for all members of the community. However, Joppe (1996) alludes to the fact that it is important to understand that there exists a fundamental division between conventional community development and community economic development (CED) models.

While conventional economic development focuses on the attraction of new businesses to the community (seen as an outward-directed approach to development), conversely a CED focus is on being small, green, and social, and is more inward in its orientation by striving to 'help consumers become producers, users become providers, and employees become owners of enterprise', through the principles of economic self-reliance, ecological sustainability, community control, meeting individual needs, and building a community culture.

Tourism is increasingly seen as a key community development tool in the 1990s, with the recognition of its economic contribution in bolstering stagnating economies and diversifying existing sectors, and its ability to unify community members. Such is the case in the Shetland Islands, Scotland, where tourism is being relied upon to sustain an economy that was once dominated by North Sea oil development, or the Finnish island of Åland, where all tourism initiatives are owned or controlled by local people.

With this realisation, researchers have begun to explore community development as it relates to tourism and ecotourism from many different perspectives. As an example, Christensen (1995) examines the role that tourism can play in securing quality of life within the community. At the foundation of any tourism development strategy is the realisation that

If tourism development is to be viable as a long-term economic strategy, these concerns [social and ecological] must be addressed, and the resource base must be protected in the process. The host community is the economic, social, cultural, and infrastructural resource base for most tourism activity, and resident quality of life is a measure of the condition of the resource.

Christensen proposes a community quality of life framework that addresses both objective and subjective indicators, at the individual and community scale. A tourism development project is said to affect change in the quality of life of members of the community, which in turn cause impacts at different social scales. Such impacts need to be evaluated both by individuals and by the community, depending on the scale of reference to the individual. There is a deliberate hierarchy established with respect to agents of change, suggesting that appropriate solutions need to be implemented at the individual social scale first, followed by neighbourhood groups, coalitions, responsible industry, policy, and governmental regulation.

The tactical approaches used by regions (local or national governing bodies) will make or break how ecotourism is perceived by local people, according to MacKinnon (1995). She sites a number of examples of communities in Mexico which have adopted or been identified to develop ecotourism in the country. One such community is Tres Garantías in the Yucatán peninsula. This region was initially set out as a hunting reserve by an international development team, but the area's residents found that non-consumptive recreation was more attractive to tourists than consumptive forms.

The project, however, was conceived using a top-end approach, and even though there have been isolated benefits derived from ecotourism, MacKinnon suggests that social integration within the community is not complete, and will not be complete until benefits are more widespread and the perception of ownership is given to the community.

MacKinnon further uses the example of Los Tuxtlas, Veracruz, to illustrate that ecotourism has been successfully integrated into a community through more of a grassroots approach (initiated through the efforts of a local woman who set out to build empowerment slowly and deliberately). In this latter case, the community has been more quickly able to realise benefits which have been spreading on a more regional scale.

According to MacKinnon, the traditional mass tourism development model perpetuates the widening gap between rich and poor in countries like Mexico. Conversely, community-based tourism 'lends itself to being environmentally sustainable. Locals are the first to recognize the benefits of conserving their natural-resource base—much more so than large developers who don't live in the area'. While the interests of the community from a social standpoint are certainly paramount in the development of small-scale ecotourism, Williams (1992) feels that all factions within the community need to cooperate effectively in ensuring that a high-quality product is delivered without diminishing the ecology of the resource base. He advocates the development of an institutional structures strategy with the capacity to respond to tourism development before such development runs out of control.

This strategy includes the following:

- Development of a grassroots planning process, driven by local interests and including aboriginal involvement;

- Understanding and appreciation of ecotourism market requirements;
- An inventory of the region's resources to determine areas that are suitable for ecotourism and ones that are not;
- The establishment of goals and objectives in line with concerns related to the cultural and natural impacts of ecotourism, with the creation of a vision statement to act as a control mechanism for the future; and
- The establishment of a formal Tourism Management Board, to work with both the operators and the public, with the responsibility of monitoring change, communication, local benefits, etc.

Despite the fact that there will be direct and indirect beneficiaries and participants in the ecotourism industry, it is important to recognise that the entire community should be involved to some level. Participation therefore plays a key role in the initiative, as it empowers people to play a role in the decision-making process, where in many cases it is only those who are politically connected or affluent who are involved in the control and management of the enterprise.

Such involvement can take the form of community representatives who speak for various elements of the population. This 'management committee' is very much like the proposed Tourism Management Board outlined by Williams (1992). The community ecotourism initiative needs to be founded on the notion of trust and transparency.

Actions and decisions need to be communicated to the community through bulletin boards or other means. Money and finances are identified by Sproule as critical elements in dividing a community. To be open about expenditures and to share information in an attempt to dispel feelings of mismanagement or corruption is to be transparent in one's approach to management. Specifically, Sproule's community-based ecotourism (CBE) refers to ecotourism enterprises that are owned and managed by the community. Furthermore, community-based ecotourism implies that a community is taking care of their natural resources in order to gain income through operating a tourism enterprise and using that income to better their lives. It involves conservation, business enterprise and community development.

A final example of how management may be used to control the development of ecotourism initiatives within a community is outlined by Drake (1991).

She defines local participation as 'the ability of local communities to influence the outcome of development projects such as ecotourism that have an impact on them'. Important in this process is the demonstrated benefit to the community both through community members' participation and through their realisation that some aspect of their community has been treated or protected (e.g. natural resources).

The following is proposed as a model of local participation in the development of ecotourism projects:

- *Phase 1: Determine the role of local participation in project*: This includes an assessment of how local people can help achieve set goals through efficiency, increasing project effectiveness, building beneficiary capacity, and sharing project costs.
- *Phase 2: Choose research team*: The team should include a broad multidisciplinary approach and include people in the social sciences and those within the media.
- *Phase 3: Conduct preliminary studies*: Political, economic, and social conditions of the community should be studied in the context of the environment, from existing documents, and by other survey-related work. Identification and assessment of the following is important: needs, key local leaders, media, the community's commitment to the project, intersectoral involvement, traditional uses of the land, the type of people interested in the project and why, the role of women, who will manage and finance the project, land ownership, and cultural values.
- *Phase 4: Determine the level of local involvement*: Local involvement occurs along a continuum from low-intensity to high-intensity involvement. This must be determined in addition to when the involvement is to occur. In cases where government is not supportive of local government, intermediaries (e.g. NGOs) can be used to facilitate local participation.
- *Phase 5: Determine an appropriate participation mechanism*: This is affected by the level of intensity of the participation, the nature of existing institutions (e.g. government, NGOs, citizens' groups), and the characteristics of the local people (how vociferous they may or may not be). This phase may include information sharing and consultation, which usually takes the form of a citizen advisory committee with representatives from many groups within the community. The committee is charged with the task of commenting on goals and objectives or other project-related aspects.
- *Phase 6: Initiating dialogue and educational efforts*: The use of the press is important in this phase as a means by which to build consensus through public awareness. Key community representatives can be used in this process. The ecotourism team should explain the goals and objectives of the project, how the project will affect the community, the values of the area, any history of threats, and the benefits of the project. Various audiovisual techniques should be used to emphasise these points. Workshops or public meetings could be organised to identify strengths and weaknesses of the project.

- *Phase 7: Collective decision-making*: This is a critical stage that synthesises all research and information from the local population. The ecotourism project team present the findings of their research to the community, together with an action plan. Community members are asked to react to the plan, with the possible end result being a forum through which the team and local people negotiate to reach a final consensus based on the impacts of the project.
- *Phase 8: Development of an action plan and implementation scheme*: In this phase, the team and community develop an action plan for implementing solutions to identified problems. For example, if members of the community express the need to increase the community's standard of living, the team may respond by purchasing agricultural produce from local people at market rates or on a contractual basis. They may also develop a variety of positions to be occupied by local people including gift shops, research positions, park management positions, and private outfitting companies for the local people. This local action plan must then be integrated into the broader master plan of the project.
- *Phase 9: Monitoring and evaluation*: Monitoring and evaluation, although often neglected, should occur frequently and over the long term. The key to evaluation is to discover whether goals and objectives set out early in the project's life cycle have been accomplished or not.

Community development initiatives have a better chance of being accepted by local people if developers begin to acknowledge the fact that different groups within the community want different things, depending on their role in, affinity within, and utilisation of the community. This perspective is discussed by Jurowski (1996), who feels that because the impacts of tourism are not the same for all residents, residents' individual values need to be recognised by tourism developers in order for their projects to be successful.

The first unique group identified by Jurowski is the 'attached resident'. Such a person is likely to be a long-term resident or an older individual who loves living in the community because of its social and physical benefits. To these people, control over the form and function of their community is important. In general, tourism developers can gain support for their projects from this group by involving citizens in the planning process, establishing a focal point and common theme, developing projects that emphasise heritage themes, and showing that the project has social and ecological benefits for the community.

The second type established by Jurowski, the 'resource user', typically includes people like anglers and other recreationists who, although ambivalent about the economic impacts of tourism, can be won over by developers. The developers can gain their support by providing skill opportunities for youth, involving this group in events related to their interests (e.g. bike races), protecting 'their' sites for participation, and allocating tourism funds for the development of facilities and services they desire.

The final group outlined by Jurowski is the 'environm-entalist'. Although this group is the most likely to focus on the negative aspects of the development, it is in the best interests of development teams to do the following:

- Provide information on how the project will protect the environment;
- Incorporate ecological education programmes;
- Encourage the participation of environmentalists in development; and
- Prompt citizens to develop their own educational programmes for tourists. Projects that reflect the interests and concerns of the community, therefore, are said generally to stimulate volunteer activity and minimise conflict.

This research is attractive because it acknowledges that people residing in the local community are indeed different from one another. This is in contrast to much tourism research which considers the local community as one homogeneous group. A key principle underlying the process of community development is the element of leadership.

Mabey (1994) suggests that unlike the older model of leadership, seen as an individual influencing a group towards an end, newer leadership paradigms involve collaboration and partnerships between community individuals, groups, and organisations.

This means devolving power to the followers, according to Mabey, and being fluid in the connection of people and resources. Belasco and Stayer (1993:18) likened this new style of leadership to what happens in a flight of geese:

I could see the geese flying in their 'V' formation, the leadership changing frequently, with different geese taking the lead. I saw every goose being responsible for getting itself wherever the gaggle was going, changing roles whenever necessary, alternating as a leader, a follower or a scout.... I could see each goose being a leader.

This example illustrates the importance of a common purpose in removing obstacles and establishing responsibility within the community ecotourism initiative. In essence the process of empowerment—holding the will, resources, and opportunity to make decisions within the community—allows people, either internal or external to the community, to step in and provide assistance in a respectful manner, while allowing local people to shape and control the pace of tourism development within their communities.

Where this is especially relevant is in marginal places where there exists a tremendous void between those who can and those who cannot access information and resources. As such, education must play a key role in this empowerment process of revitalisation through ecotourism (e.g. providing the needed means to enable people to be informed of certain choices).

An excellent example of education's role in empowerment lies in the Community Baboon Sanctuary project of Belize. Through education and partnerships, local farmers have stopped their conventional practice of clearing and denuding the land for agriculture purposes in favour of a land management strategy that is more environmentally sound. In so doing they have been able to attract international tourists fascinated by the ecological and cultural diversity of this part of the world.

Education, therefore, helps to rekindle people's love and appreciation of the land, which is indeed important for both community-building and nation-building. A similar case study involves the Havasupai reservation adjacent to the Grand Canyon National Park in northern Arizona, where education and tourism have played a significant role in diversifying the local economy.

PARTNERSHIPS

A partnership, as defined by Uhlik (1995:14) is 'an on-going arrangement between two or more parties, based upon satisfying specifically identified, mutual needs. Such partnerships are characterized by durability over time, inclusiveness, cooperation, and flexibility.' More specifically, Uhlik (1995) developed a six-stage model of partnership development that concentrates on the conditions that will lead to a successful partnership agreement.

These include:

- Education of self and others;
- Needs assessment and resource inventory;
- Identifying prospective partners and investigating their needs and inventories;
- Comparing and contrasting needs and resources;
- Developing a partnership proposal; and
- Proposing a partnership.

Clements *et al.* (1993) suggest that because tourism is starting to be recognised as a community development tool, development must be sensitive to the requirements of many stakeholder groups, including tourism providers (e.g. hotels), public providers (e.g. recreation and park providers), and residents. Their view is that partnerships must be struck to ensure that a high-quality product is delivered, and is based on the notion that tourism experiences rely on all aspects of the community.

The overall effectiveness of the delivery system is only as strong as its weakest link, and communities intent on the development of a tourism industry will increasingly rely on the positive benefits of partnerships in being accountable to the local and non-local public. The partnerships developed for ecotourism, according to Sproule (1996), must also fit into systems that have been developed at regional and national levels. There are potentially many partnerships that can be struck to facilitate an atmosphere of cooperation and trust.

Potential partners include:

- Organisations within the established tourism industry, particularly tour operators;
- The government tourism bureau and natural resource agencies, especially the park service;
- Non-governmental organisations (NGOs), especially those involved with environmental issues, small business management, and traditional community development;
- Universities and other research organisations;
- Other communities, including those with a history of tourism and also those that are just beginning; and
- Other international organisations, public and private funding institutions, national cultural committees, and many others; the tourism industry literature is replete with examples of stakeholder groups that have conventionally been at odds.

In Canada, the United States, Australia, and many other countries around the world, there exists a significant degree of incompatibility between parks and aboriginal peoples.

McNeely (1993) feels that despite what has occurred in the past, partnerships must be forged between these two groups in order that both may prosper in the late twentieth century and beyond.

He feels that the following ten principles must be followed in order to help the cooperative efforts of these stakeholder groups:

- Build on the foundations of local culture.
- Give responsibility to local people.
- Consider returning ownership of at least some protected areas to indigenous people.
- Hire local people.
- Link government development programmes with protected areas.
- Give priority to small-scale local development.
- Involve local people in preparing management plans.
- Have the courage to enforce restrictions.
- Build conservation into the evolving new national cultures.
- Support diversity as a value.

Rather than emphasise what has not worked in the past, the partnership ideal must embrace the present and future needs of the groups involved in any transaction. For those in the realm of parks it may be biodiversity and the establishment of more protected areas. From the perspective of aboriginal people, decision-making and culture may be issues that top the list.

ABORIGINAL INTERESTS

As outlined above, the relationship between parks and aboriginal people has often been one based on conflict, and stems from the physical displacement and socio-economic fragmentation of aboriginal people. In Canada, the relationship has been one of mistrust, where peripheral lands (occupied by aboriginals) have been run outside the control and sphere of influence of local native authority.

This in itself is a perpetuation of the rift that has existed between Ottawa in the south and those living in the 'north'. Part of the problem exists because the concept of 'park' never existed in aboriginal languages, at least in North America, and the fundamentals of our Western view of park management (i.e. balancing recreational use with preservation) are completely alien to aboriginal culture, as oulined by Notzke:

The distinction between work and leisure is largely an artifact of industrial society. The fragmentation and compartmentalization of life and environment which is part and parcel of western culture, is totally alien to aboriginal cosmologies, which view the world in an essentially holistic and unified manner.

This view is supported by Sadler (1989), who suggests that aboriginals think of space primarily from a holistic perspective, which is contrary to the dichotomous Western perspective associated with conservation. Park management therefore proceeded to exclude Aboriginals entirely from the park planning process. This has led to an indifferent, even hostile, attitude towards the existence of parks close to or adjacent to aboriginal lands. The Clearwater River Provincial Park in northwestern Saskatchewan is an example of this indifference.

Even though there is an abundant population of indigenous people in the vicinity of the park, there is little use of park resources (e.g. fish, game) by such people, in large part because of the park's political status (B. Wilson, personal communication, December 4, 1996). In order for parks to become accepted by the aboriginal population, therefore, some feel that a revision must be made to the preservation mandate that currently exists in some types of parks, changing it to one that is conservation oriented, which will be more consistent with the social, economic, and ecological requirements of the First Nations people in Canada.

CASE STUDY

THE STRUGGLE FOR KAKADU

According to Fox (1996), territories rich in resources provide more options for their use. This is the case with Kakadu National Park in the Northern Territory of Australia, which is a World Heritage Site and a place of immense ecological and cultural significance. Kakadu is owned by the Aborigines of the region, who lease it to the National Park Service. Legally, mismanagement of the resource may lead to the tenure being terminated. Ecotourism is thriving in the park, so much so that according to the Aborigines, there is no longer a distinction being made between the effects of mining and tourism; both are contributing to the degradation of the park.

Some Aboriginal people, according to Fox, recognise that while mining will ultimately end, tourism will continue to grow and grow, and has manifested itself in the form of planned multi-million dollar tourism projects for the park. The issue of most concern to Aborigines is that their fundamental values are not consistent with current development philosophies in the park.

According to Elliot (1991), the example of mining and tourism in Kakadu is a perfect example of the competing and overlapping environmental values that various stakeholders have.

For example, would it matter if our actions caused a species to become extinct? Would it matter if our actions caused the death of individual animals? Would it matter if we caused widespread erosion in the park? Is the extinction of a species an acceptable price to pay for increased employment opportunities? One would imagine that miners, the tourism industry, Aborigines, the park service, and other interests would all differ along these fundamental lines.

The element of control is critical in analysing any relationship between the ecotourism industry and indigenous people. For tourism development to be successful, aboriginal people must be allowed to take control of it despite the social and political forces that often work against them. This has been a problem in the restructuring of South Africa, where there remains a legacy of poor education and lack of training for black people. The result is that the whole touristic experience is one that is inherently foreign to the poor in South African society.

Given that part of the government's tourism vision relates to addressing the need to improve the quality of life of every South African, Swart and Saayman recognise the need for significant changes in legislation to benefit all people.

Keller (1987), as discussed earlier, recognised that the Northwest Territories (NWT) has struggled with the development of its tourism industry, largely owing to the real lack of control of the industry at the local and regional levels. Keller's conclusions imply that the people of this peripheral region must have decision-making control and act to limit development to a scale of growth in tune with the social, ecological, and economic climate of the region.

However, at least in some places in the NWT, Inuit, Indians, and Metis people have started to realise that their varying social, ecological, and economic needs can best be met through cooperative action with other agencies. The vehicle that is enabling them to do this is national parks, territorial parks, heritage rivers, and the tourism opportunities that emerge from such areas. For example, Scale (1992) suggests that two rivers, the Thelon and the Kazan, were easily designated as within the Canadian Heritage Rivers System owing to the fact that the project planner lived within the community with his family for 18 months, in an attempt to educate and work closely with local organisations such as the Hunters and Trappers Association and the Elders' Society.

Scale believes that continued success will be contingent upon recognising the importance of conservation, tourism, and the needs of aboriginal people in Canada's north. In particular the following factors need to be considered:

Community involvement:

- Involvement of First Nations people in all aspects of tourism and conservation planning.

Community benefits:

- Continued and/or exclusive access to biophysical resources of the protected area for subsistence purposes.
- Provision of technical and professional training opportunities relating to positions in tourism and in conservation agencies.
- Priority status in hiring programmes undertaken by tourism interests and conservation agencies.
- Priority status in the licensing of businesses to be operated in the park or protected area.
- Compilation of traditional knowledge and heritage values of the aboriginal societies by the conservation jurisdiction, for use both by the communities themselves in strengthening their societal traditions, and by the conservation agency in managing the protected area and in giving to its visitors a heightened appreciation of the traditional society.

Scale:

- Ecotourism and adventure tourism can be accommodated much more readily than mass tourism, where control of such tourists (numbers and use patterns) will be in the communities' best interests socially and ecologically.

Land ownership:

- Tourism and protected areas will be accepted much more readily by aboriginal societies if the legal status of the land in question is first settled to their satisfaction.

Sensitivity to needs of area residents and visitors:

- Ecotourists must be informed as to what is and what is not acceptable behaviour in the north, in recognising that the quality of their experience depends in part on their compliance to accepted norms.

- Traditional societies and conservation organisations need to come together to establish patterns in which visitors and locals can meet in circumstances of mutual respect.

Increasingly, however, examples in the literature are emerging that demonstrate the positive signs of local indigenous control in the ecotourism industry.

For example, Hitchcock (1993) illustrates that the semi-nomadic pastoralist people of Purros in Namibia have been able to develop a successful ecotourism industry. Ecotourists are asked to pay the equivalent of about US$12 to enter their tribal area, with all the money generated from tourism being divided equally among members of the community.

Other aspects of the ecotourism initiative include:

- The fact that tourists must abide by structured guidelines (developed by the local people);
- Tour guiding and handicraft prices are set, so as to avoid undercutting; and
- Programmes to educate tourists on resource use in the area have been set up.

Such community action, according to Hitchcock, is definitely on the rise in the developing world. Following point 1 above, Colvin (1994) proposes a code of ethics for the indigenous-sensitive ecotourist.

Code for the indigenous-sensitive ecotourist:

- Who operates the programme. Is it indigenous-run? If so, is it operated communally or do only a few individuals or families profit?
- If not indigenous-run, do local communities receive an equitable share of the profits or any other direct benefits, such as training? Or do only a few individuals/families benefit?
- Learn as much as you can about the local culture and customs. Visit local indigenous federation offices for information and materials with an indigenous perspective.
- Do not take photographs without asking permission.
- If you want to give a gift, make it a useful gift to the community rather than to an individual (e.g. gift to a school). Most indigenous communities function communally.
- Refrain from tipping individuals. If you are with a group, everyone can contribute to a gift to the community.
- Be aware of the boundaries of individual homes and gardens. Never enter or photograph without permission.
- Bring your own water purification tablets. Don't rely on boiling water exclusively as it depletes fuelwood and contributes to forest destruction.

- Pack out what you take in, and use biodegradable soaps.
- Be sensitive to those around you.
- Don't make promises you cannot or will not keep—for example, sending back photos to local people.
- Do not collect plants or plant products without permission.
- Wear appropriate and discreet clothing (e.g. many cultures are offended by women in shorts even though they may go topless).
- Respect local residents' privacy and customs. Treat people with the respect you would expect from visitors to your own home.

The issue of control in the development of ecotourism was at the centre of an incident between the Kuna Indians of Panama and the Panama national government. Chapin (1990) writes that in the 1970s the government of Panama had the specific aim of working with multinational corporations in the development of a tourism product in the region of the Kuna (around Carti on the Caribbean side of the country): 'In return for their services as tourist attractions, the Kuna were to be given employment as service staff'.

According to Chapin, the Kuna were unwilling to comply with the feasibility team and collectively forced the tourism industry influence out of the region. While plans for the development of casinos had to be discarded, one operator had his boat confiscated, and another individual had to endure being shot, set on fire, a hanging attempt, and a pummelling at the hands of many Kuna youth.

Conversely, the small hotels of the region that currently exist in the area are all run by Kuna and cater to a small and manageable number of tourists on the basis of Kuna ownership and Kuna law.

Communities are therefore cognisant of the importance of sustainable development and are striving to achieve it, but under the following conditions:

- They must have control of the industry;
- Projects must be small in size and therefore manageable; and
- There must be equity and dialogue among the various stakeholders.

The importance of training and education appears to be a common thread that links the literature on ecotourism and indigenous development. Wearing (1994) emphasises that at any level of hierarchy, 'ordinary' people are perfectly able to solve their own problems if given the chance. Through an analysis of ecotourism and local indigenous communities, Wearing believes that experiential education and training are crucial in allowing such communities to develop ecotourism so that it is not just another commodified product where benefits are exported and natural resources are abused.

'Concrete experiences' are important in acting as cornerstones to teaching and learning in many indigenous communities. Aboriginal people can contrast this with the 'formation of abstract concepts and generalisations' attitude, which is more akin to the Western approach, and provides the means by which to bring a more conceptual foundation to the learning process. 'Observations and reflections' and 'testing implications of concepts in new situations,' represent the integration of Western and local traditions that may be desired of an ecotourism experience, with the former representing a traditional method of learning in aboriginal cultures and the latter representing more of a Western scientific approach to problem-solving.

A significant body of research has surfaced in Australia on parks and Aboriginal involvement, where despite many years of agreements and talks, there still exists uncertainty regarding the role that Aboriginals must play within protected areas.

In Kakadu, Cobourg, and Uluru national parks, reported to be the model of Aboriginal-national parks relations in Australia, co-management strategies have not been successful in integrating and protecting indigenous values and rights, despite the fact that land in these areas has been given back to Aboriginals as freehold title.

Davey (1993) reports that the models break down by failing to involve the aboriginal landowners in policy and planning, by not having majority Aboriginal representation on park boards, and by the lack of training and skills to enable Aboriginal people better to understand their role within the park setting.

Notwithstanding these failures, Australians have endeavoured to overcome some of these problems through research initiatives designed to develop Aboriginal skills and training. Baker *et al.* (1992) suggest that Aboriginal people can contribute equally to park management by applying Aboriginal ecological knowledge—which is based on generations of accumulated knowledge—with conventional biological surveys to overcome the time and finance constraints normally associated with research.

In addressing the need to enhance Aboriginal skill levels, De Lacy (1992) discusses the development of a number of Aboriginal employment programmes in Australia in the 1980s, including the initiation of many courses and skills that are currently available at selected universities within the Australian system.

Similar training opportunities have been reported by Liu (1994) in the American Affiliated Pacific Islands, where support of indigenous ecotourism entrepreneurs is thought to be critical in achieving sustainable economic growth.

Liu suggests that government needs to take the lead in providing financing, development and operational support, and training programmes to develop appropriate marketing and business skills for this population. This is supported by King and Stewart (1996), who feel that national level controls are needed, in concert with local involvement, as a means by which to coordinate ecotourism development with the aim of reducing the effects of commodification of local indigenous cultures.

SITE DEVELOPMENT

The tourism industry has long been recognised as a formidable agent of social and ecological change, some say in a positive context through increased education, renewed pride in culture, the conservation of heritage, and of course economics, while others say in a negative sense, at the expense of people and the resource base. For example, hotel developments in Spain and Turkey have been identified as being excessive in their impacts on beach environments.

In other cases, improper development and the lack of sewerage systems hamper the tourism industry to such an extent in places in Mexico and Brazil that tourists are told not to swim in the ocean owing to the pollution. In such cases tourism development is strongly affected by what does not exist (i.e. no sewerage systems) or because such systems are unable to keep pace with the ongoing increase in tourism visitation and associated development.

The style and extent of tourism development in the 1990s has been tempered by the trend towards the increase in the recent past, in mega-development projects designed to cater to a growing market of travellers looking for self-contained, hassle-free vacations. Fennell (1989) writes that this mega-resort boom began in the mid-1980s, and includes sites such as the 31,000-acre resort community of Waikoloa in Hawaii and the 1,200-acre Sanctuary Cove mixed-use resort between Brisbane and the Gold Coast. Yet while most of the development has been centred in what have been politically stable democracies, management consultants have been looking to the untapped markets of the Far East.

In the midst of this mega-development push there has emerged the move towards more responsible travel and development, in response to the green movement (pressure from various groups including academics, ENGOs, and the general public), and in keeping one step ahead of the competition.

The response to the changing emphasis has meant that even some of the major hotel chains have endeavoured to experiment with ecologically sound rooms through recycling, washing sheets only at the request of visitors, cutting down on the use of electricity, and so on.

However, where this changing focus has become the most noticeable is through the variety of small-scale initiatives that have developed in urban (bed-and-breakfasts), rural (farm tourism) and back-country (ecotourism developments) settings.

SUSTAINABLE DESIGN AND ECOLODGES

Over the past few years, several documents have emerged that analyse the development of ecolodges and ecotourism facilities on the basis of principles of sustainability. However, there appears to be some confusion on the scale and magnitude of development of such areas according to Epler Wood, who reports that ecotourism continues to be misunderstood in resort advertising schemes, while the term 'ecoresort' has yet to be appropriately defined (Shundich 1996). For instance, a tourism industry trade publication recently wrote that 'Another recent and perhaps surprising region for ecoresort development is India.... There is interest in genuine cultural experiences within the country.

One man has proposed a historical tour of India by rail.' Interest in sustainable ecotourism design took flight in the early 1990s in part as a result of a US national park service publication dedicated to the principles of sustainable design. Two events took place in the United States that prompted the development of this book. The first was the National Park Service Vail Symposium in October 1991 which discussed, among other things, the severity of environmental stresses within parks; while the second was the Virgin Islands National Park initiative in November 1991, which specifically dealt with issues related to sustainable design in parks and protected areas.

The latter publication explores interpretation, natural and cultural resources, site design, building design, energy management, water supply, waste prevention, and facility and maintenance operations in its overview of sustainable design. Of particular importance is its extensive checklist for sustainable building design that emphasises and respects the many interrelationships of all parts of the natural and cultural aspects of the site.

However, these were not the first attempts to integrate the developments of humankind with the natural world (especially parks), as evident in the seminal work of Miller (1976, 1989) on ecodevelopment.

Although the US Department of the Interior book is devoted to facility design and construction *in parks,* there is a more generic section that deals specifically with sustainable tourism development. Here the authors advocate using the principles of Aesculapia, which is the Greek place of healing. From this perspective, 'nature is respected for its restorative qualities.

The human experience is set in harmony with the environment, and an opportunity is created to allow a reconnection of human needs to the natural systems on which all life is based' (US Department of the Interior 1993:58).

This type of design principle would then strive to meet the following criteria, according to the authors:

- Provide education for visitors on wildlife, native cultural resources, historic features, or natural features;
- Involve indigenous populations in operations and interpretation to foster local pride and visitor exposure to traditional values and techniques;
- Accomplish environmental restoration;
- Provide research and development on, and/or demonstration projects of, ways to minimise human impacts on the environment;
- Provide spiritual or emotional recuperation;
- Provide relaxation and recreation; and

- Educate visitors to realise that knowledge of our local and global environment is valuable and will empower their ability to make informed decisions.

Russell *et al.* (1995:x) define an ecolodge as 'a nature-dependent tourist lodge that meets the philosophy and principles of ecotourism'. Although they underscore the importance of the ecolodge concept from an educational and experiential perspective, they suggest that it is the philosophical tie with ecological sensitivity that must define these operations.

The importance of ecology is also underscored by the Ecotourism Society, which feels that such lodges promote an educational and participatory experience while at the same time being developed and managed in regard to the local environment in which it exists. Russell *et al.* distinguish between traditional lodges and ecolodges using the 12 points. They further distinguish between the ecolodge and the nature-based lodge, with the latter being associated with fishing, skiing, and luxury retreats.

The philosophical issue related to ecolodges identified above is one considered by Andersen, who feels that along with environmental codes of ethics, a low-impact approach to the design of ecotourism facilities needs to be employed for such facilities to be truly sustainable—an approach that he suggests would entail a complete reworking of the conventional design of architects. Andersen's work is well publicised in the field of ecotourism, especially his advocacy of a number of principles which, broadly defined, include organisational issues (e.g. has an analysis been done of the area's ecological sensitivity?), site planning issues

Table. Traditional Lodge Versus Ecolodge.

Traditional	Ecolodge
Luxury	Comfortable basic needs
Generic style	Unique character style
Relaxation focus	Activity/educational focus
Activities are facility based (e.g. golf, tennis)	Activities are nature based (e.g. hiking, diving)
Enclave	Integrated development with local developmentenvironment
Group/consortium ownership common	Individual ownership common
Profit maximisation based on high guest capacity, services, prices	Profit maximisation based on strategic design, location, low capacity, services, price
High investment	Moderate/low investment
Key attractions	Key attractions are surroundings and facility

are facility and surroundings	
Gourmet meals, service, and presentation	Good/hearty meals and service-cultural influence
Market within chain	Market normally independent
Guides and nature interpreters non-existent or minor feature of operation	Guides and nature interpreters focus of operation

(e.g. minimise trail crossing points at rivers and streams), building design issues (e.g. maintenance of the ecosystem should take priority over view or dramatic design statements), energy resource and utility infrastructure issues (e.g. consider the use of passive or active solar or wind energy sources wherever practical), waste management issues (e.g. provide facilities for recycling), and evaluation (e.g. whether accommodation is made for older guests and physically disabled individuals).

Andersen has been able to operationalise many of these design features in his Lapa Rios Resort development on the Osa Peninsula of Costa Rica's Pacific coast. This development has a main lodge in addition to 14 private bungalows which were built by local engineers with the removal of only one tree.

Given the low-capacity and low-impact philosophies of ecotourism development, a logical question is: at what scale does the ecolodge model *not* apply? That is, when is a development considered too big? This question, at least peripherally, has been addressed by Ayala (1996).

As an international ecoresort developer, she believes both that ecotourism is becoming a segment of mass tourism, and that it is not incompatible with beach tourism. She supports this view by suggesting that there is the need to diversify the vast number of sea, sun, and sand products through the addition of ecotourism (but not at the exclusion of other hard-path experiences). Ayala feels that the line between ecotourists and conventional tourists is least detectable in long-haul travel, citing similarities in their levels of education, household income, and their occupations.

Interesting is the fact that:

- The ability to travel long distances is directly related to one's wealth, and
- Wealth is directly related to education and occupation.

Ayala fails to discuss other factors (e.g. psychographics) that determine differences in travel types. For example, the assumption being made is either that all long-haul tourists are ecotourists, or that all ecotourists are simply long-haul travellers. Ayala further writes that many of the mega-resort chains in Africa and Central America go so far as to donate money to conservation efforts.

However, if the link is being made to ecotourism, which is the focus of her article, then one wonders what percentage of the revenue from the hotels stays within the local communities and what percentage flows back to North America or Europe. Could such an initiative by the big companies be an appeasement mechanism or marketing scheme designed to look green?

It is not easy being sceptical about published work in this area, but increasingly scepticism is what is needed to address some of the issues related to the philosophy and implementation of ecotourism, especially as they relate to ecoresorts. Will ecotourism's fall from grace be directly attributable to the belief and practice that it fits very nicely as a form of mass tourism, and that mega-ecoresorts are the solution to bring ecotourism to the masses? Is this the rationale for their development—the intrinsic need to not deny the masses their place in the sun (or rather rainforest)?

Or rather is it simply that from an extrinsic motivational perspective, it is big business making money the old-fashioned way? Having seen some of these developments first hand, one merely has to dig a bit more closely at some of the unsustainable features of the development. For example, an ecolodge in Mexico recently developed by a large international company used grass and other materials not indigenous to the area in the design of the facility. In addition, no interpretive programmes had been developed to enable tourists to learn about or experience the natural and cultural attractions of the area.

Such develo-pments are merely cosmetic, often with few educational and sustainable features, which presumably are important to this segment, and undermine what Hawkins (1994) and others have suggested about ecotourism as being minimum density and low impact. Even in cases where ownership is in the hands of one or a handful of individuals, local ownership is rare.

CASE STUDY

GREYLOCK GLEN ECOTOURISM RESORT

This recently approved project is a consortium of state, local, not-for-profit agencies, and private interests which have come together to build a demonstration site for the concept of sustainable development in the region of the Berkshire Mountains region of Massachusetts. The developers hope that this site will be a prototype for similar developments throughout the world.

The resort will operationalise the concepts of sustainable development in offering educational, recreational, and conference-oriented programmes. In particular, visitors will be able to enjoy a golf course (developed from the Audubon Society's guidelines for environmentally sensitive golf courses), a nature centre (a year-round environmental education facility), hiking,

Nordic skiing, biking, camping, tennis, swimming, horseback riding, and other recreational activities. In addition to a 200-room resort, 800 acres will be designated as open, recreational land. The developers (Greylock Management Associates) have specified that the following approaches to sustainability will be followed:

- *Natural resources*: The maintenance of forest integrity and animal preservation will guide all development decisions at Greylock; a natural resource inventory will be compiled.
- *Cultural resources*: All cultural artefacts (e.g. farming fields, old roads, orchards) will be preserved and highlighted.
- *Energy management*: Energy meters will be present and interpret energy usage at the centre.
- *Water and sewerage*: Water-efficient toilets and shower heads will be used. Visitors will be presented with guidelines to help them cut down on water consumption.
- *Waste management*: A recycling programme will be implemented, in addition to composting.

ECOLODGE RESEARCH

As outlined earlier in this chapter, ecotourism and the ecolodge concept have been misused by resort advertisers in the past. For this reason research needs to play a stronger role in providing leadership in this area. The following few examples serve to illustrate some of what exists in the area of ecolodge research.

Russell *et al.* (1995) undertook an international ecolodge survey of 28 operators in nine regions around the world (Belize, Costa Rica, Peru, Brazil, Ecuador, the state of Alaska, Australia, New Zealand, and Africa). This study discovered that many of the lodges were found in or adjacent to protected areas, with outstanding natural beauty acting as a key to success of the operation.

Most of the ecolodges sampled were small in size, accommodating about 24 guests, with some successful operations in Amazonia catering up to 100 guests. Prices for accommodation (single night), meals, and local transportation were approximately US$130-170. The authors felt that although most of the ownership had been typically small scale and independent, corporate ownership was becoming more common.

They cited the P&O line in Australia and the Hilton in Kenya as two examples of this recent phenomenon. Finally, they suggested that very few such lodges exist in North America owing to the existing reliance on camping and other, more comfortable recreational lodges. This finding is supported in a recent market study of ecotourism in Alberta and British Columbia.

However, according to Wight (1995), this is not necessarily what is happening. She feels that market research does not indicate that such a trend is due to market preference, but rather it is due to the demand for a range of accommodation. To Wight, a better question would be to ascertain the range of accommodation types supplied by the region or destination area, where, she feels, there is an abundance of the conventional hotel/motel opportunities. She does, however, feel that there is a distinct lack of adventure-type, small-scale, fixed-roof accommodation.

The hard aspects of ecotourism can be identified, at least in part, by non-permanent types of dwellings, including tents and hammocks. The ecotourism experience grows continually softer through fixed-roof units (cabins and lodges) on-site, and through fixed-roof dwellings off-site, usually in the form of hostels, hotels, and resorts.

This hard-soft accommodation continuum relates in part to the work of Laarman and Durst (1987), at least in part, who suggested that one of the hard and soft dimensions of ecotourism was the physical rigour of the trip. Those who were prepared to walk extensively in back-country regions, sleep in camps or crude shelters, or tolerate poorer sanitary conditions were said to have been interested in more of a hard-path ecotourism experience.

If this continuum is to apply to North America, it is logical to ask whether or not such operations are applicable to consumptive or non-consumptive forms of recreation. This issue has not been adequately addressed in the literature, at least from the Canadian perspective, and is an issue that is of the utmost importance as outfitters and operators wrestle with how to refit their enterprises to accommodate the changing recreational focus in the north, because, as Anderson/Fast (1996a:5-4) suggest, 'depending on the characteristics of the package and the participating tourists, outfitter camps [the only form of accommodation in many remote regions of Canada's north] may or may not be appropriate'.

Finally, literature on ecoresorts seems to indicate that accommodation, although important, is not the overriding motivation for visiting regions. ARA (1994), for example, places accommodation below the natural setting and wildlife viewing (of primary importance), and other secondary activities related to the experience. To this, Wight (1995) adds support by suggesting that accommodation is an enabler of the overall ecotourism experience; basically tourists select the experience, then choose the accommodation.

Often, though, prearranged package tours dictate much of the on-site experience, including choice of accommodation, restricting the opportunity for ecotourists to choose lodging, and reinforcing the point that there is an element of ambiguity as to just what ecotourism entails. According to Grenier *et al.* (1993:9), 'one person's ecotourism dream may be another's touristic nightmare'.

One of the unfortunate realities of ecotourism is that despite its altruistic intentions, to date there is little evidence that it is less intrusive than other types of tourism development. It is indeed frustrating that we continue to talk of appropriate means by which to control development, yet have very few successes to report on. Those who do report success have perhaps not been operating long enough to let, for instance, the destination life cycle unfold. In many localities around the world, local initiatives are chipping away at the conditions or circumstances that continue to plague ecotourism development. It is within the local arena that such change must occur.

There does seem to be pressure from international development firms to integrate the concept of ecotourism at a grander scale. While there certainly appears to be the opportunity to provide the tourist with a degree of the ecotourism experience at such a scale, caution needs to be used in promoting such areas as true ecotourism sites.

Where this relationship between mass tourism resorts and ecotourism breaks down seems to be in relation to the elements of ownership and control at the destination, with international or multinational domination of the industry still in existence. Regions intent on the development of ecotourism must be able to secure both consensus within the community and the means, i.e. the decision-making responsibilities, to move away from many of the conventional global tourism development dysfunctions that are so prevalent within the industry.

SOCIO-CULTURAL CONTEXT OF ECOTOURISM

In the past decade or two ecotourism has become increasingly visible and significant in a number of ways. It is commonly referred to as the fastest growing sector of the tourism industry; estimates of the amount of money it generates annually range from $30 billion to $1.2 trillion. Early in the 1990s, the organization that became the International Ecotourism Society, a combination of trade organization and advocacy group, was founded. That same period saw the appearance of the Journal of Sustainable Tourism, and in 2002 the Journal of Ecotourism appeared.

More spectacularly, the United Nations declared 2002 the International Year of Ecotourism. The growth of the industry is not hard to understand, for its expressed goals and image are laudatory.

Ecotourism involves travel to enjoy and engage with attractive and interesting surroundings—often identified as 'natural'—in a way that does not degrade those surroundings. It also involves travel to enjoy and engage with attractive people and their activities—often identified as 'indigenous' or 'exotic'—in a way that respects and supports them.

More materially, ecotourists are seen to be more likely than regular tourists to make use of locally owned accommodation and services, and consequently to benefit the local economy. Further, they are likely to pay user fees that support parks and other conservation projects.

As the executive director of the International Ecotourism Society put it, ecotourism 'should:

- Protect and benefit conservation;

- Benefit, respect, and help empower local communities; and
- Educate as well as entertain tourists'.

In these descriptions of ecotourism is an implicit, and at times explicit, favourable contrast with regular tourism. For instance, the executive director of the International Ecotourism Society said that ecotourism is 'a profound, indeed revolutionary, concept, challenging the mass tourism industry and travel as we've known it'. Some have expressed unease about this contrast and the laudable construction of ecotourism that it includes.

Here we focus on two aspects of that unease. One revolves around the definition of ecotourism, which is so elastic that it may be close to meaningless. This elasticity is manifest in the divergent estimates of ecotourism expenditure presented above; the difference between them would seem to reflect widely divergent definitions of ecotourism. The other is the tendency to conceptualize ecotourists and ecotourism in what may be termed an 'ecotourist bubble'. By this we mean viewing ecotourism in a way that ignores its context.

Perhaps because of the positive and commercially valuable perception of ecotourism, more and more tourist facilities apply the label to themselves. While there are endless attempts to produce a standard definition, this means that the ecotourism industry ends up including, at one extreme, firms that cater to deep-green conservationist hikers in the Appalachians or the Pennines and, at the other extreme, package tour operators who include an optional afternoon snorkelling or even sunbathing in a park near the tourist hotel.

This fluidity of definition in practice is apparent in an influential review of ecotourism by the International Union for the Conservation of Nature. In it, Ceballos-Lascurain (1996: 20) invokes a fairly strict definition, effectively as sustainable tourism with a low environmental impact. However, when he produces estimates of the economic value of ecotourism (1996: 46), he invokes without reservation a study that states that 40-60 per cent of all international tourists are ecotourists, which would seem to employ a much looser definition. The result of this fluidity is an appropriation of the label by interested parties, so that 'ecotourism' becomes a brand used to promote tourist destinations just as it is used by tropical countries as a label for their tourism development policies.

From one perspective, this has led to the complaint that 'far too much gets labeled as ecotourism' while, from another, the divergence of definition is seen to spring from differing understandings of the environmentalism with which ecotourism is associated. There is a tendency to see and experience ecotourism in what we said is an 'ecotourist bubble'. Regular tourists are often said to travel in a 'tourist bubble' that manages them and insulates them from important parts of their destinations. We think that there is an analogous bubble apparent in the ways that ecotourism is presented and understood.

This ecotourist bubble focuses attention on the interaction between ecotourists and the particular nature or culture that they are visiting, which induces ignorance of the context of the visit, the antecedents and corollaries that we describe in this chapter, which are relatively invisible because they are outside the bubble. Obviously this bubble is not uniformly present or of uniform effect; the existence of much of the critical literature on ecotourism is evidence of this. However, we think it fairly common, and worth critical attention.

The nature of this bubble and its exclusions became apparent to one of us in communication with a woman who identified herself as an environmentalist. She pointed out that when she visited Antarctica she was careful not to step on any of the local plant life because it was so fragile.

Although made only in passing, her statement illustrates the effects of this ecotourist bubble because it construes her tourist activity in a way that ignores the environmental effects of the infrastructure and operations that got her from her home in the Northern hemisphere to Antarctica, guided and supported her through that continent, and returned her home again. These antecedents and corollaries can be significant. Consider the typical Northern-hemisphere ecotourist visiting a tropical country, who normally travels by air.

Gossling (1999) calculated that, on average, getting such a visitor from home to destination and back again used 205 kg of aircraft fuel and generated about 650 kg of C[O.sub.2] emissions (for data on travellers to New Zealand, a growing ecotourist destination. This environmental cost routinely is excluded from the ecotourist bubble by those who discuss—and especially those who support—ecotourism.

This bubble has socio-cultural aspects as well which are unsettling given ecotourism's expressed respect of and support for local cultures. There is a substantial body of work that points to the ways in which local populations can be dislocated and disadvantaged in the creation of ecotourist destinations like parks and reserves.

Equally, there is substantial work on the ways in which local people can be led to staging authenticity in their dealings with tourists as well as on the local strains and disruptions that can be induced by catering to ecotourists. Ecotourism does not inevitably harm the natural environment and local people. When removed from its bubble and viewed in the round, some ecotourism may have beneficial effects on the environment—Gossling (1999) says that the C[O.sub.2] emissions may be less harmful than alternative uses of the environment that ecotourists travel to see—and for local people. Moreover, we do not mean that the environment and local people should be seen as properly or naturally existing in some stable, untouched state.

However, the existence of the ecotourist bubble means that the tourists and the industry that serves them are approached by many advocates and commentators without much attention to their antecedents and corollaries. This inattention is unsettling given the professed environmental and socio-cultural claims made for this form of tourism. We want to disperse the bubble by showing parts of the context in which some ecotourism exists; in particular, the effects of ecotourism on local people's relationship with their surroundings, effects that often do not accord with ecotourism's socio-cultural claims. These effects have interested others.

They are worthy of further consideration because they shed light on the cultural underpinnings and institutional context of ecotourism, and on the way in which ecotourism affects the local populations whom the industry is said to support and respect. Our concern here is the relationship between the nature of ecotourism and the ways in which it is presented. Although we present some material on ecotourists themselves, their experiences and understandings are only tangential to our central argument.

THE SETTINGS

We pursue our analysis through a consideration of two coastal sites in the Caribbean that have national parks visited by many tourists. One is the village of Bayahibe, a relatively new tourist destination that Macleod studied in 1999-2000 and again in 2001. It is in the Dominican Republic and is on the periphery of the Del Este national park. The other is the city of Montego Bay, a tourist destination for over half a century that Carrier studied intermittently in the late 1990s. It is in Jamaica and is the site of the Montego Bay Marine Park, one of the first of the country's national parks. As will be apparent, these sites differ in more than the historical depth of their existence as tourist destinations.

The origins of these sites, and especially of Montego Bay, in conventional tourism means that they do not match the archetypal ecotourism destination in being relatively undeveloped with nature and exotic people as the attraction. However, they represent an important sort of ecotourism which involves the marketing of the enjoyment of natural and cultural attractions as part of an otherwise conventional vacation.

Bayahibe is on the southeast coast of the Dominican Republic, about 60 miles east of Santo Domingo, the country's capital. In 2001 it had a population of about 1,800, and the population of the smaller villages nearby effectively had doubled since the middle of the 1990s, as a result of, in large part, the growth of tourism in the area. Before that the main source of livelihood had been small-scale fishing and some agriculture.

In the 1960s, the Gulf and Western Corporation bought plantation land in the area from the Puerto Rican Sugar Company (historic ownership of some of this land is currently claimed by a local family). In the 1970s, Gulf and Western sold much of this land to a private company and gave some of it to the Dominican Republic on condition that it was used to form a national park, now the Del Este park. This sale and donation helped to establish tourism and linked it to the attractions of the natural environment.

The land donated to the Dominican Republic for a park includes a small island, Saona, but not the separating sea channel, so that the park is primarily terrestrial, having no significant waters within its boundaries. During the 1980s the private company that bought the Gulf and Western land built a tourist hotel, the Casa del Mar. By 2001 five other hotels were open or under construction.

Montego Bay, on the northwest coast of Jamaica, is the country's second city, with a population of about 85,000. Unlike Bayahibe, it has a long history as a substantial city and as a tourist destination but, like Bayahibe, its population boomed in the closing decades of the twentieth century, driven by the growth of tourism. By the late 1990s it had fifty-six hotels and construction was continuing. While the labour force of Montego Bay is diverse, there is a significant and visible small-scale, in-shore artisanal fishing sector. Like Bayahibe, the city has a park, the Montego Bay Marine Park, but, unlike the park near Bayahibe, this has no land within its boundaries, and occupies much of the bay's waters.

Like conventional tourism, ecotourism is a form of environmental exploitation, one that often displaces previous forms. To consider the ways in which ecotourism affects local people's relationships with their surroundings, we will begin with a consideration of that exploitation. Doing so will burst the ecotourist bubble by showing how ecotourism developed in ways that frequently do not accord with its goal of respecting and supporting local people. After discussing environmental exploitation, we turn to environmental protection, one of the professed aims of ecotourism.

ENVIRONMENTAL EXPLOITATION IN SOCIO-CULTURAL CONTEXT

Although the Dominican Republic and Jamaica differ in many ways, they share the common weakness of Caribbean economies. Jamaica conventionally relied on primary production for foreign markets: bauxite, sugar, and bananas. Attempts in the 1970s to strike better terms with aluminium companies ultimately failed in the 1980s; Jamaican sugar has been in decline for decades, and the case of bananas is similar, especially since the attack by the World Trade Organization on the Lome convention, which had called for preferential pricing of Jamaica's conventional agricultural exports.

The result has been a marked reliance on tourism. Figures for 1994 illustrate this. In that year, Jamaica's exports of domestic goods were roughly $J39 billion, while foreign travel receipts, effectively tourism, were about $J30 billion.

The situation of the Dominican Republic is similar. By the 1970s, following the end of the Trujillo dictatorship, international loans and a buoyant sugar market helped the country's economy. However, by the early 1980s the economy was weak and external debt was high.

A devaluation of the Dominican Republic peso in the middle of the 1980s attracted foreign capital and tourists. In the early 1990s an IMF deal was arranged, calling for reduced government spending and greater efforts to repay foreign debt, and this was extended in the middle of the decade. The country sought foreign exchange by courting overseas manufacturing capital and foreign tourists. Since then traditional exports—sugar, coffee, cocoa, and tobacco—have amounted to only 40 per cent of all exports, and the country has relied on low-wage manufacturing in free-trade zones, remittances from migrants, and tourism.

The growth of tourism in the Dominican Republic and Jamaica does not, of course, necessarily mark the onset of environmental exploitation in tourist areas. Indeed, it may be less harmful environmentally than the sorts of exploitation it displaces. In the case of the region surrounding Bayahibe, this was sugar cultivation, fishing, subsistence agriculture, and forestry; in Montego Bay tourism did not noticeably displace any significant pre-existing form of commercial environmental exploitation. However, the growth of tourism in these two places, which developed the facilities that ecotourists use, affected both the natural environment and people's relationship with their surroundings.

In Montego Bay the growth of tourism and the attendant increase in the city's population put pressure on city services and, through that, on the natural environment. For instance, city waste and sewerage facilities have not expanded enough to cope, so that each rainstorm washes rubbish down the gullies and leaches effluvia from pit latrines into the bay. More narrowly, the expansion of the city and the construction of hotels entailed filling in environmentally sensitive coastal areas, including a number of mangrove stands.

It also led to the expansion of port facilities to handle increased freight traffic and larger cruise ships, which entailed extensive dredging and land fills that appear to have altered the coastal current in important parts of the bay. The effect of tourism on people's relationship with their surroundings is most apparent in the closure of significant parts of the city's beach front as the tourist hotels effectively restricted access to the beach to all but hotel guests.

The environmental consequences of this growth have affected fishers. The most general and least obvious effect has been a change in their composition and what appears to be a growth in their numbers, making them more fragmented than they had been previously. The growth of tourism, coupled with the weakness in other areas of Jamaica's economy, led many Jamaicans to move to the city. Some, unable to get a job, became 'opportunistic' fishers, turning to fishing in order to secure at least some food and money.

These fishers have been prone to take up spear fishing, which can be learned easily and requires little outlay. The other main forms of fishing in the bay are trap fishing and trawling, which require either a substantial outlay for a boat and equipment or a close relationship with someone who has these. The growth of tourism, then, ultimately appears to have contributed to a rough bifurcation of local fishers.

One group is a body of established fishers who use a technique requiring a boat. Such people tend to be relatively committed to fishing, though their level of activity varies. The other group is a fluid body of opportunistic fishers who use spear guns, though a few regular fishers also use spear guns from time to time.

There is tension between these two groups, reflecting their different backgrounds and orientations, expressed in the assertion by established fishers that the spear fishers are not 'real' fishers, and in the recurrent complaint by trap fishers that spear fishers raid their traps.

For all fishers, the growth of the city and the deterioration of the waters has led to a reduction in the size of their catches, and hence in their ability to support themselves through fishing (their fishing also reduces fish stocks). The growth of tourism has also been accompanied by a rising tension between fishers and the tourist industry, which tends to see them as an intrusion, disfiguring the coastal waters that they hope will attract tourists.

The relationship between fishers and the industry is complex, as many fishers also work in tourist facilities. However, generally they resent their low wages and the constraints and insecurity of their employment, and as fishers they see themselves as being in conflict with the industry. This conflict has been fuelled by attempts to protect the bay's marine environment.

The establishment of the Montego Bay park in the 1990s marked an expansion of ecotourism in the area, which had long been a destination for those quintessential marine ecotourists, divers. However, this expansion was on an established and relatively mature base of tourism and urban development. Consequently, the effects of expanding ecotourism are less striking there than they have been in Bayahibe.

When the Dominican Republic government accepted the Gulf and Western land to set up a park, it also appropriated adjacent land to round out its borders. Villagers had used that land in a range of ways for small-scale subsistence: grazing cattle, keeping bees, growing foodstuffs and cultivating coconut palms, hunting crabs and birds, and as a source of wood for house materials, craft work, fishing gear, firewood, and charcoal. Indeed, as a part of the tourist development process, the entire village of Bayahibe was moved to a new spot about half a mile away, and while some residents were compensated, many felt that they had been treated badly.

This move meant that residents lost an attractive beach and acquired a rocky harbour, and they lost access to the beach within the hotel's compound (and within all hotel compounds), even though Dominican Republic law says that nine metres of shoreline must remain state property. In being evicted to a new site, Bayahibe people's natural surroundings were appropriated by a tourist complex that caters to those occasionally seeking the ecotourist attractions of the Del Este park.

The tourist industry has affected these people's relationships with their surroundings in other ways as well. Tourists regularly pass through or near the village on horseback and quad-bike trips organized by the hotels, or they view it from the air on helicopter tours (though the hotels warn guests not to enter the village alone). This produces a bifurcation of people's surroundings in Bayahibe that is not significant in Montego Bay. Guests at Casa del Mar and the other hotels regularly invade village space in organized tours, while hotel guards stop Bayahibe residents from invading tourist space.

In addition, the growth of tourism has adversely affected the coastal environs in Bayahibe. What had been ecologically useful woods and wetlands got turned into lawns, beaches, and construction sites. Further, the park is a national attraction, and tourists from much of the country are brought to the area and taken by motorboat from Bayahibe to the island of Saona.

This boom in boat traffic has polluted the waters and driven fish away, so that fishers now must travel long distances to get any sort of catch. This has contributed to a decline in local fishing, and by 2001 there were only fifteen full-time fishermen in the village, though many other men fish in their spare time or while they are working as tour boat captains with their boats anchored at sea.

A typical day would see around thirty coaches arriving in the morning to park on the edge of the village. The tourists would then be chaperoned into chartered motorboats carrying up to twenty passengers each, or ferried on huge catamarans for the half-hour journey to the relatively pristine, but increasingly deteriorating, beaches on the island of Saona. The day is spent sunbathing, swimming, dancing, playing beach games, drinking, and eating at the makeshift beach bars, and generally relaxing.

Most tourists encountered were enthusiastic about the tropical setting, the white sand beach, and the particularly colourful sea displaying varying shades of green and blue enhanced by occasional glimpses of starfish, rays, and dolphins. Such visits appear to be ecotourism insofar as they are fee-paying visits to a national park. However, the failure of the park to provide tourists with environmental information, the intrusive boat traffic close to breeding grounds, and the general hedonistic air of these tourist visits all suggest that no one cares much about anything beyond the pleasurable or profitable enjoyment of a pleasing natural setting.

What Duffy said of the ecotourists she studied in Belize would seem to apply here: 'the majority of ecotourists... did not reflect on and confront the results of their own actions' (2002: 30). There were, however, other tourists at Bayahibe who were more thoughtful and engaged with their natural and cultural surroundings. For instance, Priscilla, a French woman in her thirties, was a 'backpacker', travelling independently around the Dominican Republic.

She said that the eastern part of the island was 'beautiful and interesting' and there was a 'joy and sensuality' in the people she had met.

She relished the natural environment of the island and was keen to visit the Del Este park. Perhaps because she was not part of a package tour, she had no maps or guides to the area and hence had no very clear idea of the entrance to the park. She set off along the coast one morning; after more than an hour of walking she reached the edge of the park and, finally, the entrance gate. She could not, however, enter. Entry required a ticket, which could not be bought at the gate. Her experience was not unusual among independent tourists. In fact, individuals very rarely visited the park, most visitors being tourists in coach parties that were organized by hotels or the occasional group of students organized by the national university.

Carole, also French, was in her late twenties and was also travelling independently. She visited Bayahibe in order to sail on the giant catamarans to Saona and had been highly impressed by the undeveloped nature of the village, with its wooden huts, dirt tracks, and traditional appearance, so different from the more linearly planned, modernized settlements on the island. Carole had hoped to visit the park, and did in fact manage to see a small part of it. However, because she was not able to identify a clear route through the park or get a park map, she was unwilling to explore it. She did, though, spend some time snorkelling along the coast of Bayahibe and was surprised and delighted by the tropical fish and coral so close to the shore.

Independent tourists like Priscilla and Carole found the park difficult. Most of the area was heavily wooded and largely impenetrable, and the old paths established by local people were generally overgrown. Even so, the park made little effort to cater to such tourists.

For instance, in 2000, by which time the park had been in existence for almost twenty-five years, there was no established tour of the park interior from the entrance nearest Bayahibe, and the general absence of maps and guides discouraged most independent tourists. The NGO that had recently taken over the park and its tourism development had assigned an employee to establish a trail in the park, but so far without result.

That employee, from the Dominican Republic, was a young graduate of a US university who was unfamiliar with the park: he was even unaware of the cave with impressive Taino carvings just outside the park's eastern entrance, a favourite stop for small coach tours. On one occasion he acted as tour guide for Macleod and a US Peace Corps volunteer who was interested in ecotourism development, pointing out the park's various flora, especially endemic trees, as well as rock formations and caves.

However, we saw none of the protected fauna supposed to live in the park. This young man expressed the NGO's concern that the park would find it difficult to maintain its conservationist aims while attracting tourists as the majority of tourists would come from hotels, and hotel management would want commissions and probably some control over the tours, regardless of the organization's objectives.

Another, and more successful, way of attracting ecotourists was by offering diving instruction, usually in week-long courses. There were two independent dive shops in the village of Bayahibe, and the nearby hotels commonly had their own. An Austrian couple in their late twenties is examples of the sort of ecotourist attracted by these courses. They had, they said, 'escaped' from an all-inclusive hotel for the last few days of their booked vacation and decided to go diving in Bayahibe. The woman explained that she had recurrent dreams as a young girl about diving and being surrounded by fish but that when she grew up she had become scared of going under water.

However, she said that the diving instructor was considerate and held her hand throughout the dive, giving her confidence. The dive was an exhilarating experience for her and she hoped to dive again in the future. Other divers had come to the Dominican Republic specifically for the diving, travelling around the island to various sites. Many were impressed with the diversity of coral near Bayahibe but were worried about the effects that the motorboats visiting Saona were having on the marine life and the coral.

These examples help indicate the type of ecotourists drawn to the area because of its natural attractions—the beaches on the park island, the sea, the marine environment, the park interior—and because of the cultural appeal of Bayahibe as a small, albeit diminishing, fishing village. Some of them, the independent travellers, who may well be environmentally concerned, stayed in local accommodation provided by villagers; others, especially the Saona day-trippers, who may well be indifferent, were in large hotels.

Whatever the type of tourist, however, concerned they may have been about the environment, whatever the sorts of activities they undertook at their destination, they all had to get to the Dominican Republic and to Bayahibe, and thence onwards to the island of Saona or to diving sites, and from there back to their hotels or local accommodation, and, ultimately, back to their home countries. These antecedents and corollaries of their ecotourism tend to be excluded from the ecotourist bubble, their effects ignored.

The spread of ecotourism and the development of the infrastructure that tourists use in Bayahibe has not only had effects on the coastal environment. It has also constrained and under-cut people's relationships with their natural surroundings. These constraints reflect, and hence re-create in the surroundings, a host of cultural values carried by the tourists themselves, mediated by the companies that cater to them.

These values relate to the separation of work and leisure in Western capitalist societies, a separation accompanied by particular understandings of consumption, especially of ludic tourism. They also relate to particular understandings of nature, both in itself. Put differently, commercial interests that profit from ecotourists used their powers to shape the natural surroundings of local people, reflecting values and practices springing from North American and European culture and political economy.

In both Bayahibe and Montego Bay, the growth of international leisure tourism and ecotourism have affected coastal waters so that local people now have to deal with a marine environment that is less productive than it had been. That growth has obliged local people to confront a new construction of their natural environs. What had been an aspect of their surroundings in which they worked to extract subsistence and petty commodities was presented to them as an object of hedonistic and aesthetic pleasure, in terms of which they were viewed variously as intrusions, service labour, or objects of tourist consumption.

ENVIRONMENTAL PROTECTION AND SOCIO-CULTURAL CONSEQUENCES

Although ecotourism is a form of environmental exploitation, one of its aims is environmental protection. Of course, exploitation and protection can be intertwined. In Bayahibe they are two sides of the same process, for the creation of the Del Este park was directly linked to the introduction of tourism. In Montego Bay they are linked as well, but the relationship is more complex (as we describe later). We now turn to a description of the system of environmental protection in each of our sites, to see how these systems have affected local people's relationships with their surroundings, and so how they accord with the aim of respect and support for local populations.

Our description focuses on two distinct sets of people: ordinary residents in both sites, and environmental activists in Montego Bay, the main location we discuss in this section. It may be contentious to include environmental activists and park managers as 'local people' here. However, to exclude them would be to accept only exotics as local, and so to make the ecotourist bubble even more opaque and restrictive.

In Bayahibe, the protection system was the Del Este park, run by the National Park Directorate of the Dominican Republic. It was established in the second half of the 1970s, shortly after Gulf and Western's land gift, and its boundaries have not changed significantly. In 2000, the Directorate, short of resources, entered into a management agreement with a Dominican Republic conservation organization, Ecoparque, which was given oversight of park conservation activities and was expected to become self-financing by charging user fees. Ecoparque has since changed its name to Parques in Peligro (Parks in Peril) and is closely associated with the Parks in Peril programme funded by the Nature Conservancy and the United States Agency for International Development.

The overwhelming lessons of Bayahibe are simple, and can be presented briefly. To begin with, the creation of the park involved significant dispossession of people and restrictions on their activities. A quarter of that park is on the island of Saona, with the balance on the adjacent mainland. Restrictions on land use on the mainland portion, together with restrictions on infrastructural development, effectively obliged the almost 100 people living there to abandon their settlements.

Even those not originally on land that became park have been affected, as, for instance, charcoal burning has been restricted. Life on the island was also disrupted. There were about 370 people living there in 1980, almost five years after the park was established. The bulk of those remain, but they have changed their means of livelihood away from a mix of agriculture and fishing to tourism services and fishing.

Thus, the environmental protection system has resulted in the dispossession of many local people from their homes and aspects of their livelihoods and it has changed their surroundings from the place where they lived and worked to an object of political dispute. This dispute, based on dispossession, has been fuelled by other aspects of the park operations.

For one thing, people were unhappy that the user fees went directly to the park's national headquarters without benefiting local people. Similarly, people say that when a park official stole fees, he was given a very light sentence. They took this as a sign that park management was not concerned with corruption, and it increased their alienation from the park and heightened their sense that it was being run for the benefit of its managers.

An indication of the degree of alienation is the result of attempts to organize a beach clean-up day in 1999: no local people showed up.

The Dominican Republic illustrates a case of fairly straightforward dispossession and alienation, primarily because this has been the most striking effect of the environmental protection system. This was, after all, a park controlled by and catering to outsiders imposed by a multinational corporation and the national government. As a result, local people were obliged to relate to their surroundings differently, as outsiders, for reasons that appeared to make no real sense to them.

Of course, the events described here occurred in the past and hence are not likely to be apparent to those who travel to Bayahibe to enjoy the attractions of its natural environment and local people; certainly they are not pointed out by the package tour operators and hotels. In general, local adults showed virtually no interest in the park as a protected area; they never visited it and they were not concerned with the fate of the species that the park sought to protect. This situation may, of course, change.

With the spread of environmental education in schools throughout the Caribbean, children might well end up with a different set of attitudes toward their natural surroundings, though it is not clear how this will develop or what practical difference it will make. More immediately, it may be that some who cater to ecotourists may end up adopting the Western view of nature as a valued resource. The situation in Montego Bay is more complex. There has been a long history of local agitation for a park there, so that residents are on both sides of the interaction between those who want to protect the environment and those who want to maintain their artisanal exploitation of the environs. Also, because Montego Bay is a marine park, the form of dispossession was subtler than that which occurred at the terrestrial park at Bayahibe.

In Montego Bay there had been a degree of formal environmental protection since the middle of the 1970s, when a small marine reserve was established.

However, marine protection was extended to cover much of the bay in the mid-1990s, when the park was formally authorized by the Jamaican government and the Montego Bay Marine Park Trust began to manage it. The park's efforts to protect the marine environment have affected the relationship of both local fishers and environmental activists to their natural surroundings, and have done so in ways that do not seem to accord with the ecotourist goal of respecting and supporting local peoples. As is the case with Bayahibe, these effects mostly came about in the past, or have come about in other ways that mean that they are likely to be excluded from the ecotourist bubble.

For fishers, one important effect is that they have been displaced from the waters that they had hitherto exploited. One form of displacement is material. The park divides its waters into zones and limits the activities that can be carried out in each, though spear fishing is prohibited in all. Displacement also takes place in the management of the park. While there was some effort to consult fishers when formulating the zone system, there has been little effective communication concerning the park's operation.

This is common in the Caribbean, where local users routinely are consulted about the initial decision to establish a park or reserve, but are much less likely to be consulted about management strategies or the mechanics of park or reserve operation. Displacement takes other forms as well. For instance, the park has not offered compensation to fishers in return for restricting their access to fishing grounds. Legally, fishers lost no property, but they see themselves as being denied access to valued resources.

Further, it is plausible that these Jamaicans see the waters as a part of their patrimony, something like the 'family land' common in the Caribbean. This is land that belongs to all the descendants of the ancestor who acquired it—archetypally at the end of slavery—and having it marks a person as belonging to a particular group of kin. However, it also has an economic aspect, for it is a resource that can be tapped when one is truly down and out. Olwig puts it thus: 'For the greater part of family members, the land has been a place where they might go whenever they are in need, but not a place where they actually have chosen to live' (1997: 151).

When the park imposed its management system, it redefined the bay, denying its status as a resource that people could draw on in time of need simply by virtue of being Jamaican. Fishers were also displaced because they were subordinated to the interests of tourism. The park was anxious to generate user fees, which meant attracting tourists and the support of the tourist industry; indeed, the park was brought about to a significant degree by those involved in the tourist industry.

For fishers, this association between the park and tourism was particularly apparent, and galling, in park environmental management which focused on fishing. Fishers said that fishing harmed fish stocks, but argued that the main problem was the deterioration of the bay's waters brought about by the twin growth of the city and of tourism. Thus, fishers said that they were being told to give up an important basis of their livelihood while the tourist industry escaped criticism. Indeed, many fishers argued that the basic purpose of the park was to make the bay's waters attractive to tourists, and so benefit the tourist industry.

There was much basis for this view, but it is also the case that the park's formal authority was restricted to the sea. Many activists became concerned with the bay because of their personal experiences. For instance, one important early activist ran a tourist diving company in Montego Bay in the 1970s.

One aspect of his orientation to the waters was commercial capitalist, but his relationship with the bay was more complex than this for he also had a clear personal relationship with and pride in these waters, which were not just a commodity but the place in which significant events of his life took place.

As he became an activist, he began to talk to and work with environmental scientists, and so acquired a second and complementary view of the bay, one that construed it in terms of the neutral and objective rhetoric of the scientific knowledge of natural processes. His story is fairly common among important, long-term supporters of the conservation of the bay's waters.

The situation became more complicated once their activism resulted in the establishment of the park. Limited state resources meant that while the government established the park, it did not adequately fund it. In 1996 its operation and management budget was US$85,000; state funding in 1999 and 2000 was about US$15,000 per year.

So, the park had to look for other sources of funding, and tried two different but intertwined ways: applying for money from international donors and charging user fees. The main international source of money for conservation projects in Jamaica is the United States Agency for International Development (USAID), which obliged the activists-turned-managers to relate to the park and its waters in distinctive ways. The core of this was portraying the park as a rational bureaucratic organization, most visible in the requirement that it draw up management plans.

Such plans obliged these people to ignore their personal histories, and hence the understandings of the coastal waters that sprang from them. Instead, they were obliged to think in terms of things like biodiversity, ecosystem and consultative groups. Therefore, the need to produce these plans obliged these people to engage with their marine environment in new ways; what had been a feature of personal history and scientific knowledge became also an object of administrative planning.

The park also tried to get money by attracting ecotourists. This is not a new idea, for the Caribbean was awash with tales of the ways that ecotourism could generate money, and there were published reports that pointed in the same direction. In a study of possible sites for marine parks in Jamaica, carried out late in the 1980s, ecotourism was an important consideration in the evaluation of the different locations considered.

The report stated that marine parks can be pretty much self-supporting through a number of activities: snorkelling, SCUBA diving, glass bottom boat tours arranged for a fee. Usually the marine park organization will leave most of these activities to commercial diver operators and water sport centres. In that case, however, substantial revenues may be obtained from concessions (O'Callaghan, Woodley & Aiken 1988: 37). Using this criterion of potential ecotourism revenue, the report selected Montego Bay as the prime park location, for it was then, as it continues to be, by far the largest tourist location in Jamaica.

Thus, activists and managers had to present the park not just as a bureaucratic, rational organization, but also as a commercial organization. Appropriately, of the five action plans in the park 1998 management plan (Montego Bay Marine Park 1998), the longest is the fifth, 'Financial sustainability', with the goal of becoming 'financially sustainable through utilizing all possible sources of revenue, cost sharing and partnerships'. In other words, people were induced to relate to their marine environment as a commodity, access to which was to be traded for money. Thus, senior park management were concerned to enhance those aspects of park waters that they thought would attract ecotourists.

Probably they would not have stated what they were doing in just this way, but they embraced any opportunity to learn about consumer demand, especially the demand from divers, a particularly salient body of ecotourists: what are they looking for in a dive site? One activist with a substantial history of involvement in conservation in Jamaica made the commercial point bluntly. The tourist industry should pay a levy for environmental protection. He said that their situation is 'Just like in any business. It [the environment] is a maintenance cost'.

Certainly the activists did not respond to these pressures by relating to the bay's waters only in commodity terms. Rather, their personal orientations, supplemented by scientific ones, became supplemented in turn by bureaucratic and commercial orientations. And activists appear to have seen these institutional pressures as an intrusion, and complained about them often in the form of stories about the USAID and the iniquities and idiocies of its policies and projects.

For these Montego Bay activists and managers, as for fishers there and local resource users in Bayahibe, the national parks that help make these places ecotourist destinations do not mark just an effort at conservation of the sort that accords with ecotourism's environmental image. In addition, they mark an intrusion on people's relations with their natural surroundings, which would appear to conflict with the socio-cultural side of ecotourism. Most obviously, these parks have had the material effect of restricting people's access to those surroundings. Moreover, they have had a more cultural or symbolic effect, imposing new meanings on those surroundings, whether as nature to be celebrated or as commercial resource to be managed.

The questions that concern us revolve around the ways in which ecotourism commonly is presented. Ecotourism is said to have two main aspects: the celebration and protection of the natural environment and of local people.

However, understanding ecotourism in this way seems to follow from placing it in a bubble that obscures the contexts in which the industry exists. Our two Caribbean case studies help 'burst' the bubble and make these contexts more apparent.

Our analysis has focused primarily on the socio-cultural side of ecotourism, its celebration of and support for local people. We argued that, at least in these two sites, the bubble excludes from visibility the socio-cultural consequences of ecotourism that seem not to accord with its socio-cultural objectives. For both locations, the establishment and operation of the facilities that are used to attract tourists have disrupted and constrained local people. These disruptions and constraints are embedded in the foundations of these ecotourist destinations.

This is clearest in Bayahibe, with its tale of dispossession, physical dislocation and local dispute attendant upon the fairly recent construction of hotels and establishment of the Del Este park. In Montego Bay these disruptions and constraints are less obvious; they are fairly far in the past, or less visible in the present. Those disruptions concern who fishes and why, where they fish, in what way, and how productively they do so, and how environmental activists understand their surroundings.

We point to these problematic events and processes for two reasons. First, they sit uneasily with the ecotourism goal of respect and support for local people. Second, they are excluded from view by the ecotourist bubble, which restricts attention only to the here and now of the ecotourist's visit.

Just as the environmental and social aspects of getting those ecotourists from their homes to their destinations and back again are excluded from the bubble, so too are the environmental and social aspects of constructing and maintaining what they use, see, and do at those destinations. Certainly we do not mean that no ecotourists are aware of this, any more than we mean that no analysts or commentators are aware of it; but that awareness comes in spite of, rather than because of, the common image and presentation of ecotourism.

To put this in broader and more portentous terms, in excluding ecotourism's context, the ecotourist bubble fetishizes ecotourism and the travel and consumption that are being sold to potential ecotourists. Famously, Marx (1929 [1867]) posited a tendency to the fetishization of commodities in capitalist systems, the tendency to present the commodity for sale in a way that obscures the social relations and situations that bring it into existence and to the attention of the potential buyer.

That fetishism, expanded to include an environmental dimension, seems to be at work in ecotourism. From within the bubble's confines of the here and now of the ecotourist's visit, it makes sense to say that one is careful not to step on plants in Antarctica; from a less fetishized perspective, the relationship between that claim and the assertion that one is an environmentalist is more dubious.

The fetishism of the bubble is perhaps clearest when considering the environmental dimensions of ecotourism practices and their relation to the goal of protecting the environment. We have pointed to another area where it seems to exist: local people's relations with their surroundings. There is yet another and possibly more subtle manifestation of it in the way that local people appear to be rendered in ecotourism. The phrase 'local people' does not mean what it appears to say on its face, people who live in a locality.

Rather, from an ecotourism perspective the phrase seems to mean people in the locality who bear a distinct set of cultural practices, such as styles of clothing, house design, songs, foods, and artefacts. It is the distinctiveness of their practices and artefacts that made, for instance, Mayans (Medina 2003) a suitable ecotourist attraction, a set of local people to be respected and supported. Where is the fetishism in this? In focusing on the practices and the artefacts, the ecotourist bubble excludes from view the social relations and situations that bring them into existence and to the attention of the ecotourist. Local people, then, are reduced to material expression, the context of which is occluded.

This opens the way for staged authenticity and so raises yet another question about the distinction between ecotourism and mass tourism. It also, however, makes the ecotourist bubble more self-sustaining: if the material manifestations are there, it is not necessary to attend very much to the social relations that underpin them, or to ecotourism's effects on those relations.

We have presented an extensive set of questions concerning ecotourism's professed goals of support for the environment and for local people. This questioning should be placed in the context of some of the observations made at the start of this chapter. Ecotourism advocates contrast it favourably with mass tourism, and the rapid rise of ecotourism is said to mark a radical change in tourism toward environmental and social responsibility.

We do not doubt that there are responsible ecotourists, no more than we doubt that there are responsible firms in the ecotourism industry. However, the fluidity of the definition of ecotourism means that there seems to be a tendency to include within it the sort of ecotourism that occurs at Bayahibe and Montego Bay. As we have argued, this ecotourism is responsible only if seen within the confines of the bubble. Until that bubble is burst, observers are poorly placed to speak of who is or is not an ecotourist, the responsibility of this form of tourism, and what the existence of the sector might say about the changing nature of tourism.

ECOTOURISM AND ENVIRONMENTAL FUTURES

Monte Verde, Costa Rica, has recently become a popular tourist destination among North American, European, and Costa Rican ecotourists desiring to experience rain and cloud forests. The resplendent quetzal, a migratory bird with colorful plumage and mythical connotations, figures as a central icon and spectacle in Monte Verde's cultural economy of tourism. This chapter explores how the practices of producing and consuming quetzals are embedded in and reflect contested interpretations of forest landscapes, authentic experiences, and environmental histories and futures.

As spectacles around which touristic experiences are often organized, quetzals are invested with nostalgia and hopes for the future. By focusing on the various social contexts in which quetzals are produced, viewed, and explained, this chapter examines some of the processes by which transnational and local discursive and capitalistic formations, increasingly organized under the banner of ecotourism, claim the authority to fix the meanings, histories, and futures of Monte Verde landscapes and nature more generally. (Ecotourism, Costa Rica, environmental activism, tourist spectacles)

Several weeks after he began a new job as a maintenance worker at a small cloud-forest preserve in the Tilaran highlands of Costa Rica, Manuel Azofeifa (a pseudonym) invited me to walk with him through the forest. Located in the Monte Verde region, one of Costa Rica's most renowned sites of nature conservation and ecotourism since the 1970s, the Reserva Santa Elena where we took our walk was a relatively new reserve, opening in the early 1990s. Manuel explained that as a career cattle rancher he had paid relatively little attention to the establishment and expansion of forest preserves and the growing numbers of foreign tourists visiting this remote mountainous region in which he and his family have lived and farmed for 50 years.

He decided to work at this preserve not so much because he wanted a change of career or to participate in the tourism economy, but out of a desire to support his son's high school, which had acquired the cloud-forest preserve in 1995 to fund its daily operations. We carried machetes and our lunch, as is typical on long walks like this, but Manuel viewed this walk differently from others he had taken, and not simply because he had not been in this forest since it was formally protected in the late 1970s, or because he now worked here as an employee.

The shift in Manuel's approach to this walk was reflected in the camera he carried, a small point-and-shoot that he rarely used except for special occasions like parties or family trips. This was the first time he had taken a camera with him into a forest.

Manuel explained that he brought his camera because he wanted to take a picture of a waterfall he had heard was in a remote section of the forest to show his wife and daughters, since they would never come this far into the forest. When we found the waterfall he posed for a picture in front of it, donning my cowboy-style hat, for he said he wanted to look like he was on an aventura (adventure).

Walking away, Manuel talked excitedly about waterfalls, saying that they are particularly what Costa Ricans enjoy when they visit forest preserves. Then, on hearing the call of a resplendent quetzal, he hurried ahead to see it. When I caught up to him, he was pointing his camera up a tree at the quetzal and making noises to get its attention. He snapped a photograph, turned to me, and announced, "You know, five years ago, I might have shot at this bird with a gun, probably just for the hell of it. But, you see, now I shoot it with my camera."

ECOTOURISM AND THE CONTESTED GROUNDS OF NATURE

A characteristic act of tourism is to insist on difference and mark it by various techniques of observation, including photography. That Manuel judged the waterfall and the quetzal as different enough to mark with photographs suggests that for him these sights stand outside his ordinary, workaday experience. But this is not necessarily as obvious as it may seem, since while quetzals and waterfalls may not be everyday occurrences to Manuel, a cattle rancher, they are at least not as exotic to him as they would be to an infrequent or first-time visitor to a Costa Rican cloud forest.

The fact that a year and a half later, as we reviewed his family photo album, we landed upon the pictures of that day—a blurry image of dark green with no obvious bird and a picture of Manuel in front of the waterfall with my hat—reinforces the idea that at the very least, these sights were worthy of remembering and showing to friends and family members.

When I asked why he kept these photos in his album, particularly since one of them did not really seem to show anything, Manuel told me that it was a way to remember "la aventura que tuvimos aquel dia" (the adventure we had that day). Aventura, he explained, included visiting places he had not seen before. But he must have gone to places before that he had not previously visited, yet had not felt compelled to take pictures of them, much less put them in the family album. So what was different about this occasion?

If we take into account, following Simmel (1971:197), that "adventure, in its specific nature and charms, is a form of experiencing. [But t]he content of the experience does not make the adventure, " then perhaps the difference Manuel sought to mark with these pictures was a different way of experiencing the forest and its attractions than he had practiced before. He was approaching the forest with new eyes (literally, with a camera), and he may have been eager to demonstrate to himself, to me, and to anyone who would see his pictures that he could properly interpret a cloud-forest landscape and recognize its attractions in terms of some of the ideologies and practices of environmental conservation and ecotourism, both relatively new and significant socioeconomic forces in Monte Verde. In fact, by some definitions he was being an ecotourist that day; insisting upon going on an adventure into a cloud forest with a camera to see certain things, like the other ecotourists with whom he was having increasing contact in his new job.

Although it seems a modest and commonplace object to carry on a walk through a tropical forest, the fact that Manuel recorded attractions through a camera lens represents a significant conceptual and practical shift in how he relates to Monte Verde landscapes.

Manuel's shift in perspective is bound up with several political-economic and cultural processes through which Costa Rican forests are being resignified as, simultaneously, laboratories for biological science and biotechnology, reservoirs of economic development through tourism, and refuges for touristic inspiration and learning in which certain universalized behaviors are commonly assumed to be more appropriate than locally specific behaviors.

This chapter about those processes in Monte Verde tries to account for certain emergent uniformities in ways of experiencing and knowing tropical landscapes, for it is no accident that Manuel chose to shoot a picture of a quetzal and show it in his album. Touring itself is constituted by the search for photogenic or memorable images from multiple angles, and a strategy for accumulating photographs. But this only partly explains Manuel's actions, for it does not recognize the highly specific reasons he took pictures of what he did; that is, of himself in front of a waterfall and of a quetzal in a tree.

In Monte Verde's emerging complex of touristic images and activities, the resplendent quetzal, a migratory bird with colorful plumage and mythical connotations, figures as a central icon and spectacle of consumption. As events around which touristic experiences are often organized (not only for those who travel to Monte Verde but increasingly for those who live there), viewing, photographing, and representing quetzals exist within a densely moral arena in which the positive and negative aspects of ecotourism and environmental conservation in Monte Verde are assumed, expressed, and opened for reflection.

As synechdochic references for the emergence of ecotourism, quetzals are invested with nostalgia, representing real, imagined, or desired natural and social histories, as well as economic, environmental, and cultural futures. The quetzal therefore represents a key site (and sight) in ongoing struggles over how to view, comprehend, and interact with Monte Verde's landscapes.

There is tension at the heart of producing and consuming quetzals as touristic spectacles, related to their temporal and spatial dynamism: on the one hand, as touristic object, the quetzal is fixed in time and space, as a site/ sight to register within a quest to register other sites/sights (at certain times of the year, when its migrations bring it to Monte Verde), and on the other hand, timeless, affirming the moral imperatives of pristine and undisturbed landscapes. Embedded in the processes of knowing and representing quetzals, then, are such contradictions that are mediated by competing conceptions of chronological priorities and their spatial manifestations.

The natural and social histories of quetzals are not based on neutral chronologies, for they translate into certain uses for forest spaces (such as preserving them in perpetuity) and carry specific ideas of who can use the spaces and when. In other words, quetzals are appropriated by, and are appropriate representatives of, processes by which the relationships between rural Costa Ricans, foreign tourists, and Monte Verde tropical forests are being restructured.

By focusing on various social contexts in which quetzals are produced, viewed, and explained, this chapter examines some of the processes in which transnational and local discursive and capitalistic formations, increasingly organized under the banner of ecotourism, claim the authority to fix the meanings, histories, and spatial boundaries of Monte Verde's tropical forest landscapes.

Attention to these details reveals that within the context of Monte Verde ecotourism there is no single definition of or commitment to incorporating and comprehending nature, but ongoing encounters between multiple ways of thinking about and relating to natural and social histories in a context of uneven relationships of power and authority.

THE RESPLENDENT QUETZAL AS TOURISTIC SPECTACLE

In Monte Verde, several potent signs dominate the grounds of what counts as worthwhile for tourists to view and how to make sense of these views. Culture, insofar as it is understood as human inhabitants and their social relationships or traditions, is not the central target of most touristic viewing. For the most part, campesinos such as Manuel represent an obligatory, usually awkward, culturally vapid, and ecologically threatening backdrop typical of many Third World landscapes. But in their explorations, ecology seekers also seek culture, and Monte Verde does have its own cultural icons: North American Quakers who settled in the region during the early 1950s. Rejecting U.S. militarism and pioneering a peaceful agrarian lifestyle, at least some of the Quakers also brought with them preservationist convictions, reflected in the protection of a forest watershed that is now the Monteverde Cloud Forest Preserve, an internationally renowned research and tourism destination.

The Quakers have been fully integrated into the mythology of visiting Monte Verde, and many foreign (especially U.S.) tourists arrive with expectations of participating in their social experiment of peace and natural resource conservation. But for the most part, for the over 60,000 visitors to Monte Verde each year, seeing a Quaker, much less interacting with one, is a remote possibility.

The reason for this lack of interaction between Quakers and tourists is partially explained by the fact that Quakers themselves are not stereotypically identifiable. They do not look like "the Quaker on the oatmeal box" (as one British visitor commented to me), nor do they actively present themselves as touristic curios.

More important, however much tourists wish to see living Quakers, viewing people and their culture is marginal to touristic practices in Monte Verde, whereas viewing cloud forests and certain animal species is central. Just as Monte Verde environmentalist fundraising efforts have been tied to certain charismatic animal species, so have Monte Verde touristic practices; indeed, the two are mutually determinate. For example, the golden toad and resplendent quetzal, promoted internationally by Monte Verde environmental activists as unique and endangered (the former mysteriously not seen since 1989), have been used as justifications for the preservation of cloud- and rain-forest ecosystems as absolute nature preserves.

Tourists and other visitors, including individuals like Manuel, have participated in and reinforced the potency of these images—especially of quetzals—as they have moved through Monte Verde social, commercial, and physical spaces. Indeed, for some tourists the very reason to visit Monte Verde and its cloud-forest preserves is to view the quetzal that they have come to know as bird watchers, television-documentary viewers, or in some cases as donors to the international fundraising campaigns of the Monteverde Conservation League, the Monteverde Cloud Forest Preserve, and their philanthropic allies (World Wildlife Fund, the Nature Conservancy, etc.).

For some Monte Verde environmental activists who promote ecotourism as a central strategy for the long-term viability of rain- and cloud-forest preservation, tourism to view quetzals represents a central reason to preserve such forests in the first place.

Conservation and tourism have motivated an important realignment of economic possibilities and political activities in Monte Verde. While dairy cattle and cheese production once dominated the regional economy and local political processes, these activities now coexist and sometimes compete with the interests of tourism entrepreneurs and environmental nongovernmental organizations. Indeed, in the space of five years, tourism emerged as a major economic force in Monte Verde: during the late 1980s, milk production represented as much as 67 per cent of regional income, but by the mid-1990s, tourism represented approximately 65 to 70 per cent of regional income.

Resplendent quetzals are migratory birds, and during the times of year that they are passing through and nesting in Monte Verde's forests and cattle pastures, one is likely to find tourists asking for them and scrambling through forests and pastures to view them.

The number of tourists demanding the experience of viewing a quetzal is not insubstantial, since the quetzal's nesting period coincides with tourism's high season (March-April). During this time, when several hundred tourists may visit Monte Verde's most popular forest reserves each week, it is not uncommon to encounter small crowds of tourists craning their necks to view a quetzal nest.

This is partly related to the fact that, much like visitors to a theme park, visitors to Monte Verde and its forest preserves expect to view things that are outside of normal human sight, a condition the quetzal fits well because of its much-acclaimed beauty. In a context where animals are difficult to see through the intense profusion of botanical life that are cloud (and to some extent rain) forests, the male resplendent quetzal represents an unusually spectacular sight, with its long tail and emerald-green and red colors.

The quetzal is not by essence spectacular (even if many would claim it is on aesthetic grounds), but it is so in a theoretical sense: its presence is an event or performance that is co-opted by tourism, and around which tourism is organized. "Spectacles, great and small," MacCannell (1989:235) points out, "are productions of moral-aesthetic equations and ratios which provide evaluative frameworks for the full range of human qualities and accomplishments."

In this sense, viewing, recording, and representing quetzals have significant moral connotations, but these activities carry different significance and represent different dreams, chronologies, opportunities, and responsibilities for participants in the Monte Verde tourism economy.

At their most spectacular, quetzals are paradoxically both fixed in time and timeless. They represent the redemption of nature by the triumphant efforts of international (mainly North American and European) environmental activists who have raised money to purchase Monte Verde's cloud and rain forests. The act of viewing a quetzal fixes it in a specific time and space as a sight to consume within a quest to register other sights.

In other words, the desire to view quetzals exists within a universal and structured process of bringing nature under human management and purview, and reduces their viewing to one moment in that process. This is possible because the highly specific socioeconomic conditions that created the possibility of the viewing are obscured by the intense visibility of the bird, distracting attention from the wider conditions of its production. At the same time, the quetzal represents timeless and transcendent nature, inhabitant and representative of an Edenic tropical landscape of closed canopy forest. One North American biologist and environmental activist who resides several months of the year in Monte Verde explains, "The fact that there are quetzals here in Monte Verde is a reflection of healthy habitat, and the necessity of maintaining that habitat in its undisturbed state if those quetzals are going to remain here."

In fact, significant research has been undertaken in Monte Verde on quetzals and their migrations under a similar assumption, and their movement through extensive geographical space has justified the purchase of anthropogenically undisturbed forests by the Monteverde Conservation League, even as the time they are in these forests is circumscribed by their migration. Monte Verde's forests are therefore not viewed in isolation from other Costa Rican forests, and the absence of quetzals in Monte Verde does not signify that they are forgotten.

Evidence that they breed in Monte Verde's forests justifies that at the very least these forests remain intact as closed canopy forests and preserved in perpetuity. Environmental activism to save and touristic desires to view quetzals are redemptive and nostalgic in another, more mystical sense: they connect the modern with a premodern and sacred past. Naturalist guides and bird advocates often point out that the quetzal was sacred for the ancient Mayas.

In this sense, searching for and viewing quetzals reaffirm the moral imperatives of forest and pristine wilderness preservation, or saving things as they have always been (or at least were when the ancient Mayas were around), since these creatures would not survive without forest cover. Quetzals, in other words, represent a dream of authentic and undisturbed landscapes, and viewing them is participating in a form of time travel and nostalgic mysticism (a sacred journey), referring to the time before the anthropogenically/campesino-motivated fragmentation of their habitat.

Furthermore, the reconnection to a sacred past lays the groundwork for a resacralized present and future, except that it is not from the vantage point of ancient Mayas, but, ironically, modern science.

The result will be that unlike what happened to the ancient Mayas (i.e., that, according to current theory in environmentalist circles, they destroyed their habitat because they overused their resource base), the future of modern humanity's relationship to the environment will be based on sustainability and a new cultural sensitivity toward nature, mediated by environmental experts.

If successful, there is a deliberate transcendence of time itself, a reconstituted timelessness for unpeopled nature. At the outset, it must be noted, this perspective is based on a dismissal of local Monte Verdean ways of knowing and relating to forests' social and economic histories, assuming (often inaccurately) that campesinos represent a unilateral tendency to deforest and destroy habitats, and therefore offer no practical methods or ethical foundations for forest preservation.

3

Towards the Future Tourism Marketing

INTRODUCTION

For most hotel companies, it was only during the 1980s that the word *marketing* was anything more than a euphemism for sales. Indeed, in the competitive landscape of the not too distant past, an aggressive and knowledgeable sales staff could accomplish most activities that related to putting guests in rooms. In the competitive environment of the present time, this has become impossible. Hotel companies that design and market a sophisticated inventory of hospitality services need a similarly sophisticated scheme for letting potential clientele know about their services.

For most hotel companies in the twentyfirst century, true marketing has evolved to reflect this sophistication. This development also acknowledges increased sophistication on the part of guests and potential clientele.

Business travellers, travel agents, and meeting planners who represent and book group and convention business are educated and informed consumers.To serve this clientele, hotels have had to develop marketing efforts and product segmentation, first to interest the market, and second to allow people representing that market to make intelligent choices among competitors.

Increasingly, individual consumers and small businesses are becoming more sophisticated in arranging their own travel plans over the Internet. This represents yet another challenge to hotel marketers: How do we market most efficiently to all groups? Good question.

Marketing has become an umbrella term that covers a number of strategic and tactical activities designed to tell the clientele the story of the hotel's services and to encourage that clientele to make choices based on how one hotel's marketing message matches their needs better than the available alternatives.

In any given hotel or hotel company, marketing includes a range of sales activities, public relations, advertising in all media, design of symbols and images, and the departments of convention services, reservations, revenue management, and, perhaps, catering. It should be noted that research plays a major role in designing marketing strategies and tactics. The monograph presented in this edition by Bianca Grohmann and Eric Spangenberg has a research orientation at its core.

It is designed to assist managers in choosing and generating data that are useful to staying successfully competitive. It is important that managers understand the range within which this data may be interpreted and applied. Successful managers and high-quality organizations are always seeking information and data that allow them to make accurate decisions and design effective marketing and managerial efforts.

These data can take a number of forms but, for the most part, deal with the characteristics of the hotel's target market segment that affect their choice of hotels. In this case, the research seeks to understand how consumers make choices among hotels based on the value of their various attributes.

Among other data that hotels find mechanisms to accumulate and interpret are these kinds:

- *Geographic:* What sorts of communities are represented; what parts of the country or world; how far people travel
- *Demographic:* Age, sex, occupation, income, ethnicity, family, education
- *Psychographic:* Client's self-image, social or peer group, lifestyle, personality traits
- *Behavioural:* Whether the hotel choice is a routine or special occasion; what guest seeks in terms of quality, service, economy; user status; usage rate; loyalty.

While many of the specific details or programmes implied under the marketing umbrella may be farmed out to agencies that specialize in advertising or public relations, the genesis of the hotel's strategic marketing plan must be within the hotel organization itself.

The object contributed to this part by Fletch Waller provides a strong argument for broadening the definition of *marketing* to include all operational aspects of the hotel.This object is an excellent overview of the marketing process. Waller shows the relationship between marketing and operations as a "continuing process" without which hotels probably cannot remain competitive.

Yield management, long a practice of the airline industry, has found total acceptance by hotel marketing and reservations systems. Indeed, it has become an industry standard.The object in this part by Paul Chappelle can be read in conjunction with that by Quain and LeBruto for a comprehensive primer on yield management.

Together, these objects explore various aspects of that practice from the viewpoint of Chappelle, current practitioner. Chappelle lives the theory of yield and revenue management on a daily basis and provides insights about how it works in practice. As the revenue manager for over 30 hotels,

Chappelle has the experience to back up the theory. The Sinclair thesis on hotel pricing should be read in the context of the issues and suggestions raised by the contributions on yield management. But it goes beyond that. Drawing on Sinclair's deep experience in hotel operations, particularly sales, this contemporary work on pricing is up to date and useful not only from a conceptual standpoint but a practical one.

Shaw and Morris bring their collaborative talents in academe and industry to the thesis on the organization of the sales function in hotels. Because, as noted elsewhere in this text many times, the potential markets for a hotel's services and the types of hotel are so numerous, sales efforts can be complicated. Shaw and Morris present this complex departmental function in a clear, straightforward fashion that is both theoretically relevant and operationally practical.

Traditionally, the function of public relations for any organization, particularly hotels, was oriented towards the generation of favourable— usually free—publicity and the suppression or management of bad news. Louis Richmond proposes the different and expanded but not necessarily contrary position that public relations activities can positively enhance the hotel's sales and marketing efforts.

He discusses his experiences in the case of the Seattle Sheraton Hotel and Towers.Using that example, he argues that through creative cooperative efforts with local charity, cultural, and volunteer organizations, hotels can serve the activities of those groups' fundraising efforts and simultaneously position themselves to show the arbiters of potential business how well the hotel can perform.

His examples are instructive. Richmond, who is president of his own very successful public relations firm in Seattle, retains the Sheraton and other hospitality concerns as clients. All in all, the strategies, tactics, activities, personnel, and concepts described in objects and thesiss in this part provide an overview that only hints at everything important to effective management of the marketing function.

Marketing is perhaps the most written-about topic in hospitality literature. Because of the great diversity of opinion, it can be argued that there is no one "right" way to market, nor is any single piece of literature generally considered seminal to hotel marketing. The reader is urged to consider the references cited by contributing authors, the suggested readings, and active perusal of recent hospitality journals to achieve greater understanding of this fascinating process— and, by extension, its management.

BUILDING MARKET LEADERSHIP: MARKETING AS PROCESS

The hotel business has changed enormously over the last 30 years, embracing special niche forms of lodging, new ways of segmenting markets brand proliferation and consolidation, new tools for acquiring customers distribution innovations and globalization. These changes in markets and in ways hotels relate to and capitalize on them have put new demands on marketing.

Marketing, as addressed herein is not the sales and marketing department; I mean marketing in its broadest sense of how hotels respond to and seize on market opportunities.

Definition? Marketing is a process of creating and sustaining productive relationships with desirable customers. Its goal? To produce such relationships more effectively than competitors do. Let's examine the definition and its implications.

Marketing is:

- *A process*: A process, a series of functions and actions for approaching and dealing with opportunities. *Marketing,* as used herein, is not a job but a way of proceeding to create and operate a hotel focused on customers and competitors, a way that incorporates all members of the hotel staff and its support.
- *Of creating*: The essence of marketing is creation: imagination, insight, willingness to change and evolve, and, yes, discard.
- *And sustaining*: Loyalty over time and repeat customers are the key to productivity and optimal contribution margins.
- *Productive relationships*: A relationship must be two-sided, with benefits for both partners in the relationship. In the case of customers, the benefits are wants and needs consistently fulfilled and full value received; in the case of staff, professional satisfaction and operating profits sufficient to fund improvements provide attractive compensation, and provide returns on investors' or owners' capital.
- *With desirable customers*: Not all customers are equally desirable; we want those who are willing to pay, growing in numbers, making multiple purchases, and whose needs we are able to fully satisfy. And the goal?
- To produce such relationships. *Production* implies inputs, outputs, and the measurement of productivity. Marketing productivity has been lagging for the last decade; the rising costs of acquiring customers must be reined in.
- More effectively than competitors do. Marketing success is judged in relative terms, using competitors and similar hotels as benchmarks. As a creative process, especially in a field like hospitality wherein innovations are unprotected and easily copied, the benchmarks and goals are always moving targets. Besting the competition is the constant challenge.

It will be clear that successful marketing of a hotel requires the orchestration of a wide variety of talents and skills, of which sales and marketing personnel are only a part. Chain hotels approach the process one way; independents must do so another. But in either case, market success depends on an effective integration of marketing and operations at the property level under the direction and leadership of a marketdriven general manager.

THE MARKETING PROCESS

BACKGROUND TO EXMAR

Professor Malcolm McDonald of Cranfield University School of Management, a world authority on marketing planning, has produced numerous publications on the marketing planning process over the last 10 years. His best selling book, *Marketing Plans - How to prepare them: How to use them,* now in the Fourth Edition, describes *The Ten Steps of the Strategic Marketing Planning Process* as follows:

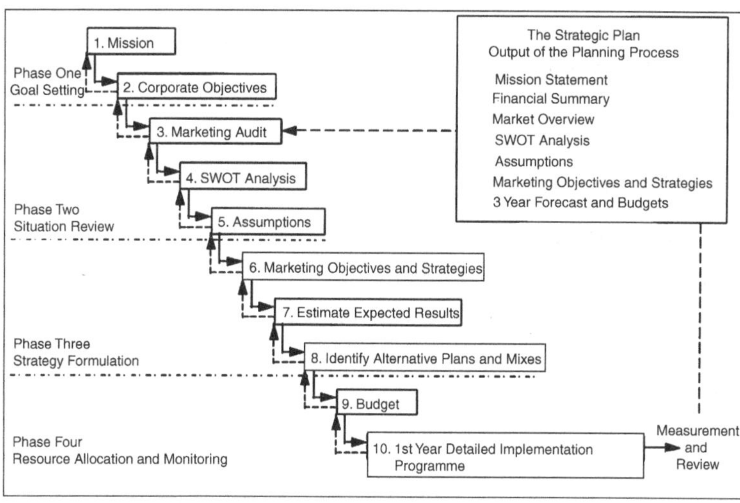

Fig. The Ten Steps of the Strategic Marketing Planning Process

In order to assist companies with the implementation of an effective Strategic Marketing Planning Process many of the techniques were implemented in software programmes. Several prototypes were developed at the Cranfield School of Management, which were widely tested in a variety of commercial environments over a number of years, in order to produce a complete and robust specification of the requirement.

EXMAR

PRODUCT DESCRIPTION

EXMAR is a process, supported by a set of associated services, for developing Strategic Marketing Plans.

It assists companies by:

- Guiding them through a logical marketing planning process
- Prompting and defining key data requirements
- Displaying information graphically to aid understanding of the business
- Providing advice at key stages
- Allowing 'what-if ' analyses
- Automatically outputting the report resulting from the analysis.

There are a number of techniques and methodologies incorporated in EXMAR including:

- Gap Analysis
- SWOT Analysis
- Ansoff Matrix
- Boston Box
- Directional Policy Matrix
- Market Segmentation
- Perceptual Maps
- Porter Matrix
- Objective and Strategy setting.

BENEFITS OF EXMAR

The competitive differentiation derived from EXMAR has been the subject of extensive research by Cranfield School of Management and can be summarised as follows:

- Provides a planning framework which ensures consistency across divisions and each division covers all the key aspects of the planning process
- Takes the 'number crunching' out of marketing analysis
- Gives new insights into the markets particularly through the market segmentation techniques
- Gives powerful graphical display which makes large volumes of data understandable
- Enables easy 'what-if ' iterations as strategy options are explored
- Facilitates team work and multidisciplinary involvement in the marketing planning process
- Improves marketing skills within the company
- Focuses planning on the customer
- Gives a clear vision of markets and the company's position in them
- Adds value to marketing database investment.

IMPLEMENTATION OF THE STRATEGIC MARKETING PLANNING PROCESS USING EXMAR

The successful introduction and implementation of the Strategic Marketing Planning Process within an organisation is dependent on management commitment and high quality process consultancy and training, as well as the EXMAR process support tools. This ensures that key members of staff are familiar with, and trained in, all the marketing processes and integrated techniques that have been developed in conjunction with Cranfield School of Management, and that a first class strategy is produced.

Experience has shown that the most efficient and beneficial method of implementing the Strategic Marketing Planning Process supported by the EXMAR software is to follow the steps shown below:

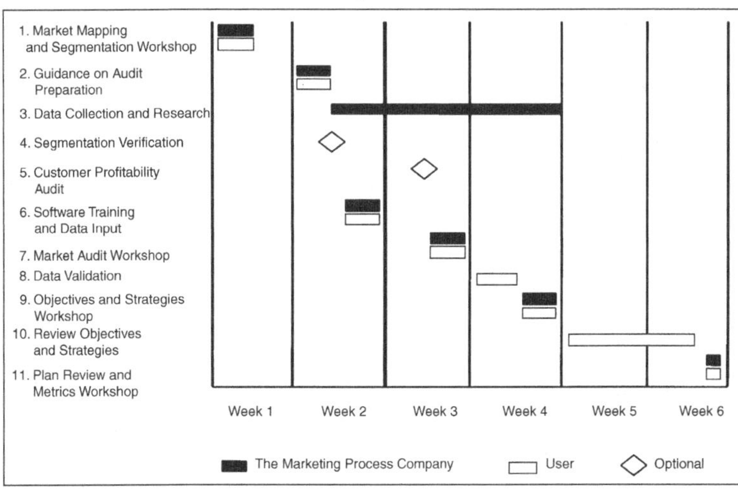

Fig. Project Plan for a Strategic Marketing Planning Process Implementation

MARKET MAPPING AND SEGMENTATION WORKSHOP

The objective of the workshop is to produce a structure for the defined market, which clearly identifies the different requirements that customers look to be satisfied. These different requirements can then be used to develop the alternative strategies that need to be implemented to better access the segments and tune the product offers to suit the customer requirements. It should be noted that most organisations do not have access to the information to produce a definitive segmentation structure that is 100% accurate. However most organisations do have sufficient internal knowledge to produce something that is 'roughly right' and a reasonable starting point. Where this is not the case, the process makes it very clear where the information holes are and the importance of that information. If research is required, the process ensures a rigorous and very targeted brief can be produced.

Market Definition

A market is defined in terms of a need that can be satisfied by the products or services customers' view as alternatives. Once this is clear, the boundaries for the segmentation project can be set.

Market Mapping

A market map defines the distribution and value chain between supplier and final user, which takes into account the various buying mechanisms found in a market, including the part played by 'influencers'.

Market maps help focus attention on key decision makers within a market, and identify key target market segments within a market segmentation project. Market channels and the key players within channels can be easily identified with the help of a graphic presentation of a market. A market map can help deliver key customer and consumer insights, and ensures full awareness of the the total market place.

Market Segmentation

Market segmentation is a concept in economics and marketing. A market segment is a sub-set of a market made up of people or organizations with one or more characteristics that cause them to demand similar product and/or services based on qualities of those products such as price or function. A true market segment meets all of the following criteria: it is distinct from other segments, it is homogeneous within the segment; it responds similarly to a market stimulus, and it can be reached by a market intervention. The term is also used when consumers with identical product and/or service needs are divided up into groups so they can be charged different amounts for the services.

The people in a given segment are supposed to be similar in terms of criteria by which they are segmented and different from other segments in terms of these criteria. These can be broadly viewed as 'positive' and 'negative' applications of the same idea, splitting up the market into smaller groups.

Examples:

- Gender
- Price
- Interests
- Location
- Religion
- Income
- Size of Household

While there may be theoretically 'ideal' market segments, in reality every organization engaged in a market will develop different ways of imagining market segments, and create Product differentiation strategies to exploit these segments. The market segmentation and corresponding product differentiation strategy can give a firm a temporary commercial advantage.

Bases for Segmenting Consumer Markets

- Geographic segmentation
- Demographic segmentation
- Psychographic segmentation
- Behavioural segmentation

Geographic Segmentation

The market is segmented just as to geographic criteria- nations, states, regions, counties, cities, neigborhoods, or zip codes. Geo-cluster approach combines demographic data with geographic data to create a more accurate profile of specific

Psychographic Segmentation

Psychographics is the science of using psychology and demographics to better understand consumers.Psychographic segmentation: consumer are divided just as to their lifestyle, personality, values. People within the same demographic group can exhibit very different psychographic profiles.

"Positive" Market Segmentation

Market segmenting is dividing the market into groups of individual markets with similar wants or needs that a company divides into distinct groups which have distinct needs, wants, Behaviour or which might want different products and services. Broadly, markets can be divided just as to a number of general criteria, such as by industry or public versus private. Although industrial market segmentation is quite different from consumer market segmentation, both have similar objectives. All of these methods of segmentation are merely proxies for true segments, which don't always fit into convenient demographic boundaries.

Consumer-based market segmentation can be performed on a *product specific* basis, to provide a close match between specific products and individuals. However, a number of generic market segment systems also exist, *e.g.* the system provides a broad segmentation of the population of the United States based on the statistical analysis of household and geodemographic data.

The process of segmentation is distinct from positioning. The overall intent is to identify groups of similar customers and potential customers; to prioritize the groups to address; to understand their Behaviour; and to respond with appropriate marketing strategies that satisfy the different preferences of each chosen segment. Revenues are thus improved.

Improved segmentation can lead to significantly improved marketing effectiveness. Distinct segments can have different industry structures and thus have higher or lower attractiveness Once a market segment has been identified, and targeted, the segment is then subject to positioning. Positioning involves ascertaining how a product or a company is perceived in the minds of consumers. This part of the segmentation process consists of drawing up a perceptual map, which highlights rival goods within one's industry just as to perceived quality and price. After the perceptual map has been devised, a firm would consider the marketing communications mix best suited to the product in question.

Behavioural Segmentation

In Behavioural segmentation, consumers are divided into groups just as to their knowledge of, attitude towards, use of or response to a product:

- *Occasions*: Segmentation just as to occasions.we segment the market just as to the occasions.
- *Benefits*: Segmentations just as to benefits sought by the consumer.
- Users status: nonusers, ex-users, first time users, etc.

Using Segmentation in Customer Retention

The basic approach to retention-based segmentation is that a company tags each of its active customers with 3 values:

1. *Tag No.1*: Is this customer at high risk of canceling the company's service? One of the most common indicators of high-risk customers is a drop off in usage of the company's service. For example, in the credit card industry this could be signaled through a customer's decline in spending on his or her card.
2. *Tag No.2*: Is this customer worth retaining? This determination boils down to whether the post-retention profit generated from the customer is predicted to be greater than the cost incurred to retain the customer. Managing Customers as Investments.
3. *Tag No.3*: What retention tactics should be used to retain this customer? For customers who are deemed "save-worthy", it's essential for the company to know which save tactics are most likely to be successful. Tactics commonly used range from providing "special" customer discounts to sending customers communications that reinforce the value proposition of the given service.

Process for Tagging Customers

The basic approach to tagging customers is to utilize historical retention data to make predictions about active customers regarding:

- Whether they are at high risk of canceling their service
- Whether they are profitable to retain
- What retention tactics are likely to be most effective

The idea is to match up active customers with customers from historic retention data who share similar attributes. Using the theory that "birds of a feather flock together", the approach is based on the assumption that active customers will have similar retention outcomes as those of their comparable predecessor.

Niche Marketing

A niche is a more narrowly defined customer group who seek a distinct set of benefits. Ýdentified by dividing a segment into subsegments,distinct and unique set of needs,requires speciallization, and is not likely to attract too many competitors.

Price Discrimination

Where a monopoly exists, the price of a product is likely to be higher than in a competitive market and the quantity sold less, generating monopoly profits for the seller. These profits can be increased further if the market can be segmented with different prices charged to different segments charging higher prices to those segments willing and able to pay more and charging less to those whose demand is price elastic.

The price discriminator might need to create rate fences that will prevent members of a higher price segment from purchasing at the prices available to members of a lower price segment. This Behaviour is rational on the part of the monopolist, but is often seen by competition authorities as an abuse of a monopoly position, whether or not the monopoly itself is sanctioned. Examples of this exist in the transport industry where business class customers who can afford to pay may be charged prices many times higher than economy class customers for essentially the same service.

Ansoff Matrix

To portray alternative corporate growth strategies, Igor Ansoff presented a matrix that focused on the firm's present and potential products and markets. By considering ways to grow via existing products and new products, and in existing markets and new markets, there are four possible product-market combinations. Ansoff's matrix is shown below:

Table. Ansoff Matrix

	Existing Products	New Products
Existing Markets	Market Penetration	Product Development
New Markets	Market Development	Diversification

Ansoff's matrix provides four different growth strategies:

1. Market Penetration - the firm seeks to achieve growth with existing products in their current market segments, aiming to increase its market share.

2. Market Development - the firm seeks growth by targeting its existing products to new market segments.
3. Product Development - the firms develops new products targeted to its existing market segments.
4. Diversification - the firm grows by diversifying into new businesses by developing new products for new markets.

Selecting a Product-Market Growth Strategy

The market penetration strategy is the least risky since it leverages many of the firm's existing resources and capabilities. In a growing market, simply maintaining market share will result in growth, and there may exist opportunities to increase market share if competitors reach capacity limits. However, market penetration has limits, and once the market approaches saturation another strategy must be pursued if the firm is to continue to grow.

Market development options include the pursuit of additional market segments or geographical regions. The development of new markets for the product may be a good strategy if the firm's core competencies are related more to the specific product than to its experience with a specific market segment. Because the firm is expanding into a new market, a market development strategy typically has more risk than a market penetration strategy.

A product development strategy may be appropriate if the firm's strengths are related to its specific customers rather than to the specific product itself. In this situation, it can leverage its strengths by developing a new product targeted to its existing customers. Similar to the case of new market development, new product development carries more risk than simply attempting to increase market share.

Diversification is the most risky of the four growth strategies since it requires both product and market development and may be outside the core competencies of the firm. In fact, this quadrant of the matrix has been referred to by some as the "suicide cell". However, diversification may be a reasonable choice if the high risk is compensated by the chance of a high rate of return. Other advantages of diversification include the potential to gain a foothold in an attractive industry and the reduction of overall business portfolio risk.

GUIDANCE ON AUDIT PREPARATION

The objective of these two days is to ensure that the data required has been identified in detail and the format of the data is consistent.

DATA COLLECTION AND RESEARCH

The following information needs to be collected and input into EXMAR for each product-market as defined in the Ansoff Matrix. This information is then used to drive the market audit.

For each product-market the following information is required:

- Market size and growth Volume
- Revenue
- Market share

Current figures are requested. Historical data is also useful, as far back as available. If only some of these data items are known, the system will estimate data values where possible. In order for EXMAR to construct the Boston Box and the Directional Policy Matrix, it is necessary to define and gather the following information:

- Market Attractiveness Factors - defined once for the business unit
- MAF scores
- Critical Success Factors
- CSF scores for yourself and important competitors.

Segmentation Verification

Often our clients sell products and services into horizontal segments. In these cases, the product-offer maps onto how the customers run their business, and segments are often hard to identify in a way that will give maximum leverage in the marketing plan. To help solve this problem, we have developed a set of tools and processes for analysing existing and potential customer data, and generating and sizing segments.

CUSTOMER PROFITABILITY AUDIT

This is an optional audit and will develop a more realistic view of Customer/Segment Profitability as opposed to Product Profitability. It is often the case that a few segments generate more than 100% of the profit and it is important to identify which segments are actually profitable.

SOFTWARE TRAINING AND DATA INPUT

Two days of hands on training are provided on the EXMAR software including the use of the extensive help system. Data from your company can be entered into EXMAR at this stage.

Market Audit Workshop

The objective of this workshop is to produce the Market Audit and Trend Analysis, *i.e.* What will happen if we do nothing over the plan period?

For each product-market the following information is analysed:

- Financial performance
- Market share
- Relative strengths and weaknesses
- Competitor strategy

- Relative costs
- Market attractiveness trends
- Opportunities and threats
- Assumptions and sensitivity analysis.

Additionally the portfolio of products and services is analysed using various tools including the Directional Policy Matrix and the Boston Box.

Data Validation

The sensitivity analysis on assumptions, whether they be in terms of relative strength, market growth, or profitability are used to highlight those areas where it is most important to verify the data, as wrong assumptions could lead to inappropriate strategies being developed. This may require highly focused Market Research studies on the particular issues identified.

OBJECTIVES AND STRATEGIES WORKSHOP

The objective of this workshop is to set the overall strategies and those that operate at the product-market level. Objectives are defined as the financial performance and market share required from each product market. Strategies are defined as the set of costed actions required to improve competitive performance in order to reach the objectives. It also includes assigning responsibility for the actions.

The process is iterative and can result for example in the identification of generic problem areas, where one set of actions and investments can affect competitive performance in several productmarkets. These usually provide the best ROI.

Additionally the output of the workshop often results in several scenarios, each with its own investment profile, *i.e.* these are the anticipated results of this level of investment as opposed to a larger or smaller sum. These can highlight the implications of the spread of the investment and resources.

REVIEW OBJECTIVES AND STRATEGIES

This phase of the project involves the Client in performing a 'sanity check' on the strategies. This can be both in terms of the viability of implementation, given the internal processes and constraints on the organisation and investment available, as well as a management review.

PLAN REVIEW AND METRICS WORKSHOP

On completion of the project, a day is set aside to review the Strategic Marketing Plan and to identify key metrics for monitoring the implementation and success of the strategies. For example, if 'service levels' are an important Critical Success Factor, then key performance indicators need to be defined that can be measured, such as 'response times to customer requests' or 'adherence to committed delivery schedules'. If required we can offer our

Clients further services to help them design and implement appropriate KPIs in their organisation.

DECIDING WHAT TO BE AND WHAT TO OFFER TO WHOM

In an existing hotel, the developer and architect already may have decided many of the things it is—high-rise or resort, in the business center or on the edge of town, large rooms and baths or smallish, one restaurant or several, wood or marble, with ballroom or not, and so on. Even so, the management team must still consciously examine what they intend the hotel to be and offer to whom. The type of customer originally in mind may not be available now in enough numbers to support the hotel.

Perhaps a competitor has come in and taken away a piece of the market. Perhaps the business center has shifted to another part of the city. Perhaps new customers from Korea or California have replaced the original ones from Europe and the East Coast. Even though the owner has provided a basic envelope within which to operate, there still are options—many things the hotel team can control, many choices to be made on what to offer and to emphasize to various market segments. Is the hotel the place to be seen or the place that guards privacy? Is it better to stress family style or crisp, professional business style? Should the hotel add services, like a Japanese breakfast, to meet the needs of one particular group? Should the team put in meetings express and add more small meeting spaces to tap the short-lead-time corporate meetings market? Should it drop some services the market no longer wants to support?

The answers to what to be and offer are found by studying the marketing situation, which comprises three parts:

1. Strengths and weaknesses,
2. The kinds and numbers of customers available in the marketplace, and
3. The other hotels with whom this hotel competes for these customers.

Careful analysis yields a picture of which segments the hotel is best able to attract and serve. These become the *target markets*—the "to whoms"—and their needs and wants become the "what to be's." The key to successfully deciding what to be and offer to whom is a matter of strategic selection of, focus on, and commitment to a well-defined set of markets for whom the hotel is best suited to compete. Trying to be all things to all potential customers is a guarantee of ineffectiveness.

A good example of focus and targeting is Starwood's W. At risk of turning off a sizeable portion of the business and leisure travel market and leaving families well behind, Starwood focuses tightly on a lifestyle segment of professional and business people, with remarkable success.

The talents required to assess the marketing situation, create a data model of the market's segments, calculate a feasible share of each, and select the targets on which to focus are comfort with data, the ability to observe and infer, creativity, patience with detail, comfort with the hypothetical, and an analytic curiosity. Usually, such analyses are uncomfortably foreign to people with backgrounds in sales, and often to operators as well. It is essential that we teach, motivate, and reward curious, careful, insightful analysis of history and market information—skills that are not natural to those typically attracted to hospitality management. the *target markets*—the "to whoms"—and their needs and wants become the "what to be's."The key to successfully deciding what to be and offer to whom is a matter of strategic selection of, focus on, and commitment to a well-defined set of markets for whom the hotel is best suited to compete. Trying to be all things to all potential customers is a guarantee of ineffectiveness.

A good example of focus and targeting is Starwood's W. At risk of turning off a sizeable portion of the business and leisure travel market and leaving families well behind, Starwood focuses tightly on a lifestyle segment of professional and business people, with remarkable success.

The talents required to assess the marketing situation, create a data model of the market's segments, calculate a feasible share of each, and select the targets on which to focus are comfort with data, the ability to observe and infer, creativity, patience with detail, comfort with the hypothetical, and an analytic curiosity. Usually, such analyses are uncomfortably foreign to people with backgrounds in sales, and often to operators as well. It is essential that we teach, motivate, and reward curious, careful, insightful analysis of history and market information—skills that are not natural to those typically attracted to hospitality management.

SETTING PRICES

Having decided what to be and offer and to whom, the next most important decision is price. Pricing is a critical decision because it determines, first, whether or not the intended customers will purchase, and second, whether they will be satisfied with the value offered and, thus, be willing to return. Third, it determines whether the hotel will be financially healthy enough to maintain itself and reward its employees so customers can once again be satisfied when they do return.

Three factors must come into consideration in pricing—the Three Cs of pricing, if you will: costs, competition, and customers' comfort zones. In F&B, costs drive pricing of menu items and beverages. Drucker says American industry has too much cost-driven pricing, and that it needs more price-driven costing.

Doesn't F&B have the opportunity to build and test menus to discover where price points should be set, and is not the chef challenged to manage ingredients and portion size to deliver the cost and margin structure desired? Yet the cost-driven practice continues.

In rooms, competition is most often the dominant factor. Costs play a role, but changes in variable cost of an occupied room are generally small and rooms' contribution margins are large, typically 65 per cent or better. Moreover, hotel accounting does not measure discounts from a standard price, as do almost all other industries. So there is no visible cost in reducing price to meet competitors. Remember: Any damn fool can cut his price, and some damn fool always will.

Must everyone follow? No. The key is to get in the head of the customer. The truly controlling factor is customer comfort zones, and all too often hotel management leave money on the table because they don't know what those comfort zones are. At what price does the offer attract and deliver value? That is the key question in setting prices.

Price setting requires talent and skill in data gathering and analysis, accounting and building pro formas, interpreting and drawing inferences, and decision making. Do not let salespeople set prices; do not let controllers set prices. Only one person—the GM—can pull together the inputs of sales, control, operations, reservations, and the rest, and make this crucial judgment call. Also, build at least three price scenarios and have the controller and marketing director agree on occupancy impacts. Then run a GOP pro forma on each.

Out of that exercise will come a sense of the best pricing approach to take. Setting prices is the one task the GM cannot delegate, for he or she must live with and be accountable for all that results from this critical decision.

CREATING AWARENESS AND STIMULATING DEMAND

Herein are the typical roles of the marketing department: using sales, communications, and promotions to attract the target markets. But creating awareness is not only marketing's job. Everything the public sees and hears about the hotel—its name or brand, its signs, its restaurants, the public activities of its managers, its charitable support and festivals—all create a meaning, a picture of what this hotel means and offers.

Starwood's W again offers an example: Every element of their presentation expresses the "to whom" they target. In decor, uniforms tone, and attitude, they focus and send a coherent message. It is critical that every department understands the target markets and agrees on the idea, the meaning the hotel intends to have for each of the target customer groups. This is called *positioning;* it's something done not to the product but to the mind of the prospect.

The team should prepare written positioning statements, including a compatible but individual positioning statement for each market segment they intend to target. These statements are the blueprint against which each ad, promotion, and sales call is tested to assure consistent messages are being sent.

And those statements should be shared with all employees.When all parts of the hotel are sending a coherent and consistent message of what the name or brand means and what underlying promise is being made, the hotel establishes a clear position in the mind of the prospects—ideally, one that is attractively distinctive from competitors.

Marketers can use a variety of tools to create awareness and stimulate demand—for example, sales blitzes, telemarketing, newspaper ads, Internet sites and ads, partnership alliances, radio ads, and price promotions. The marketing mix is the range and balance of tools selected and resources devoted to each to achieve the hotel's marketing goals.

In most hotels, direct selling is still the primary marketing tool used to create awareness and stimulate demand.There are two parts of effective direct selling: sales skills and sales management. Consider one the weapon, the other the shooter.

Sales skills are not natural; enthusiasm may be natural, liking to meet people may be natural, but selling is a process that anyone can learn and that must be practiced. Make sure your salespeople are taught how to research their prospect, to listen for needs and purposes, to acknowledge that they have heard the prospect, to transform relevant features into benefits and to sell the customer's success, to anticipate objections and prepare responses, to negotiate, to ask for the order, and to thank the customer and facilitate delivery.

Sales management is quite another thing; often the top salesperson does not make the best sales manager. The sales manager must be able to select salespeople; reinforce their training; coach, counsel and motivate them; assign them to prospects and market segments; set goals, manage compensation, review performance; and troubleshoot. He or she must also be the gatekeeper on contracts and rates, making sure that inventory Compensation of salespeople need not be complicated. *First principle:*Tie compensation to goals set in terms of what you want them to do—that is, produce contracts and roomnights.

Don't just set room-night goals; add measures of relationship or share of a specific customer's business. Have salespeople suggest their own goals for the coming year; participation builds commitment. *Second:* Provide them near-term reward and reinforcement, not postponed rewards. Pay out bonuses quarterly.

Third: Build teamwork so that one salesperson supports and encourages another. Add a team bonus multiplier to personal performance measures. *Last:* Separate performance bonuses from overall job appraisal. No one attends to suggestions for performance improvement if he or she has just received a big check for exceeding goal.

Many full-service hotels are overresourced in group sales and underweighted in transient market tools. Sales efforts should be balanced with other parts of the marketing mix—advertising, publicity, and promotions.

The range of communication options increases geometrically with proliferation of new media—cable television, news magazines and national papers, the Internet, and direct mail and telemarketing. But the eyeballs are not growing apace, meaning the audience for any one medium is steadily shrinking, putting increasing demand on measures of productivity, care in allocating resources, and creativity to get through the clutter. As audiences of prospects become increasingly expensive to reach through advertising, the tools of publicity, the Internet, and direct marketing are increasingly the media of choice.

The Internet is a demanding medium for communication; use professional help to design, maintain, and market the hotel's website as though it were, itself, a product for which awareness must be created and demand stimulated. To draw audience to the site and manage its visibility in search engines are skills beyond the property team. Set specific goals for the site:They might be to attract qualified prospects, to sell services, to provide customer service. Don't just have a site. And measure the experts against those goals.A passive, unmanaged, and undermarketed site is a waste of money.

Promotions can powerfully stimulate demand, but too often, price promotions are resorted to as a last-minute attempt to prop up a weak demand period. Promotions should be planned, justified on a breakeven basis, and used sparingly. Not all promotions need be price promotions; customers invest energy and time in transactions, too: value-added promotions that offer nonmonetary savings can be used to avoid habituating consumers to buying only on sale or shopping only on price. Well-forged alliances for copromotion can increase both productivity and absolute sales volume.

The skills and talents necessary in a comprehensive effort to create awareness and stimulate demand include:

- *In sales:* Initiative; being goal-directed; listening with empathy and imagination; time management; self-confidence.
- *In sales management:* Coaching and counseling; quantitative skills; priority setting, time management, and sense of urgency; leadership and problem solving; ability to manage incentive programmes.
- *In communications:* Ability to write clearly; ability to select, engage, and manage professional creative talents; ability to evaluate and allocate resources among options; comfort with and appreciation of the Internet and the Web.
- *In promotion:* Ability to analyse breakevens; creativity; anticipation; conceiving and selling partnerships and alliances.

MAKING THE HOTEL AVAILABLE

Once a person in one of your target markets is interested in buying, how does he or she reach you? Your hotel's reservations office, the central reservation system, airline global distribution systems, corporate sales offices, and your property sales office are all parts of a distribution network. Travel agents, corporate travel managers and secretaries, meeting planners, and travellers themselves reach your hotel through this network.

Travel industry distribution channels are in chaos by virtue of the shift of travel agencies from commission to fee-for-service models, the rise of the Internet as a consumer's direct booking channel, and online thirdparty intermediaries like Expedia and Travelocity.

Increasingly, the Internet will become your key distribution channel, but in the meantime, you must manage two parallel systems, the traditional central reservation and travel agency channels and the new electronic channels. Are the rooms you want to offer available in both systems, with helpful and upto-date information? Are your prices sensible in each outlet? Making the hotel available is no longer a passive stance but an active part of your marketing.

In other industries, distribution channel revolutions have brought efficiencies that benefit both consumers and suppliers. In the travel distribution revolution now underway, the consumer has benefited, but costs to hotels—the suppliers—have skyrocketed. Since 1993, full-service hotel costs of distribution more than doubled, to $1,377 per occupied room per year in 2002.

Along with these new channels and thirdparty room merchants has come pressure on prices. In the downturn of 2001–2003, this was devastating. Price comparisons are quick and easy for the consumer. Packagers and auction sites unconsciously cultivate the destructive idea that a hotel room is a commodity, as is an airline seat. But hotels are not commodities; each differs in location, features, and benefits. A hotel team must resist the idea that a room is a room is a room, must emphasize their hotel's distinctive positioning, and must resist the urge to simply match the lowest price offered.

For the foreseeable future, both the traditional and Internet-based distribution systems will coexist and have to be managed. This raises a new question:What channels do you want to encourage, and what ones discourage? Conventional wisdom, in recent years, has been to make the hotel's inventory and rates available via as many channels as possible so as to capture from anywhere in the world the last drop of demand for arrival on a given day. Given their sharply differing costs, however, and the difficulty of managing coordinated presence in these new and overlapping channels, the time may be coming for a new strategy.

One possibility is to starve undesirable channels with limited information and access while being fully open and transparent to others. Another approach might be to price differentially among channels to reflect their different costs. A large Hawaiian resort group is already doing that by explaining to consumers what comparative options and costs are. Other chains advertise a guarantee that the lowest price will be found on their own website, which is a low-cost channel for them.

Reservations, revenue, and channel management constitute the fastest-changing part of hotel management today. Channel management requires a comfort with and interest in technology and systems, and a knack for problem solving, anticipating, and risk taking.

CLOSING, CONFIRMING, AND MANAGING REVENUE

How one commits space—a room, meeting space, ballroom, or even a restaurant table— and at what price—determines the revenues and financial health of the hotel and determines the customer's expectation of value.

Revenues must be managed to optimize financial returns and customer satisfaction— that is, the customer's willingness to return. No one department controls the tools of revenue management. They are shared among salespeople, catering and banqueting managers, front desk agents, reservation agents, and so on.

To manage properly requires frequent and open conversation between managers, good forecasting, skillful selling by customer contact people, and an appreciation of each week's goals and targets for the hotel. Poor forecasting, inflexible inventory policies, and conflicting approaches by different departments with whom the customer deals can undo all the best advertising, selling, and promotion.

Through the same forecasting disciplines, hotel teams manage their revenues to maximize the productivity of the hotel and assure its financial health. Revenue management tools and increasingly affordable yield systems can have a major and salutory effect on the financial health of the hotel.

Another part of revenue management is incentives for reservations upselling, conversion of callers, and average rate increases, and for front desk agents upselling. In the same way, F&B staff should be viewed as salespeople and given training on suggestive selling. Inventory policies for tier price quotes by forecast levels of occupancy, for stay-through restrictions, for same-rate substitutions and upgrading to clear demand inventory categories— all these are tools through which reservation and revenue managers optimize the RevPAR performance of the hotel.

It is in the area of revenue management that chains, especially multibrand management companies, have achieved significant advantage over independent hotels and franchisees that do not participate in cluster or regional revenue management.

Decisions on pricing are still the domain of the property GM, but with a centralized expert staff collecting data and forecasting, the advice and guidance available has brought yield and RevPAR premiums to the chain member properties.

Revenue management requires attention to detail and analytic and forecasting skills; tolerance for ambiguity and comfort with change; and managing, training, leading, and motivating reservations agents. This is one of the most critical and dynamic areas of hotel management, one with which every aspiring general manager or director of sales and marketing should take pains to become familiar.

PREPARING TO DELIVER AND DELIGHT

A marketer of a product can count on the factory quality-control system to deliver a consistent product for sale. When the sale is closed, the customer takes the product away and uses it. In a service business, however, the product is human Behaviour, and the customer uses the product in the hotel. Because we are humans, both customers and employees, our interactions are never the same one time to the next. The job of the marketer is to help employees understand what the customer will want, need, and expect, and to sell employees on doing their job with enthusiasm.

In a full-service hotel, the conference services department embodies this preparing idea as its primary function. Conference service managers are the essential group business brokers between sales and operations. Conference services people can create loyal and repeat meeting planners; the job requires empathy, attention to detail, willingness to work unusual hours, action orientation, internal relationship building, and persuasiveness.

Preparing the hotel to fully satisfy and regularly make customers happy is as much a marketing task as attracting customers in the first place.What makes marketing hospitality services harder than marketing a tangible product is that for every market segment there must be two marketing programmes, one directed externally to customers, the other internally to employees.

RETAINING CUSTOMERS

The key to both financial health and market leadership is retaining a higher proportion of customers than do any of your competitors. Retain more customers than others do, and over time your costs drop—because of efficiency, lower advertising and selling costs, better forecasting—and your occupancy and rates rise. Numerous studies validate the high correlation between profit leadership and customer retention.

Frequent-stay rewards are often mistaken for retention programmes. They are not. Rewards can motivate returns only as long as the customer values the points or airline miles or whatever. But they do not create loyalty.They are valuable only insofar as they give employees the opportunity to come to recognize and satisfy the guest, and insofar as they give the marketing department information on who the customer is and where he or she is coming from.

Retaining customers takes more than just doing the job well. Guests and customers must come to know they are valued. Management must build relationships—the tie that binds regardless of a new hotel opening in the market or a hot promotional offer from across the street. Relationships are built on recognition and familiarity, on trust, and on appreciation.Thus, guest and customer retention must be a planned and creative activity that involves both sides of the relationship— the customers and the employees. It takes more than just smiling and trying hard. Among the talents and skills needed are analytic skills, curiosity, direct marketing planning, and management of data retrieval and direct marketing service providers.

MEASURING SATISFACTION AND EVALUATING PERFORMANCE

If the purpose of the business is, in part, to keep customers, does a financial statement of rate, occupancy, revenue, expense, and profit give enough information? No. Also needed is a scorecard of customer satisfaction, of how likely customers are to return or tell others about your good hotel. That scorecard is the guest satisfaction survey. Accounting statements tell of the hotel's financial health; a guest satisfaction scorecard tells of its reputation's health. The scorecard also helps management spot changes in expectations.

Customers are not the same from one visit to the next. Experience with a new hotel, perhaps even in another city, may raise a customer's standards. To measure satisfaction, one needs quantitative skills for tracking, analysing, and reporting data, and the ability to manage the logistics of repetitive distribution, collection, and processing.

The information helps management figure out what the hotel needs to be and to offer next in order to remain competitive and keep customers. Note, now, the return to the first step of the marketing process.

THE CIRCULAR MARKETING PROCESS

In other words, the marketing process isn't the straight-line, step-by-step process, a continuous circle around which management must go again and again as competition improves and as the customer segments in the market change. Only by reviewing and renewing the marketing process will a hotel get ahead and continue to be the leading hotel in its market. This model of the marketing process applies to both the whole hotel and to any revenue or profit center within it. Use it like a checklist when thinking through improving the revenue and competitiveness of any operation.

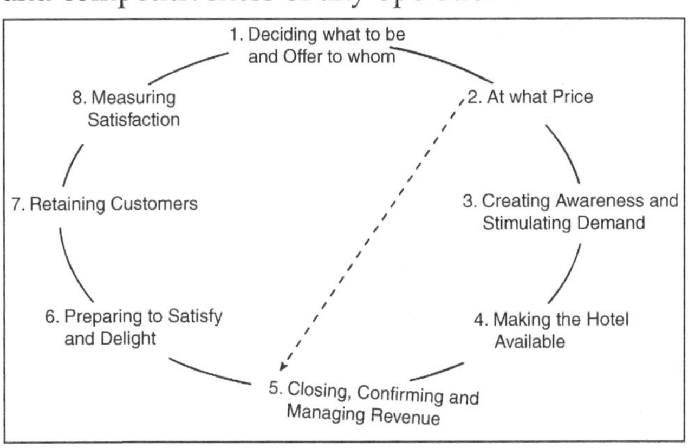

Fig. The Hotel Marketing Process

THE MEASURES OF MARKETING

The health of the marketing process should be measured over a longer time than a month or quarter or fiscal year, and it should be measured by more than just profit and loss data.

A healthy marketing process results in:

- Rising room revenues per available room and rising F&B revenues per available seat and catering space.
- Rising market share to a share index over 100—that is, a larger share of a competitive set's occupied rooms than the hotel's share of the set's available rooms, which is its "fair share."
- Falling costs of acquiring customers, not on a percentage-of-revenue basis but as dollars per unit of sale—for example, dollars per occupied room, dollars per cover, and so on.What is the acquisition cost? The total of the advertising and business promotion budget, plus commissions, reservation costs, franchise fees, and marketing fees. These costs in times of inflation may not actually decline but at least should grow more slowly than do gross operating revenues.
- Rising customer satisfaction ratings. • Increasing retention rates measured by the percentage of business from repeat customers.
- Growing top-of-mind awareness among target customer segments and, if the hotel can afford to measure it, preference by segment rising to number one among your competitive sets.

Management and owners should ask for an annual report card on the health of the marketing process—of the hotel, of a chain, of a franchise group.

MANAGEMENT OF THE PROPERTY'S MARKETING PROCESS

As should by now be clear, the marketing process is larger than any one individual's job. Further, no hotel can afford the myriad talents and skills that must be orchestrated to create and sustain a healthy marketing process; a single hotel is simply not a large enough business to afford having all those talents on staff.

Franchise companies and managed chains have the mass to employ a large proportion of those talents at headquarters, but even they must call on outside services in design, database management, advertising, direct marketing, and so on. But the chains' ability to invest in new tools and hire diverse talents has led branded chains, both management companies and franchisers, to collect increasing numbers of hotels under their umbrellas. The trend towards centralizing marketing functions to serve several hotels in a region, often even hotels of different brands, is accelerating, especially with the advent of Internet-driven information sharing.

The advantages are the ability to integrate multiple sources of information, to hire experts that a single hotel might not be able to afford, to share the cost of sophisticated systems for forecasting, revenue management and customer relationships, and to reduce the expense of marketing to individual properties.

Independents must counter such attractions with cooperative activities and aggressive local marketing. The Internet has leveled the playing field somewhat, allowing independents to be found and reviewed by consumers and travel agents in a way not possible when GDS systems were the only means of access.

PROPERTY RESPONSIBILITY FOR ITS OWN MARKETING

To optimize performance, a property can neither abdicate its marketing to a chain or franchise group nor passively rely on location and presence to bring customers to the door. Each property, whether flagged or independent, must be responsible for creating and managing a marketing process tailored to its particular marketing situation—that is, its available customers; its inherent strengths, weaknesses, and employees; and its competitors. Each marketing situation is unique, even among cookie-cutter chain properties. Each has its own location, competitor, and customer dynamics.

So, given the wide range of talents and skills that must be orchestrated to create an effective marketing process, who is to lead it? Directors of sales and marketing cannot, for the process is much larger than the marketing department. Only the general manager can lead his or her marketing process; only he or she can integrate chain supports, operating departments, human resources, the controller, and—yes, marketing and sales.

THE GM AS LEADER OF THE MARKETING PROCESS

General managers must come to see themselves as the leader of their marketing process and be comfortable in the role. This does not mean becoming expert in all tools and disciplines; it does mean seeing the whole and appreciating when to bring in what talents, when to apply what tools, and how to judge the effectiveness of the process. It means using the marketing process as an organizing concept for creating the management team and a unified viewpoint of mission and challenge.

When a hotel is led by a general manager who sees herself or himself as leader of the marketing process, when that process is thoughtfully conceived and well executed, when all employees see themselves as joint operators/ marketers, that hotel becomes customer-centered, competitive, and a leader in its markets.

Few GMs are trained to do this. Many come to appreciate that location and flag are not enough; many intuitively pick up a smattering of sales, distribution, advertising, and customer retention. But it is the rare GM who weaves these parts into a coherent whole and thinks through the challenge of creating and leading the marketing process. As marketing continues to develop more complex tools and as marketing productivity becomes a more pressing matter, owners, universities, and chains must address this issue of how to develop GM candidates who are comfortable with and capable of leading a comprehensive marketing process.

THE MARKETING PROCESS MODEL AS A PROBLEM-SOLVING TOOL

One last word: The circular model of the marketing process is presented here mainly in terms of rooms marketing. But the model can be applied to every revenue department—to food and beverage outlets, catering, the health club, the business center, and even the laundry. The model can be used for planning, for business reviews, for presentations to lenders and owners, for troubleshooting, and as a checklist when preparing proposals for new services or facilities.

Use the model, make it part of your bag of management tools, and get your team to see their role in terms of this holistic and never-ending marketing process. If you achieve that, you will have gone far to create a customer- and competitor-focused organization, one in which employees see themselves as operators/marketers rather than just "in operations" or "in marketing" or "in HR."

The few hotels that achieve and nurture a well-tuned marketing process and whose employees see themselves as integral parts of it become leaders—in market share, in customer and employee loyalty, and in financial returns to owners.

CONSUMER DECISION RULES AND IMPLICATIONS FOR HOTEL CHOICE

Consumers' choices are influenced by the goals they attempt to achieve. Once a person has recognized a need, such as the need for accommodation when traveling for business or pleasure, he or she engages in an information search to identify alternatives from which to choose. Understanding how consumers evaluate competing alternatives in their purchase decision processes enables marketers in the hospitality industry to design better advertising and promotional campaigns leading to a more favourable evaluation of their offerings in travellers' eyes.This is an important step in increasing the likelihood that consumers will choose their offering as opposed to that of competitors.

Given that most travellers' destinations offer several hotels, how do people choose among them? The answer to this question lies, in part, in research on consumers' attitudes and their relation to purchase intentions and subsequent purchase Behaviour. This stage describes several methods consumers may use to make choices based on the evaluation of identified alternatives.

Attitude is the tendency to respond in a consistently favourable or unfavourable manner towards a target. Important to marketers is that, if measured accurately, attitudes are predictive of Behavioural intentions and relatively stable over time.

Simply put, consumers generally form intentions to choose a hotel brand towards which they hold positive attitudes. Behavioural intentions, however, do not always translate into corresponding Behaviour. For example, although some consumers have preferences and therefore form intentions to stay at Fairfield Inn when traveling across the country, they might end up choosing other forms of accommodation from time to time.Why would they act inconsistently with their intentions?

Traveling with friends who have different attitudes and preferences, temporary price reductions of competitors, or the fact that a Fairfield Inn is not readily available in a specific area might be reasons for inconsistencies between Behavioural intentions to stay at a Fairfield Inn and actual choice Behaviour.

Despite situational factors sometimes influencing travellers' choices, attitudes are ultimately useful in predicting actual Behaviour; changing or strengthening the basis of consumer attitudes may therefore increase the likelihood of consumers engaging in desired Behaviours. In order to change attitudes and subsequent related Behaviour, marketers must understand a few basic decision rules associated with consumer attitudes. We introduce decision rules likely to be implemented by different segments of consumers under varying market conditions.

DECISION RULES

Decision rules are strategies consumers use to choose among alternatives. Several factors can influence what decision rule consumers ultimately apply in a specific situation.

Typically, the more important and less frequent a purchase decision is, the more time and effort consumers are willing to expend making that decision. Choosing a resort at which to spend a twenty-fifth wedding anniversary, for example, is a decision most consumers face only once and therefore are likely to take a relatively long time to make, and they are likely to be careful and thorough in evaluating alternatives.

On the other hand, a salesperson traveling frequently in a familiar territory likely chooses a hotel using a routine process where far less time and consideration are given to alternatives. Further, brand-loyal customers might choose to stay with the same hotel chain whenever possible, thereby avoiding a situation where they are forced to choose among alternatives. In general, the stronger a consumer is motivated to search and the greater the risk associated with a choice, the greater the complexity of the decision rule he or she implements.

Another important characteristic of modeling decisions is the fact that people often do not attempt to optimize choice. If a person's goal is optimal choice, considerably more time and effort is typically required to identify and evaluate alternatives.

Therefore, consumers often choose a satisfactory alternative in order to save time and effort. The use of decision rules in these instances enables people to take shortcuts in making decisions in the face of the apparently unlimited or overwhelming amounts of information available regarding all possible alternatives. Consumers usually work with a consideration set so they do not have to work as hard cognitively when required to make a decision in a given product category. They then make a final decision from this reduced set of alternatives.

Such decision rules are referred to as *heuristics* or rules of thumb. Employing heuristics, people save time and limit complex information processing while still making reasonable or satisfactory choices based on the few brand attributes or characteristics most important to them at the time of choice. In the context of hotel choice, brand attributes are things like location, room rates, and availability of a swimming pool, restaurant, and so forth.

Although the number of consumer decision rules is almost infinite and likely varies by consumer, basic categories and a few specific examples serve as useful tools in modeling and predicting traveller decisions.

Two general categories of decision rules are:

1. Compensatory and
2. Noncompensatory.

Compensatory Decision Rules

Compensatory decision rules model consumers as deriving an overall brand evaluation such that alternatives performing poorly on one attribute can *compensate* for their respective shortcomings by positive evaluations of other attributes. For example, a high-priced hotel might not be perceived positively on the dimension of room rates by some travellers; however, these same travellers might be willing to spend more money knowing they will receive better service or that the hotel is conveniently located—that is, in this example, service and location compensate for the perceived disadvantage of high room rates. The multi-attribute attitude model described in the next part is perhaps the most popular compensatory decision rule.

MARKETING IMPLICATIONS

Once consumer evaluations of salient attributes are determined and their beliefs regarding a hotel brand's offerings are known, managers can use this information to improve their hotel's competitive positioning in the market. The goal of any marketing strategy is to increase positive attitude towards the offering or to encourage the use of certain decision rules, thereby increasing the likelihood of being chosen by consumers. When consumers use a compensatory decision rule, the overall attitude towards a hotel is determined by the sum of the products of evaluations multiplied by beliefs regarding salient attributes associated with the offering.

Consequently, travellers' overall attitudes towards a hotel can be rendered more positive by strategies targeted at increasing the evaluation of an attribute in consumers' decision making, or by changing consumers' beliefs about a hotel's offerings.

Travellers' attribute evaluations can be influenced by stressing the attribute in advertising. This strategy of influencing attribute evaluations is effective in attitude change and also relatively easy to pursue. It is, however, not a strategy always recommended for changing consumers' attitudes when they are using a compensatory model. The potential problem associated with this approach is that attribute evaluations are constant across brands in a consideration set.

Travellers evaluating importance of the availability of an indoor pool is the same for all hotel brands, E, F, G, and H. If Hotel H were successful in a marketing message in increasing the evaluation of an indoor pool with a segment of consumers, say to a rating of _3, it would increase consumers' overall attitude towards its brand. At the same time, however, consumers' overall evaluation of Hotel G would increase by the same amount, as both brands do not differ with respect to consumers' beliefs about their having a great indoor pool. In the end, the attempt to increase consumers' overall attitude towards Hotel H would also benefit some of its competitors.

Thus, sometimes a more effective strategy for improving consumers' overall attitude towards a hotel's offerings is to improve consumers' brand-specific belief ratings. For example, Hotel F could strive to improve consumer belief that it offers a pleasant indoor pool by providing a picture of the pool on its website, or by stressing the availability of the indoor pool in advertisements. While consumer brand-specific beliefs are then likely to increase, Hotel F's competitors will not benefit from its strategy, and Hotel F thereby improves its competitive position.

Assuming that Hotel E cannot do anything to increase consumers' belief that it is not located in proximity of a skiing area, a strategy it may employ to increase consumers' overall attitude towards the property is to add a salient attribute to the set of attributes consumers consider when making hotel choices. For example, Hotel E could provide free accommodation for children staying with their parents.

It is likely that parents would consider this option important when choosing a hotel. As long as other competitors do not offer this service, Hotel E enjoys some advantage in the choices made by its target market. It is essential that when adding a new attribute, marketers consider the following: First, the attribute added must be important enough to the hotel's target market to be included in consumers' subsequent decision making. Second, the belief that a particular hotel possesses this attribute must be stronger than the belief that any of its competitors do.

This marketing strategy, often referred to as a *strategy of differentiation,* is likely to be successful when these conditions are met. Differentiation, however, is unlikely to be sustainable— that is, over time, competitors identify what added attributes successfully attract customers and copy them, thereby creating consumer belief regarding their own properties. Thus, the hotel that introduced the new salient attribute often can expect to lose its differential advantage over time unless it maintains a unique characteristic like a special location or a fabulous chef in the kitchen.

Increasing belief strength for a hotel's attributes is not always a successful strategy, assuming a compensatory model is being used. For example, consumers may find it relatively unimportant whether the hotel offers low room rates or not.

The importance rating for low room rates is _2—that is, consumers in this particular target segment evaluate low room rates negatively, perhaps because they associate low rates with low quality or with small, underfurnished rooms. In this case, stressing that a particular hotel offers low rates, thereby increasing the strength of consumers' beliefs, may adversely affect consumers' overall evaluation of a property. If you compare Hotels F and H, you will see that the strong belief that Hotel H offers low rates negatively affects its overall evaluation. Hotel F, on the other hand, benefits from consumers not being aware of low rates.

It is important to note that importance weights associated with attributes vary across market segments. For example, while business travellers on corporate expense accounts or consumers on a once-in-a-lifetime vacation, such as a honeymoon, may attach less importance to low rates, more price-sensitive market segments usually weigh low rates more heavily in their hotel choice. It is therefore important for marketers to carefully define the targeted market segment prior to conducting their research and applying evaluation weights and beliefs to similarly disposed consumers.

In general, it is crucial to find out what attributes targeted consumers feel are most salient to their decisions and, in response, increase performance regarding these attributes and commensurately inform market segments of this stronger position. The resultant positive attitude towards the offering should then increase the likelihood of the hotel being chosen by travellers using a compensatory decision-making model. Alternatively, as a strategic move, particularly for special niche properties, marketers may want to encourage consumers to abandon the linear compensatory model. Niche market segments may exist or may be created through marketing communications; these target markets might be better served by hotels focusing on one or more of the noncompensatory decision rules presented.

For example, a segment of highly price-sensitive customers predominantly using a lexicographic decision rule with low rates as the most important attribute may constitute the primary target market for a property. In this case, travellers can be targeted by offering low prices and/or frequentstay loyalty programmes. At the same time, services deemed unnecessary or unimportant by this customer segment can be eliminated or minimized. The fact that some customer segments expect a minimal level of performance on several attributes when they use an elimination-by-aspect or conjunctive decision rule, however, implies that focusing performance and/or marketing on a single attribute may be inadequate for some segments of travellers. A hotel would then benefit from creating a level of "at least acceptable" attributes in addition to providing stronger packages of the same attributes offered by competitors targeting the same market segment.

Overall, knowing how consumers make decisions should help hotel managers to design better properties, packages, and services, and help them market those offerings to their respective target segment, thereby improving competitive position.

HOTEL PRICING

TRADITIONAL APPROACH

The single most important criterion of success in any business, including hotels, is profit.The purpose of this object is to discuss the importance of hotel pricing and its influence on yield or revenue management, especially in terms of profit generation, and because of inherent dangers to the industry worldwide, integrity of the established pricing structure.

Historically, price has been determined by the triangular relationship of cost and demand in the context of competition.

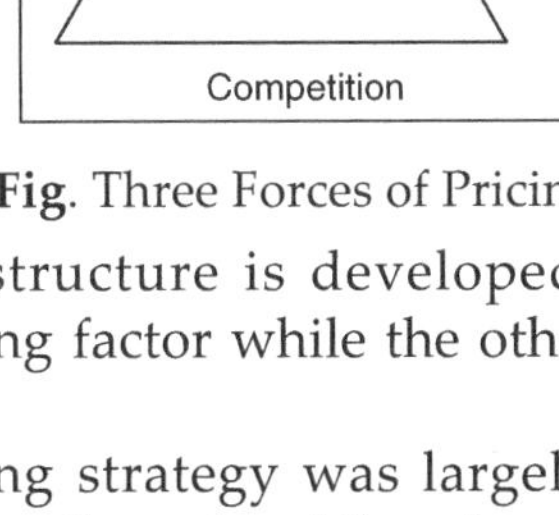

Fig. Three Forces of Pricing

The actual pricing structure is developed with one of these three components as the deciding factor while the other two play supplementary roles.

The traditional pricing strategy was largely cost-driven. Many hotel operators tended to favour the rule-of-thumb method. This approach, also called the $1 per $1,000 rule, states that hotels should charge approximately $1 per night for every $1,000 of room cost, based on an average 70 per cent occupancy.

Although popular in its day, the calculation of cost was commonly misunderstood. Another widely used quantitative method was the Hubbart Formula, developed in the late 1940s as a guideline issued by the American Hotel Association. It focused on computing an average room rate that would cover operational costs and yield a reasonable return on investment. These quantitative methods are fairly static and therefore suited for a stable economic environment. Qualitative pricing approaches, such as percentage increase of previous-year rates adjusted for inflation, payroll increases, and new cost of supplies, reflect more realistically the projected cost.

Other qualitative techniques are less exact but, by being competition-oriented, they offer more flexibility. The Pied Piper or Follow-the-Leader method uses competition as the basis for rate setting, while the Gouge 'Em approach tries to lure business away from other properties by undercutting their prices. If there is no competition to speak of, Hit or Miss fluctuation of rates tied to profitable occupancy levels could be employed. The drawback of competition-driven pricing is its sole focus on rate comparison, ignoring differences in operating expenses and customer- perceived value. An effective approach, therefore, calls for a mix of methods adjusted for different situations. The fundamental question remains:What should be the driving force in formulating a sound pricing strategy? In today's dynamic business environment, which discards the traditional view that market demand for room rates is largely inelastic, demand orientation seems to provide the best fit.

Table. Traditional Room Rate-Setting Methods

Quantitative Methods		Qualitative Methods
$1 Per	• Determine the cost of Gouge 'Em the property (building, furnishings and equipment). • Divide the total by number of rooms. • Divide the calculated cost per room by $1,000. • Estimate at 70% Hit or Miss average occupancy.	• When demand is $1,000 low, set rates below the market level. • When demand is high, set rates at a premium. • Record occupancy at each pricing level.
Hubbart Formula	• Calculate operating expenses. • Add taxes and insurance. • Add expenses for asset depreciation.	• Analyse the collected information periodically to determine which level was most profitable.

	• Deduct income from sources other than room revenue. • Divide the total by number of rooms in the hotel. • Adjust the calculated Percentage room rate for estimated Increase occupancy.	• Set the rate at the most profitable level. • List the rates that were charged in the previous year. • Calculate rate of inflation, payroll increase, the new cost of supplies. • Convert the increased cost into percentage increase. • Increase previous year rates by the calculated percentage increase.
Pied Piper	• Set rates according to what other hotels in the area are asking for comparable accommodation.	

CURRENT PRICING CRITERIA

"Our pricing is market-driven, not costbased," says Scott Farrell, corporate director of distribution with Fairmont Hotels and Resorts, a Toronto-based chain of luxury properties. When the chain is setting its prices, it starts with comprehensive market research. Based on the data, the correct price for each marketplace is determined. If there is a major shift in a market, then the prices will adjust for that. However, if there is a major shift in a demand curve, then a shift of price may have no effect.

It may actually leave more money on the table. For example, if the airlines go on strike, a significant shift in the demand curve would result. Under such conditions, decreasing the rate by $50, for example, would only result in a $50 loss. If there is an opportunity to go after a new targeted market with a specific offer, enabling the chain to capture a greater market share, then lowering the rate serves its purpose. Generally, however, lowering rates across the board is not the preferred pricing strategy.

PRICING: WHO IS IN CHARGE

While independently owned properties make their own pricing decisions, in case of a chain it is usually corporate headquarters (HQ) that sets pricing guidelines. Often, individual properties are still responsible for the actual pricing. Because they are held accountable, they must balance corporate guidelines with their autonomy to set their prices. Caroline Shin, member of the revenue management team at Starwood Hotels and Resorts Worldwide, which operates a number of upscale brands, such as Sheraton and W Hotels, stresses the cooperative nature of this relationship.

Successful pricing strategies arise from an ongoing interaction of both sides. Corporate HQ provides sophisticated tools and in-depth market analysis that would be beyond reach of individual properties. Property managers, on the other hand, offer their experience and knowledge of regional specifics that may have gone unnoticed by the corporate team."The people who have been in the property understand the dynamics of that market, and they have developed pricing intuition," explains Shin.

Some experts view intuition as a valuable part of the pricing mechanism, and even managers who are technically savvy check the numbers against their gut feeling.

PRICING: SCIENCE, ART, AND INTUITION

Pricing distribution and revenue management techniques are a mix of science and art. Recent research shows that two-thirds of managers making strategic decisions under pressure and time constraints use a combination of analysis and intuition.

The advent of modern technology, such as yield management software packages, has further strengthened this link. "Even the most sophisticated analytical model for forecasting, may it be for hotel pricing or for thermal dynamics of a nuclear plant, still needs variables based upon assumptions," says Shin, who used to work as a nuclear engineer.The more business- savvy hotel management becomes and the more they understand the hotel dynamics and the market, the more can be gained from training them how to define their experiencebased intuition and put it into numbers. In this respect, an interaction between the corporate revenue management team and individual hotels is paramount. "Every time I go out to a property, I learn something new. It only helps me when I build my analytical models to almost translate what they know into numbers," confirms Shin. The better hotels can do that, the better models they can develop. Nonetheless, inaccurate historical data remains a major limitation.

No model is ever going to be perfect, though.What seems to work best is to teach hotel managers how to use the model and to understand the direction of the pricing decisions they need to make. That is the scientific part.The art piece comes into play when they infuse the model with their knowledge and intuition.

Staff training is an important part of this process. "We can't just have Ph.D.s sitting in one room coming with all these models and we just roll it out. At the same time, we can't just have people with intuitions run around and set prices," says Shin.

Revenue management teams must make sure that hotels understand how to employ the models in their daily pricing decisions. When science is applied, the revenue team can go to their experts, ask probing questions, and get solid results. Even though intuition is a part of this process, it is based only on a hypothesis that could have been triggered by a discussion with a customer, knowledge of what is happening in the marketplace, or historic trends. That is why pure intuition is not sufficient. "Managers must have reliable data to support their hunches," cautions Scott Farrell.

CUSTOMER NEEDS

Customer satisfaction is a crucial part of marketing, pricing, and yield management. Any pricing strategy established by the hotel management must attract customers willing to pay the specified rate.While price is a determinator of the customer profile the hotel is looking for, it is also an indicator of the quality of services and the market segment the hotel is competing in.

Therefore, yield management uses information about targeted customers' purchasing Behaviour and product sales to develop pricing strategy together with inventory control that delivers products that are better matched to customer needs, create greater demand, and, on that account, produce greater revenues. Lieberman states that yield management is the process of maximizing profits from the sale of perishable assets, such as hotel rooms, by controlling price and inventory and improving service through systemization.

An exact definition of the target market is essential. There is a definite and firm perception in the psyche of the customer, who views the price as the value forthcoming. Therefore, the eventual satisfaction of the customer is the paramount task of the pricing mechanism. This is the make-or-break factor of the entire hotel, especially if the value expected does not match the price.

ROLE OF TECHNOLOGY

While the approach to hotel pricing is still ruled by supply and demand, speed and sophistication of room-rate yield or revenue maximization is now much increased due to two technological factors: yield management software and Internet bookings.

Yield management software packages enable hotels to use a higher number of roomrate levels, or buckets, and to control inventory for rate availability in real time. Each level may consist of several room rates open under given conditions to yield a maximum profit. Traditionally, hotels used between three and five rate levels; otherwise, the adjustment became too complex for the human brain to work with. The introduction of software removed this barrier, and some hotel chains now use up to ten rate levels.This allows implementation of much narrower ranges for each bucket, thus optimizing price elasticity. This further means the software model recognizes the point at which the same number of bookings can be achieved at a higher rate.

Online monitoring of room inventory in real time facilitates the timing of the adjustment. So far, the biggest limitation is the reliability of historical data. Even in its imperfect form, the system has made a difference. However, hotel managers are fully aware that it takes years to develop brand recognition and quality but just a push of a button to damage or even destroy it, if the pricing is not set up knowledgeably. As the technology becomes more sophisticated, it will eliminate such questionable practices as overbooking, which aims at compensating for last-minute cancellations by taking in more than 100 per cent reservations. Besides the question of whether overbooking is ethical and, in some countries, even illegal, better technology would definitely improve the quality of service provided by properties that engage in this practice.

Another area where technological advancement had a great impact on hotel pricing is the Internet. Its use as a booking tool has created a new level of pricing transparency and tiered competition. It also penetrated the negotiation of corporate rates. Many hotels see the effect of the Internet as both good and bad.The good side is that website bookings are growing every day.

As more customers become familiar with their favourite hotel websites, hotel companies have started investing heavily in website development and upkeep, which gives them several advantages. First, the cost of online bookings is lower than for bookings made through other distribution channels. Companies do not have to pay commission because the booking is direct, circumventing all intermediaries. Online booking also provides an opportunity to monitor inventory in real time without reliance on a distributor willing to share and regularly supply data. Last but not least, it generates loyal customers by making them eligible for bonus points, which they cannot earn if they use an Internet intermediary.

That is exactly where the flip side of the Internet lies. The intermediaries are getting more powerful and growing significantly in volume. Because most of them show all hotel rates on their website, they make the information accessible to any computer user. One way to meet the challenge of more powerful intermediaries, especially if hotels need to move inventory, is to utilize auctions where the name of the hotel is not disclosed to the customer until the transaction is finalized. Such action, however, calls for extreme caution so that it does not damage a hotel's reputation or threaten its strategic partnerships.

As intermediaries become bigger, rate transparency will increase to the point where it will drive the market, especially when computer literacy and Internet access become the norm.

Moreover, the Internet allows nonbranded hotels to compete more heavily with the branded hotels because they can now be displayed just as readily. Without significant advertising expense, they can compete on price. For some markets this does not matter, especially when the brand is powerful enough to charge the premium and get the business.

In highly competitive markets, however, the competition creates an additional strain for the individual property. Many branded hotels must now compete with other brands through the traditional distribution channels and with nonbranded hotels on the Internet, which, in principle, lowers hotel rates. A frequently adopted strategy is to invest heavily in website development and customer loyalty programmes, assuring excellent website functionality and that customers are rewarded for booking directly through the hotel website rather than through the website of a thirdparty intermediary. Both Fairmont and Starwood, for example, utilize their high-quality loyalty programmes in this way.

Internet booking also changed the way corporate accounts are negotiated. Because many companies now require that their employees make business travel arrangements via the corporate website, the placement of a hotel or a brand on this booking tool is of strategic importance. Being listed first in the accommodation part, for example, may bring in a higher volume of business and thus substantiate a lower negotiated rate.

LONG-TERM STRATEGY TOR THE INTERNET

Because hotels cannot expect that Internet distributors will go out of business, they smartly conclude that a partnership with the devil is better than a fight with him. Besides using their own websites, hotel companies are also making sure that the cost of their transactions goes down continuously so they can compete even at lower rates—while maintaining a good relationship with their carefully selected online intermediaries.

There is a large number of distributors to choose from. On one end of the spectrum is, for example, Expedia, which allows participating hotels to control their rates, meaning a hotel can change its rates any time it wants.At the other end are companies, such as Hotel Reservation Network that bind hotels contractually to a locked rate that cannot be changed. Some hotel chains do not want to partner with these distributors because they like pricing flexibility and want to make sure their rates yield as much as possible.

Adaptation to new technology has been the biggest component of change for intermediaries as well. Companies that do not have the most current technology working in real time or allowing hotels to yield rates in real time are usually not considered a suitable distribution partner for some chains. On the other hand, companies that invest in real-time technology to yield rates are ideal partners because, as the industry sees it, they work with, not against the industry by permitting hotels to raise or lower rates in real time. "They work with us," says Caroline Shin. "They give data to us very frequently so that we understand the travel pattern bookings on their website.Then we compare it with what is happening on our website and also what we are getting outside the Internet to make sure that our market mix is set appropriately." Pricing flexibility, compatibility with the desired hotel image, and protection of its strategic partnerships, together with cost, play important roles in selecting an intermediary.

THE ROLE OF CREATIVITY IN PRICING

Creativity, either of an individual or a team, can and often does lead to innovative pricing ideas. However, its application must be specific, not just directional. It is not enough to state,"We have to do something about our occupancy level." A pricing campaign must target a number of sold rooms or generated revenue that is required in order to break even or to do better. This specific approach injects efficiency into allocating marketing money to areas where it is most effective and in periods when it is desired.

If there is no task direction or overall pricing leadership, the most creative idea may book only ten roomnights instead of one hundred. It may generate more customer loyalty, but that is something the hotel may not need at the moment, although it could be an acceptable outcome in a low-season month. Pricing leadership helps team members understand the hotel's current situation and direct money and creativity to do exactly what is needed. Creativity comes up with the idea, which serves as a vehicle, but spending marketing money the smart way is a matter of experience in innovation, which turns the idea into a successful product. Creativity also plays a large part in employee satisfaction, and it lowers turnover.

In a sluggish economy, some hotels start paying attention not only to profit as the bottom line but also to revenue. This means they monitor closely the accrued cost as well as the generated revenue, thus achieving the maximum yield. Interestingly, contemporary price leadership may take different forms.

It could mean, for example, elimination of smoking rooms throughout the property. Many U.S. motels are revamping rooms, ripping off cigarette-damaged furniture and carpets, and designating them as nonsmoking. This saves on maintenance and adds to overall packaging flexibility when the business is hurt by lackluster demand. This tactic means drapes, carpets, bedding, and other furnishings must be replaced less frequently; it also mitigates fire risk and enhances cleanliness and overall safety.

THE ROLE OF HUMAN RESOURCES IN PRICING

Some large chains recognize that pricing is a complex issue and that they need to get better at it.There is a new focus on analysing the culture of pricing and how it can be improved. This approach is reflected even in the kinds of people chains are hiring. Although the majority of staff involved in strategic pricing are in the hotel industry and have a background in revenue management, others are in the airline industry and have indepth travel revenue management experience.

Some chains have sought access to this experience by hiring from outside the hotel industry. This is to encourage diversification of thinking and new ways of thought—completely out of the box, as the traditional team members are joined by researchers doing a different kind of optimization analysis. The goal could be as radical as trying to manage risk or optimize towards the railroad industry and its scheduling.

On the surface, these tactics have nothing to do with revenue management *per se*.A lot of experience in optimizing difficult travel, however, can only be gained by bringing in people with different backgrounds in consulting or with in-depth Internet experience. In order to move pricing and revenue management to a different level of thought, a new mix of people is necessary. For this approach to work, adequate training must be in place.

In this respect, basic HR functions, such as hiring and training, have an impact on pricing. What is necessary is not only to train personnel in quantitative core skills but also in strategic thinking. For example, when a hotel does not want to take a specific piece of business, it must ask such questions as:What is the revenue? What is the rate? What am I displacing by this decision? Where do I think this will go? How does it help my RevPAR?

Hotel managers must become more analytical so they can use all the new tools now available. When reports are created, team members must be taught how to use them.A lot of training must be provided for corporate executives, general managers, and regional revenue directors as well. They all must be trained to think more strategically and to understand analysis and the reports so they can help their individual properties.

DIVERSIFICATION: THE IMPROVEMENT OF THE PRICING PROCESS

As noted, exclusive hotel industry experience may lead to ossification due to one-sided judgment and the inability to see beyond the familiar. From this perspective, experience is both an asset and a liability. It is human nature to take for granted the way things are done after being in the same environment for a while.

Therefore, hotel chains are continuously creating and refining pricing strategies to accommodate not only different market segments but also different situations a hotel may face based on occupancy levels. Corporate HQ tries to identify these different situations and associated variables. "It is almost like a bag of goods, a bag of pricing strategies that should be tested," says Caroline Shin.

Hotels are given the full menu and encouraged to try a certain strategy if they are in a specific situation. Depending on the region, an individual property may use one set of strategies more than another. In a weak economy, however, the chains have to work harder and be more flexible because the market is overflowing with demand.

Adapting step by step, a hotel may apply a different strategy every week.The problem for the corporate office is to identify situations a hotel might be in and seek remedy. For example, if group bookings are low this week but competitors are full, how can the property make up the difference with transient or leisure business? The general manager may ask the corporate team, "What pricing strategies can I use in order to fill my house?" Then he or she may ask, "What else worked before for other hotels, and what may work for me based on my market specifics and market characteristics?" That way he or she can test each strategy using the provided tool and personal experience.

PRICING: SUPPORT AND PROTECT

The corporate pricing structure is also in place to support and protect members of the chain in a number of areas including pricing and partnerships. The corporate office sets guidelines for hotels in terms of pricing structure and the market segments they deal with. Fairmont Hotels and Resorts, for example, focuses on four segments: transient leisure travel, group travel, business travel, and wholesale. The corporate structure provides guidelines about how the segments fit with each other, how they cross over, and where they reside in the overall pricing structure.

This information is necessary because every segment acts differently. Most market segments are dynamic and require frequent rate adjustments. One exception is the wholesale market, where pricing is still largely done the traditional way: A wholesaler provides a net rate, marks it up, and sells it to the general population.There may be a hidden cost, however, if the distribution chain includes an operator acting as a middleman between the wholesaler and the supplier.

When setting up the overall pricing structure, one starts with the retail rate, which is a bucket of premium or best available rates charged on the open market. They usually do not carry any restrictions, such as cancellation fees, and they are fully billable. Depending on the level of occupancy, one of these rates is available on any given day when the hotel is not fully booked. It is up to the yield management system to identify which BAR to offer. All other rate types, such as discount rates and prenegotiated rates, are determined in relation to the retail rate. For instance, a corporate rate for a high-volume client will be probably set lower than the BAR rate that is estimated to sell most during the period when the contract is in place. This way the rates are nested within each other in a manner that makes economic sense.

The corporate pricing guidelines follow two main criteria: to maximize revenue and to protect key partnerships.While the hotel sales force negotiates contracts with key partners, such as longstanding corporate accounts or wholesale volume accounts, they make sure to protect these partnerships and provide them value. At the same time, they take every opportunity to maximize revenue. One cannot survive without the other, reiterates Scott Farrell. However, it is up to the hotels themselves, with guidance and additional research, to determine in their marketplace what their pricing structure should look like.

A diversified corporate team, with a mix of people with a hotel industry background and others skilled in optimization modeling, fulfills an additional function. It acts as a risk prevention mechanism, a necessary prerequisite for managing the risk inherent in pricing. Any chain with a wide variety of hotels must make sure the properties are covered in all kinds of situations. One risk containment scenario might be that the chain, in response to a changing demand curve, acquires a type of business that the brand has not catered to traditionally.

Caroline Shin explains, "Sheraton did not take on airline crew business because we did not want crew members lingering in the lobby; it affected our brand image. But we thought maybe we could start taking that when our RevPAR index or occupancy slips to a certain point. So we are trying to change the standards of different market segments we are willing to take."

On the international scale, another risk management plan would be analysing operational cost and determining whether to close down part of the hotel if market research shows occupancy will not be high enough. When PESTEL (political, economic, sociocultural, technological, environmental, legal) analysis indicates demand will drop precipitously for an extended period instead of hoping for the best and running a full house with a full staff, the hotel may decide to shut down floors or restaurants and save cost until the market picks up again.

Selection of the appropriate strategy will depend on the market specifics and protection of the image. A property may opt to close down several floors over the weekend if it caters mostly to business clientele staying during the week.

It would not, however, suspend room service, although unprofitable, if that is considered an integral part of the offered product. In a worst-case scenario, the chain may decide to sell properties in global risk areas when it determines the external circumstances make it difficult to raise occupancy on an ongoing basis.

BETTER UTILIZE YOUR DISTRIBUTION CHANNELS

The Internet creates a new level of transparency as it allows the opportunity to maximize profitability.There is now a multitude of channels to choose from. Understanding the cost of each channel in relation to the value of provided service has an impact on the quality of pricing decisions. Therefore, it is necessary to determine how much revenue bookings through an Internet intermediary generate and whether or not they justify the accrued cost.There is also a tremendous risk involved.

As discussed earlier, one of key guidelines of corporate marketing is that partners are protected. Just because there is a new Internet site it does not mean a chain can use it and advertise a lower rate, which would undermine a partnership of many years. In terms of cost, the chain must review its pricing strategy not only by market segment but also by distribution channel. "Several years ago, we would not consider the cost of distribution in our ROI.Today we do," concedes Scott Farrell.

Another challenge is to keep up with new Internet sites. The chains must reevaluate constantly and prioritize their yield so as to choose which channels to keep or drop. Fairmont Hotels and Resorts, for example, applies the 80–20 rule. They focus on the 20 per cent of the online wholesalers that capture more than 80 per cent of the business. As Scott Farrell puts it,"Why would I play with the other 10–12 per cent? I only have so many hours in a day to manage. I may as well work with the lion's share."

QUALITY ABOVE ALL?

Criteria for selecting an online distribution partner vary by price levels as well. Budget and economy properties are driven mostly by financial considerations, while upscale and luxury hotels are more concerned with compatibility.

As for chains, they ask two basic questions:

1. How can the partnership increase our brand recognition or a brand reach, and
2. How much is it going to bring us in terms of revenue or profitability?

Their choice has to match the brand first, and then it has to drive the revenue. If the brand is equaled with quality, online providers that project a connotation of cheapness will not be considered at all.The quality image refers not only to the hotel asset itself but also to how and where this asset is sold.

Fairmont Hotels and Resorts, as a quality brand on the luxury side, cannot compete on price. The quality of their product and the offering of the experience must be considered by the customer at the price being offered.

When their hotels play with price, the corporate office watches closely. Scott Farrell explains, "If our property wanted to shift their rate by $50, I would ask why? Give me the case behind it and tell me what you are going to do to make up the additional $50 you are going to lose. If they come back to me and say they are moving their rate from $300 to $250 while driving a certain volume, I would make them go through the process of determining what incremental volume they will need to make up for the $50 in loss."

In other words, pricing decisions must be driven by ROI, not only a feeling. Feelings and experience may be involved, but properties must present a strong case based on the estimated ROI and what they plan to get out of the proposed strategy. It allows them to go into the pricing change with their eyes open. They also must consider how the competition will respond.A carelessly lowered rate may lead to a price war.

SPEED AND STRATEGY

The speed and immediacy of exposure via the Internet have reshaped how marketing campaigns are conducted. Having eliminated the delay of exposure to marketing collateral material, such as brochures or newspaper advertisements, hotels can conduct targeted discount mini-campaigns on their own websites when the yield management system indicates a drop in occupancy for specific dates.

In a similar manner, brand recognition can be enhanced by a carefully orchestrated online auction. The South African hospitality group Protea was among the first in the industry using this method by offering their prospective guests the opportunity to bid on a limited number of weekend getaways in their properties that needed to boost occupancy.

By setting a minimum bidding price, the integrity of the hotel image was protected. Similar auction systems, used to encourage room-night sales during slow periods, are nowadays available in the United States and Canada via several Internet intermediaries. For chains in particular, a long-term strategy in distribution pricing is paramount. It stipulates the criteria and accepts or rejects short-term adjustments depending on what is happening in the industry, what is new in the technology, and who the new players are.

In terms of corporate hierarchy, pricing is formulated and executed on three levels:

1. Strategy,
2. Tactics and execution, and
3. Measurement.

Strategy comes first, followed by tactics meant to support that strategy and their execution. Finally, the achieved outcome is measured against the set benchmarks. If the strategy is sound, it will last longer than the other two steps. Frequently, new tactics must be implemented; these drive the execution and the measurement. This requires a development of proprietary criteria for measurement and their continuous adjustment to changing conditions.

PRICE ELASTICITY

Contrary to the traditional view that hotel rates are, in the long-term, generally inelastic, price elasticity is receiving a lot of attention nowadays thanks to yield management. Its goal is to take advantage of and to cover the entire spectrum of the customers' ability to purchase.

Price elasticity allows hotels to capture customers who do not mind paying the high rate as well as those who are more priceconscious. This can be done in a number of ways. By using different room categories, a luxury hotel can have on the same day suites available at $500 and entry-level rooms at $200. Every room rate category has a different value proposition associated with the incremental revenue. If the variance between a standard room and a deluxe room is $75, the latter should provide an adequately greater value to the customer. The result is a clear product differentiation, which can be also achieved by stay restrictions or by the use of fencing. Examples of physical differences, or fences, are room type, view, amenities, and location.

Nonphysical fences may mean different customers, transactions, or consumption characteristics. These bear many similarities with airline pricing strategies, which differentiate the product by, for example, cancellation restrictions or last-minute availability of a prenegotiated corporate rate. The result is nested pricing, allowing properties to have a very high rate available on the same day as a rate that is more attractive to the lower-end customer.

NEW AREAS OF PRICING AND YIELD MANAGEMENT

Hotel pricing strategies traditionally have been limited to setting and adjusting room rates and other ongoing activities. In order to survive in the current dynamic, competitive, and even dangerous global environment, hotels and resorts are taking on other types of business, some of which are one-time projects.

Organizing shows, festivals, and conferences or undergoing renovations requires a new type of core competency. Therefore, in addition to mastering current pricing strategies, hotel practitioners must acquire project management skills, such as those that are taught and practiced by Project Management Institute. Mastering these skills will make hotel team members capable of maximizing yield from project-type functions the same way as they optimize revenue from room rates.

HOTEL SALES ORGANIZATION AND OPERATIONS

SALES AND MARKETING

Sales and marketing are related concepts, and each is an art and a science. Sales flow from marketing. Marketing, well stated by Lewis "is communicating to and giving target market customers what they want, when they want it, where they want it, and at a price they are willing and able to pay."The primary focus of sales is on the communication aspect of marketing. It involves direct personal selling to potential customers that you and your organization have the right product, in the right place, at the right time, and at the right price—be it a hotel, a restaurant, a casino, or contract food services.

Marketing is getting and keeping a customer, a macro approach to managing a successful business. In a broad sense, marketing is the development and delivery of a successful product, that is, the development and delivery of a satisfied customer. Hotel sales comprises finding that customer and matching his or her specific needs with the right product offering, a micro or one-on-one approach to customer satisfaction. For example, a meeting planner from Texas Instruments is planning an annual sales meeting to be held in Dallas. From a macro perspective, this planner has selected the city and is searching for full-service lodging accommodations for 200 TI sales representatives for a five-day conference. From a micro perspective, he or she visits several hotel alternatives and meets with the hotel sales representatives to find the best "fit." Various aspects of the meeting being planned are discussed including dates, rates, guest room accommodations, function room requirements, food and beverage services, and so forth. It is the job of the hotel sales manager to learn the specific needs and wants of the planner and "create" the right product, place, time, and price for a successful conference.

A successful conference is what the planner is really buying, not bricks and mortar. Thus, successful selling is understanding the real needs of the buyer, communicating how your product and service can best respond to those needs, and then delivering it. In another context, McDonald's Golden Arches markets fun, simplicity, good service, and a good price.

McDonald's sells friendly service, good value for price paid, convenient locations, and those delicious golden chicken nuggets on which many of us grew up. Ronald McDonald is an ancillary product, a public relations endeavor, which augments and supports the idea or concept of kids and why they are special.

Public relations, advertising, and special promotions often support the selling effort. Advertisements for the Ritz-Carlton Hotel Company are directed to their business traveller clientele. Such advertisements incorporate both the selling and marketing aspects of this upscale hotel chain. The company is simultaneously selling hotel rooms to busy business executives and marketing a hotel that "remembers your needs," and is hallmarked by the vision implicit in their slogan "ladies and gentlemen serving ladies and gentlemen."

A travel agent, a corporate travel manager, or a secretary, however, may have handled the actual purchase of the hotel room. Thus, the Ritz-Carlton advertisements support the sale, but they do not actually make the sale happen.

SALES AND OPERATIONS

Sales is the critical link between marketing and operations.While hospitality professionals may espouse marketing, all too often it becomes ignored in the daily hustle and bustle of operations. It is the role of sales to help bridge this gap and find ways for the key customer-contact members of the hotel to keep the promise of marketing.

Selling starts by the professional sales managers prospecting, making contacts, establishing relationships with clients, uncovering their specific needs and wants. But it doesn't end there. Sales is also the host or hostess greeting restaurant patrons. Sales is the front desk clerk welcoming a guest at the local Holiday Inn or at the Waldorf-Astoria in New York City. Sales is the housekeeping staff delivering the extra set of towels requested by a guest. Sales is the sommelier in a gourmet restaurant recommending wines to complement an entrée choice. Sales is the front office cashier saying, "Thank you for staying with us. We hope you enjoyed your stay." It is amazing how a simple thank-you can express appreciation for a customer's patronage and bring them back.

All client-contact personnel of a hospitality organization perform personal selling either consciously or unconsciously. This includes staff who does not regularly have guest contact, such as the credit manager. One of the authors nearly lost a $100,000 annual account when a poorly trained credit manager called the client to collect a payment that had not yet been billed. A well-trained and motivated employee who understands how a hotel works is key to successful selling. This is accomplished through the hiring and training process, and although the many facets of human resources are beyond the scope of this stage, its importance to guest satisfaction cannot be overstated.

In this particular context, however, the hotel's human resources department can perform services on behalf of the sales department by recruiting sales associates who understand the nature of the hotel industry and its place in the broader category of the services segment of business. Services are different from products and require specialized knowledge and training to be competitive.

Because hospitality is very much a part of the services industry, it is useful to understand how services differ from products. Those characteristics that are unique to the services industry product include perishability, simultaneity, heterogeneity, and intangibility.

Perishability refers to the short shelf life of the hospitality product. If it is not sold today, the potential revenue from the sales of that product is gone. A hotel room has a 24- hour shelf life. A restaurant seat has a twohour shelf life. Manufactured goods have a much longer period of durability. If a television set is not sold today, it can be sold tomorrow or next week. The potential revenue from the sale of that product is not lost. But a Tuesday-night hotel room cannot be resold on Wednesday.Tuesday has come and gone. If the hotel guest room goes unsold Tuesday, the potential revenue lost from that vacant room cannot be recouped.

Simultaneity means that production and consumption occur at the same time. How can you produce a guest experience without the guest? Our customers, in a sense, are part of the assembly line.They need to be present for final production of the product offering.A vacant guest room produces nothing.

Yes, the carpeting is installed; the bed is made, the bathroom plumbing works. But it all just exists until a guest arrives to use it. Simultaneous production and consumption is a unique challenge for successful operations in hospitality management. The guest needs to be present, because many of the facets of the service involve performances by hotel staff. A related service characteristic in hospitality is *heterogeneity*. Heterogeneity refers to the variability of service delivery. Guest service agents have their moods. Customers have their moods. All have personalities of varying shapes and sizes.

Hospitality is a very peopleoriented business. Service personnel change from shift to shift, typically on an 8-hour schedule. Though operational manuals exist in most hospitality establishments, rarely are policies and procedures followed in an exact manner. Guests' "personalities," too, can change throughout their stay, and it may have nothing to do with how they were treated by service personnel. Dealing with heterogeneity in service operations is dealing with reality.

Mistakes will happen. But more importantly, mistakes can be addressed. Often a simple apology can win back a customer regardless of who was at fault when a mistake happens. *Intangibility* is a fourth major characteristic of service businesses. Some consider it the most important component to recognize. Intangibility refers to the highly intangible nature of the service product offering. Intangibility is a feeling; it is having a sense about something that one cannot fully articulate.

The intangible nature of the service product cannot be prejudged. Consumers cannot really see, touch, smell, hear, or taste a service product prior to consumption. They can only anticipate. One can test-drive a car before an automobile purchase is made to see what it feels like to drive. But a hospitality customer cannot test-drive a hotel weekend package or a restaurant meal prior to consumption. The intangibility aspect of hospitality emphasizes that service delivery is critical to customer satisfaction.

Most customers have an idea of what to expect. But, in the end, they are really not sure of what they are buying until the hospitality experience actually takes place. Finally, after the service has been consumed, the guest has only the memory of the performance.

The foregoing unique characteristics represent the foundational challenge to the hotel's sales staff: they must find a way to promise performance and experience in such a way that the hotel's operations departments can deliver on the promise. If the essence of marketing is finding and keeping a customer, then the sales promise is fundamental to that effort. Operations' most important role is the keeping of that promise to the customer— having that customer walk away with a positive and memorable experience and want to return again.

MANAGEMENT OF THE SALES PROCESS

Sales management is effectively directing the personal selling efforts of a hospitality establishment. It involves managing the sales process from both an individual and team perspective. In other words, sales management addresses the logistics of sales solicitation and the development of sales account executives to enhance their sales productivity.

Sales account executives need to manage their day-to-day activity, sales teams need to coordinate their efforts, and customers need to feel that they are working with a professional and well-managed organization.

There are several components to hospitality sales management. These include sales organization, sales account management, recruitment, training and development, goal setting, and performance appraisals. Sales organization refers to departmental and individual organizational issues and inventory management. The following part focuses on the sales organization aspect of hospitality sales management.

Sales Organization

Sales organization can be viewed from three perspectives. These include departmental organization, individual planning of sales activity, and inventory management. A sales department needs to be organized, and sales managers within that organizational setup need to coordinate their efforts. Sales managers need to plan or organize their individual activities on a daily, weekly, and monthly basis.

Allocating the sale of inventory to various customer segments needs to be managed, as well. These are important issues in hospitality sales management.

Departmental Organization

Organizing a sales department means determining who is going to do what. Sales solicitation needs to take place, administrative tasks need to be completed, and managerial decisions need to be made on a regular basis. In medium- to large-size hospitality establishments, a director of sales and/or a director of marketing coordinates these efforts. In smaller operations, it is not unusual to have one individual responsible for all of the above. For most bed and breakfast operations in the United States and Canada and the small boutique hotels in Europe, for example, the owner and/or manager of the establishment typically handle sales activities.

Sales organizational setup for a midsize urban hotel targeting business clientele. The sales managers in this example are organized by target market and by geographic territory. Sales manager 1 is responsible for corporate accounts located in the immediate downtown and surrounding area. Sales manager 2 is responsible for national corporate accounts. This refers to companies based in other areas that conduct business or have the potential to conduct business at the hotel. Both of these sales managers solicit group and transient business from their account base

Sales manager 3 targets meetings and convention business from national association accounts.This business may include executive board meetings, committee meetings, regional conferences, and annual conventions.

In this example, once group events have been booked they are turned over to the conference services department for service delivery. Both the sales managers and director of conference services report to the director of sales and marketing. The sales team meets weekly to discuss issues pertinent to achieving the department's sales objectives.

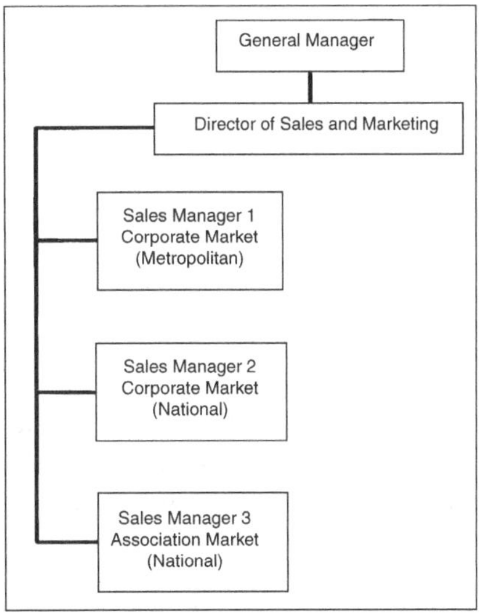

Fig. Organization of an Urban Hotel Sales Department

Weekly sales meetings are very much a part of a sales department's organizational structure, be it a sales force of two or twelve sales account executives. They are critical for effective communication within the department.

At these meetings, each team member highlights his or her weekly activity with regard to new prospects uncovered, tentative bookings, verbal definites, cancellations, etc. (Verbal definites are bookings where clients have verbally committed their meeting or function to the facility but a signed contract is not yet in hand.) In other words, sales managers share with each other progress reports on various accounts they are currently working on. Thus, each team member gets an upto- date informal report on the status of all current sales activity. For example, one sales manager may be working on a tentative booking but considers it weak because of strong competition for this particular account. Call this Group A. Another sales manager may have a new prospect with similar space requirements interested in the same dates. Call this Group B. Assume, however, that the property has the capability of booking only Group A or Group B over the same dates because of space limitations.

When these types of issues surface at sales meetings discussion will occur raising the following types of questions:

- What is the likelihood that either group will eventually book its business at the property?

- What is the estimated profitability and/or contribution margin for each group?
- Is either group a regular client?
- What is the likelihood of repeat business from either group? In other words, what is the long-term profitability for each?
- Can either group consider alternative dates? What would incite them to move dates?
- Do convention history reports match their current space allocation requests?

These are just a sampling of questions that need to be raised and answered. It is a never-ending process in hospitality sales management to search for the best fit for both the buyer and seller.

The organization of sales management is the process of directing the personal selling efforts of a hospitality establishment. It involves effectively managing the sales process from both an individual and team perspective.

Sales or account managers need to manage their day-to-day activity; sales teams need to coordinate their efforts. Sales account management involves developing, maintaining, and enhancing customer relationships. Sales managers develop expertise for specific market segments, industry segments, and/or customer accounts, and common traits among successful sales account executives include self-confidence, high energy, empathy, enthusiasm, and a sense of self-worth.

This stage introduces the foundation for hospitality sales and marketing. First and foremost, sales flow from marketing. If management doesn't have a marketing mindset, then sales efforts will be all for naught.

Marketing is giving the targeted customers what they want, when they want it, where they want it, at a price they are willing and able to pay. Sales is direct communication with potential customers letting them know we have what they want. In many respects, sales is the link between marketing and operations.

Operations is essentially the delivery component of marketing and the final determination of a happy customer. Marketing begins, transcends, and ends with the consumer. Sales makes sure it happens.

4

Scope in Global Tourism Reassessed

On the eve of the third millennium, the quest for "alternative" models is urgent; today this urgency is gaining power within the field of tourism. Many authors identify with this question. Seminars and symposia proliferate in opposing the problems of unchecked tourist growth. Alternative Tourism has become a symbol of the "Tourism of the Future."

In choosing "Theoretical Perspectives on Alternative Forms of Tourism" as the topic of its first seminar, the International Academy for the Study of Tourism invited academics and other scientists to consider all aspects of this theme. As social scientists, we must be concerned with Alternative Tourism in all its facets, actual or potential. It is the contention of the authors that the popularity of this new concept should itself be analyzed as a symptom.

The alliance of the two words "tourism" and "alternative" should alert us. It has a paradoxical resonance, an incongruity stimulating further enquiry. In this chapter, we intend to squeeze the meaning out of these words and to question the underpinnings of their use over the past two decades. Thus, ours is an essay in the sociology of knowledge and praxis.

THE PHENOMENON AND ITS CONCEPT

At several recent meetings, we have noted the perplexing nature of the term Alternative Tourism. Whenever speakers were asked to define it, their embarrassment became clear. At the International Round Table organized by URESTI, Georges Cazes (a French geographer) and Linda Richter (an American political scientist) presided over the debate on the problematics of alternative tourism in local societies. Cazes was irritated by what he considered a confusing notion and Richter proposed replacing Alternative Tourism with the term "appropriate tourism."

At Zakopane, the academicians concluded by condemning the "imprecise character of the term Alternative Tourism [as] ambiguous and hardly congruent with scientific work." Finally, at the World Tourism Organization Seminar on Alternative Tourism, the participants voted to replace the term with Responsible Tourism, purposefully defined as "relating to all forms of tourism which respect the host, natural, built, and cultural environment, and the interests of all parties concerned: hosts, guests, visitors, tourist industry, government, etc."

How can we understand the success of the term Alternative Tourism in spite of all the reservations about it?

"Alternative Tourism" has a nice ring to it. It is alliterative like an advertising gimmick. It is dynamic and provides a rallying cry. It sounds like an appeal: "Let's make the improbable a reality!" It connotes quality, responsibility, and respectability. It suggests a sensitivity that wins over the world. Yet, though attractive, the label is deceiving.

From the beginning there has been a problem of definition: where to draw the line between various kinds of tourism. The many meetings on Alternative Tourism have spawned a "discourse of good intentions." In this chapter we hope to reveal the ideological pressures behind the discourse.

There is a danger of oversimplification of the complexities of tourism: in order to avoid the dilemma of having to decide whether to reject tourism completely or accept it unconditionally, people have latched onto the easy idea of Alternative Tourism.

UNCERTAIN ORIGINS

The emergence of the word "alternative" allied with tourism throws light on its *ideological* nature. The Ecumenical Coalition on Third World Tourism (ECTWT) claims paternity. Since its establishment in Bangkok, it has aimed "to explore possible models of alternative tourism in the Third World."

In 1980, a precursor group of militant Christians gathered just before the World Tourism Organization Conference on Tourism in Manila to denounce economic imperialism, domination by transnational corporations, political exploitation, organized prostitution of women and children, the degradation of traditional cultures, and other ills.

The Tourism European Network (TEN) was soon formed in Stuttgart in collaboration with ECTWT and, in 1984, held a seminar on Alternative Tourism in Asia. In 1986 a similar international conference took place at Bad Boll, West Germany. This called for the different sectors — tourists, hosts, businesses — to participate in building a New Tourism Order. But there were broader forces and other groups also promoting Alternative Tourism.

ALTERNATIVE TOURRISM

One could also link these calls for Alternative Tourism with various "Alternative Movements" that arose in Germany or the West Coast of the United States in the 1960s. These movements wanted to promote a counterculture by rejecting consumer society. Alternative Tourism, in rejecting mass tourism, is a similar radical attempt to transform social relations and is thus part of the larger movement. Is tourism a new kind of development strategy or, more powerfully, a prime force within a new strategy of international relations? A recent congress was called "Tourism — A Vital Force for Peace." This issue of "alternatives" penetrates all domains, and tourism is but one entrée.

Thus one could envisage a sociology of "Alternative Tourism as a social movement": a force aimed at social change; a movement of people in the process of mobilizing ideas; a series of acts and speech diffused in many segments of social life, where the actors are not totally aware of their real motives.

It is only with the hindsight of history that we can speak about a real change of strategy. One should be able to analyse the actors, the channels of communication, the ramifications, and the different forces of the movement. But the believers in Alternative Tourism belong to various social groups and the issue is still unclear.

The whole question is complex. In the 1980s everybody started to talk about Alternative Tourism, but with scattered meanings and heterogenous or contradictory interests.

Alternative Tourism encompasses a wide range of connotations: tourists characterized by particular motivations; touristic practices; a touristic product; levels of technology; solutions to planning; local, regional, national, or international politics; a strategy for development.

In the last case, Alternative Tourism is the application to tourism of Alternative Development in regions where tourism has been chosen as a factor in economic development. Finally, Alternative Tourism expresses the concept of a "New order of Tourism." The multiplicity of these meanings is both a great source of confusion and a rich opportunity for in-depth study.

PROFILES OF CONCEPTUALIZATION

We may approach the problem in two ways. There is a difference between the emergence of a practical concept and the construction of a scientific concept. The analysis must go further than surveying the various meanings and denouncing the confusion, even in order to clarify them. Listing the different uses of the term and coming up with an approximate definition is easy but insufficient.

Using the methods of structural linguistics, we analyse the structure of meanings underlying the discourse of Alternative Tourism — the discourse of the tourists, professionals, politicians, scientists. We deconstruct this discourse in order to lay bare the conceptual operations from which it derives its power of persuasion. This is only a much needed preliminary step.

The expression Alternative Tourism can be baffling; to one businessman interviewed in the French Alps it meant "that the roads, the hotels, the whole place, is periodically filled and emptied!" The word "alternative," taken literally, engenders such images as ebb and flow, going and returning, leaving and arriving! But to the initiated, "alternative" (as in Alternative Tourism) is a special kind of qualifier. The whole phrase is an "autonomous syntagm"; the words are bound together like a single noun.

Using the methods of structural analysis, we look at the opposing pairs in which Alternative Tourism is used in speech. We find that Alternative Tourism always has an antithesis: commercial, conventional, mass tourism. It arises as the contrary to whatever is seen as negative or bad about conventional tourism, so it is always a semantic inversion, found at all levels of discourse.

For instance, some tourists are motivated to think that Alternative Tourism is individualized or selective, expressing their good taste, as opposed to mass tourism, which is seen as plebeian, organized, gregarious, and allowing little individual choice.

As lodging, Alternative Tourism refers to human scale, small and medium sized local, family, or community enterprises, well integrated into the area. Anything other than the usual concrete tourist establishments qualifies. Alternative Tourism connotes local artisanship, with wood and fine materials and typical local architecture.

As a tourist product, Alternative Tourism is expensive, sold by travel agents to a wealthy clientele or social leaders. "Cultural tourism" is the key word. Paradoxically, it also claims to be free of commercial circuits and capitalist profits. It appeals to advocates of "social tourism" and independent tourists alike.

As activity, it favors physical well-being acquired by good health habits, competitive sports, or strenuous outings. It implies intellectual and aesthetic attitudes, trips to far regions with unexplored cultural or natural treasures appealing to the socially mobile. It opposes mass tourism for its comfort and repetition of the "four S's" (sun, sand, ski, sex) of the average middle classes.

Finally, as planning, Alternative Tourism appears to express local wishes to bring together tourists and host communities and thereby enters into endogenous development policies concerned with local interests. Some claim that this "new model" of tourism will replace mass tourism as "old fashioned" or out of date. Thus for some, "alternative" is not just another kind of tourism, but aspires to become *the* tourism in the promotion of a new order.

THE PRINCIPLE OF THE ALTERNATIVE

In logic, an alternative is based on a judgment that there are only two possibilities. Two contemporaneous terms are placed in mutual exclusion, with an "excluded middle," that is, no other possible course is open. It is either one or the other. Thus the promotion of Alternative Tourism relies on a series of value-laden judgments: devaluation/valuation, negation/affirmation, neutralization/idealization.

Emerging from such a series of discriminating processes between"reference tourism" and Alternative Tourism, logically Alternative

Tourism becomes *the* tourism. After analyzing many texts referring to tourism, an unending repetition of these mental processes can be noted. We idealize what we promote and reject what we disapprove of.

ALTERNATIVE TOURISM AND THE CHALLENGE OF INTERNATIONAL TOURISM

To situate the Alternative Tourism movement, we must compare its goals with those of International Tourism. Within the discourse, Alternative Tourism can be seen as an opposite of International Tourism, which is itself multidimensional. Some major characteristics of International Tourism include the following.

THE PRIMACY OF ECONOMICS

International Tourism is generally defined as a particular aspect of Tourism (with a capital T), as the extension into international geographical space of a mobility originally confined within national limits in opposition to internal (or domestic) tourism.

There are, however, many ways to define international tourism. In the literature, modern international tourism is commonly linked with the Grand Tour, which began in the eighteenth century among young British aristocrats making an initiatory trip to the Continent.

As other classes were emancipated in the nineteenth and early twentieth centuries, the idea was generalized as a "vacation." In this way, the ideas of tourism and vacations are interchangeable. Thus international tourism is seen as an irrepressible seasonal mobility which crosses frontiers, as "a tidal wave, a North-South invasion, or a stampede to the sun."

Seen historically, this is a one-sided view, that of the industrialized nations. But international tourism is an "international social fact" in the sociological sense. "Not all social facts are amenable to internationalization...there are some phenomena which reflect more precisely the characteristics of one group, people, or nation; other phenomena are seen to better advantage as *exchanges* between different peoples; they surpass national territories,...they live a kind of supra-national life."

THE DUALITY OF THE CONCEPT

In the 1930s, countries in the League of Nations were aware of the assets and liabilities of international travel on the balance of payments, "petty things" which can amount to considerable sums. At that critical period, some governments protected their balance of payments by limiting travel abroad.

The League's Economic Commission, however, took a position in favour of International Tourism, with the important argument: "It is ultimately wrong to consider domestic tourism to be something essentially different from international tourism, just as it would be to forget that the economic activity of a country is indissolubly linked to its external trade". Thus tourism is divided into international and domestic but, though linked, they refer to different networks of meaning.

Domestic tourism is seen as a cultural habit increasingly widespread in industrial societies, but International Tourism has become an import/export activity reckoned in terms of international monetary exchange.

Thus International Tourism is implicitly reduced to its economic and commercial aspects, which take preference over cultural aspects. Whereas domestic and national tourism are seen as inherently cultural, International Tourism is seen as prospectively economic. Needless to say the notion of Alternative Tourism bears the consequences of this cleavage.

POLITICAL WILL: THE GROWTH OF INTERNATIONAL TOURIST MOVEMENTS

Thus tourism became first and foremost an "economic fact" for decision makers, who take this as a given in considering tourism within their overall planning. The opening of an area to foreign tourists is seen as a market phenomenon and is calculated as a matter of foreign exchange by international organizations. Countries are measured by their performance, and regions are urged to enter into this "competition." The development of tourism is seen as axiomatic.

Tourism is not just a matter of national growth, but must be conceptualized as part of international relations.

TOURISTS IN THE GLOBAL FLOWS

Reading economic forecasts gives one the impression that tourism is constantly in danger of collapse. The discourse of officials is preoccupied with signs of weakness, decrease, or loss. Thus international tourism always appears to be on the brink of a crisis, one which it in fact anticipates and resists.

The constant growth of international tourism is not spontaneous, but reflects a supernational institutional will. In the Universal Rights of Man Charter the liberty to circulate freely in the world is fundamental.

The worldwide expansion of international tourism is the subject of massive propaganda. In this regard it is noteworthy that the International Union of Official Organizations of Tourism (IUOTO), which became the World Tourism Organization in 1974, was originally founded at the Hague in 1925 as the International Union of Official Spokesmen of Touristic Propaganda.

In spite of variations during economically or politically sensitive periods, tourism has enjoyed an average growth rate of 8 per cent per annum since World War II. In 1950, 25.3 million people crossed borders as international tourists. This number reached 390 million in 1988 and is projected to grow at 4 to 5 per cent per annum through 2010. The World Tourism Organization forecasts that tourism will take first place among world economic activities, and no decline is in sight before 2000. The question is not so much whether or not there is an alternative to tourism but whether major new emerging forms of tourism will remain within the frame of reference of the dominant model or break away from it.

THE PRECONCEPTIONS OF THE IMPACT STUDIES

This question dominates the study of the effects of international tourism and is made real within the system of action where the local society — nation, region, community or ethnic group — is "targeted" by a more powerful external organization. From this point of view the impact is the target! (The word impact comes from the Latin *impingere*, "to hit a target.")

This conceptual scheme is not limited to economics; many other studies tackle tourism as an intrusion or benefit, an external variable on the one side through its side effects on the local society on the other.

This type of theory leads to a reductionist concept of the host society:

- It treats the host society as a place without specific sociological and historical characteristics, undifferentiated for the purpose of a foreign rationality.
- In its relations with tourism, "the target" is seen as limited to reacting by submitting to foreign penetration, by resisting conflicts with tourists, or by the kind of violence sometimes reported in the press. As it is opening to International Tourism, a time when tourism breeds dissent in the social order, the host society is seen as deceptively unanimous.

The problematics of the impact and the underlying system of concepts prevent us from thinking about the *processes* by which local societies are integrated into the larger political field.

Such "impact studies," therefore, never understand the nature of the changes in the economic and political systems or in social relations and attitudes brought about by International Tourism policy worldwide.

Tourism management focuses on tourism alone but actually affects the whole society and its social structure, collective memory, and perspectives in an unfolding world.

But a long term change in thinking has recently surfaced. Economists have recognized that the immediate returns from tourism may not do much for the development of the whole region. Methods of measurement and statistical data are viewed with suspicion. Growth models are discredited and the relevance of economics is challenged.

Anthropologists and sociologists are undertaking studies with a radically different awareness. As a result of local field research, in the 1980s there has been a shift from the problematics of the impact to the problematics of the alternative. Is this a real change in the problematics of international tourism? During the 1970s, planners were forced to see the limitations of their general development model and to take into account the interests of local people. The first reaction was to grant to the host society its own personality, recognizing its viability. One heard more of local dominance, participation and development.

Some have called this "the return of the local," not only in scientific research but in conceptions about planning. In a coincidence of concerns, this has become the solution to all ills. From "an area to be promoted in the marketplace," the local society has been granted its own importance, its own potentials, with its own capacity for initiative and decision making.

RETURN TO THE LOCAL/RETURN OF THE LOCAL

The "return *to* the local" as an important factor in planning has been matched by the "return *of* the local" in the form of a network of grass roots movements, much as wished by the ECTWT. The local society is no longer taken as passive but as capable of accepting or rejecting the dominant model or of coming up with its own.

"Local society" is no longer an advertising image aimed at a distant clientele also being manipulated by advertising, but has become one pole at the heart of a system of action in relation to a centre.

The local society is no longer just an end-point in a movement from "above" but a generator of impulses which can climb back up the technological chain and modify the whole. It is no longer merely a reactionary form, but as a force in negotiation, intervention, and creativity is capable of its own initiatives, with all their paradoxes.

Some would redefine tourism from local points of view, surpassing the norms of International Tourism. The idea of tourism is transformed to the point of rejecting the dominant model; according to the proponents of Alternative Tourism, the local people must be helped to take over the tourist operation, rather than just having suitable conditions defined for them. Thus one can no longer judge tourism on the basis of specific "positive" or "negative" effects but must see the phenomenon intertwined as part of a total social fact.

The problematics of the alternative becomes complicated when it tries to rethink tourism or propose new strategies of global development from the local point of view. Is this a reversal of perspective? It is up to the social sciences to examine this turning point and its methodological and epistemological foundations.

We must keep in mind the difference between an "alternative ideology" which rethinks tourism from the local point of view or in terms of local development and the scientific approach which chooses the local society as the point of observation.

The latter is concerned with constructing its object of study from field research using the inductive approach, but its foremost objective is not to increase the standing of the local community as would the Alternative Tourism movement. It is troubling to observe these efforts to "rehabilitate" the local setting after it has been flattened or evacuated by planning 112 and scientific thinking. In the Alternative Tourism problematic, the tourism production system, which carries on ever upward according to its own logic, seems to have been bypassed. In our opinion, one must work with the assumption that many parallel logics are being pushed without contradicting themselves.

After listening to the different debates and declarations, it seems that what is called Alternative Tourism while claiming to be the "good tourism" has not, in spite of its forceful declared opposition, broken radically with the "other tourism."

Alternative Tourism, still included within the promotion and expansion of international tourism, may just be another stage. Doesn't Alternative Tourism still spur the local people to preserve their customs and traditions, and then use them as tourist products to offer on the market?

At Zakopane in August 1989, the members of the Academy considered Alternative Tourism as a means to contribute to the "sustainable development" of a society, whereas by October at the WTO meeting in Tamanrasset, Alternative Tourism had become co-opted as a way to ensure the sustainable development of tourism itself. That should give us something to think about.

A POINT OF DOCTRINE

International tourism makes money and the industrialized nations are the main benefactors. Yet as early as the 1960s Kurt Krapf (1961), one of the pioneers of the economic theory of tourism, advanced a then-revolutionary idea that the developing nations should also benefit from international tourism. Soon thereafter the United Nations Conference on Tourism and International Travel proclaimed, "Tourism makes a vital contribution to the economic development of Developing Nations" (United Nations 1963).

This theory came to the fore at the very time when affluent nations decided to help "needy" societies by announcing a "Decade of Development," just when many former colonies gained their political independence.

It was reasoned that, though planting a luxury industry in such poor countries might appear shocking, the developing nations had few other resources, but they did have an abundance of natural and cultural riches and a cheap, underemployed workforce.

Tourism, a frivolous activity, could become a useful instrument in economic development. But this doctrine contains a condensation of meanings which must be untangled to avoid the pitfalls into which the doctrine of Alternative Tourism also risks sinking.

The imposition of international tourism on the developing nations suggests not only a change of scale but a turning point. International tourism is not just an international extension of domestic tourism, nor just a major contribution to foreign exchange, but is also a "transmission belt" connecting the developed and the underdeveloped worlds. Tourism policy has become part of a global project which lumps together seemingly contradictory economic interests: the organization of vacations (an idea originating in rich countries) and the aspirations for development of economically weak societies. Thus "free time" resulting from the exploitation of the surplus value of capital is put back into the calculation of economic productivity.

Societies inexperienced with industrialization are re-oriented toward "touristification"; tourism comes to be judged by economic and political criteria within the international framework, a vector for global integration. It becomes a factor in the North-South dialogue and a component of the much-discussed New World Economic Order.

THE OPENING OF DEVELOPING NATIONS TO INTERNATIONAL TOURISM

Since the 1960s, the developing nations have been persuaded to open themselves to international tourism, to give tourism a favored place in their economy, to welcome foreign capital, and to make fiscal concessions.

Many countries have responded enthusiastically, hoping to solve their problems of endemic poverty. Between 1969 and 1979 the World Bank supported twenty-four projects in eighteen countries. Immense resort projects were started on the Costa Brava and the Costa del Sol in Spain, on the Bulgarian and Romanian shores of the Black Sea, in Tunisia, the Antilles, the Caribbean, Mexico, Thailand.

Tourist resorts form a world apart, a delimited area on the fringe of ordinary life. Tourists are grouped into a hotel or complex containing all the services necessary for maintenance and pleasure, following the needs of the notorious "4 S's."

Architecturally and technically modern buildings are erected in spaces in the process of desertification or overpopulation. It sometimes happens that the local population must leave or nomads can no longer traverse the area, the land is abandoned or remodeled, or new fresh water supplies sought, all for the reception of vacationers from rich countries. Touristic mobility is an unprecedented "delocalization" movement.

TOURISM, A FACTOR IN ECONOMIC DEVELOPMENT ON A WORLD SCALE

At times of crisis, even the developed nations see tourism as a primary "export activity" worthy of subvention. In addition to the multiplier effect and offsetting foreign debts, tourism becomes one of the few remedies for never ending unemployment.

According to Organization for Economic Development and Cooperation (OEDC) experts, tourism is moving from an accessory to a major and necessary economic activity.

Rich countries are adopting policies first intended for the poor, and tourism has become a development factor in post-industrial societies. Almost all nations promote tourism development as a producer of profit, leading to envy and stiff competition for foreign exchange and tourists.

TRANSNATIONAL COMPANY NETWORKS

The tourist industry's system of production is now considered one of the world's most powerful driving forces. Through mergers and concentrations, these companies have become agents of an interconnected network penetrating many sectors.

The transnationals of tourism are the avant garde for strategies of capital internationalization. The system of tourist production has evolved into network-companies, models for transnational companies in the world economy.

Decisions for whole regions or countries are made inside one company. Yet the states or communities involved may have no veto or even influence in this "Dialogue of Monopolies and Countries". Competition is reduced by collusion, for profits grow best in homogeneous spaces. Thus culture, society, and identity become mass products when International Tourism enters a country.

These network-companies operate in an almost centralized system in which power stems from negotiations and meetings in search of consensus. This efficient organizational system, with its savoir faire and its capacity to manage behaviour and technology, is what Galbraith called "technostructure." The system relies on experts who often bring identical solutions to contrasting local conditions. Growth is external to and independent of local conditions of production.

This system also aids the integration of regions and communities into the international whole. To accept international tourism is not only to welcome foreign vacationers and their currency, it means access to international planning, technology, and finance, entering the world economy and approaching world modernity. One cannot understand Alternative Tourism without this view of reality.

THE ROLE OF THE STATE IN THE PROMOTION OF INTERNATIONAL TOURISM

It is often difficult to draw the line between the state and industry. By internationalizing tourism, the structure of the state is transformed by the arrival of officials trained in commercial technology and marketing at all levels of administration, an evolution obvious in France and many other countries.

The training of government authorities integrates local business into higher echelons. In January 1990, meetings on local development were exhorted to "think local, act global/think global, act local". Thus international tourism is one domain where the public-private dichotomy is misleading.

FROM SECTORIAL PLANNING TO GLOBAL PLANNING

International tourist planning has to do with the introduction of rational thought into management practices. Since the 1960s it has enlarged its range, from purely sectorial choices to the opening of the developing nations to international tourism.

As tourism moved from a secondary activity to a primary force in national economies, intersectorial comparisons of profitability became crucial. In addition, as tourism is inscribed in national development plans, it is justified not only by profit, but for its contributions to political aims of development. It becomes the axis on which other sectors rely, and national intersectorial planning gives way to global planning.

At the instigation of international organizations or Western, formerly colonial, powers, Third World countries cooperate and endeavor to finance their investments within a long-range set of programs. National tourist offices depend on international data.

Tourism becomes one of the vectors of inter-nationalization and thus attempts to become a generating principle for the whole society, enabling the instruments and goals of the world economy to penetrate and weave transnational bonds.

GEARING UP A SOCIETY FOR TOURISM

Marketing, long an essential tool of international tourism promotion, articulates supply and demand within a market economy, and societies embracing international tourism are plunged into this international system. Unlike other industries, the "products" of the tourist industry are a pastiche of formerly heterogeneous elements amalgamated by advertising for tourist consumption.

Combined symbiotically, they include services (lodging, dining, transportation, recreation), culture (folklore, festivals, heritage, monuments), and less palpable things such as hospitality, ambiance, and ethnicity. At last this "product" incorporates the society itself, its culture, its identity.

International tourism promotion, aimed at economic development, requires every location to offer something unique. By this logic, each country or region must produce and publicize its unique identity, with a "name recognition" that signifies its superiority.

All over the world there is a fantastic incorporation of identifying signs into touristic products: nostalgic places, historic monuments, traditional and rural heritage, the skills of ethnic groups. Populations are solicited to attract foreign attention with their talent and creativity. Everyone plays himself or herself and acts out a performance. Widespread marketing research determines what this image should be, matching aspects of local identity with the desires of potential clients. This fabrication of identity defines the seductive attributes and crystallizes them in an advertising image such that even the locals may eventually recognize themselves in it!

TOURISTIC RESTORATION/APPROPRIATION

In the analysis of the creation of "tourist attractions," cultural heritage is exploited as a "mineable resource." It must be "put to good use" by changing its purpose, and hence its meaning. It is restored along rational lines for commercial promotion and may end up looking like one in a series of reproductions rather than its own historic self.

In Europe, for example, historic landmarks and properties were often preserved by philanthropy derived from a sense of community pride. Now, however, every city restores its historic ramparts, church, or castle to attract tourists, and funding is solicited from art dealers, from cultural sponsors, and from the tourist arms of the state.

Tourism promotion is allied with marketing, and uses the quick functional "cultural engineering" perfected in the United States. Heritage, transformed into productive capital, is renovated and the profit used to repay the cost rather than for safeguarding. Tourism therefore ensures renewal.

Goaded by European unification in 1992 and the prospect of additional millions of tourists, France is now turning itself into a vast "theme park." Compared with the new EuroDisneyland near Paris, other cities and villages will appear authentic!

Castles, cathedrals, old villages, prehistoric sites, and public gardens appeal increasingly to the public. The new ecomuseums have also met with great success, as they look to older people to explain the activities and tools displayed. In disused factories, on canal towpaths, or in historic urban areas we might just meet the last person who has the skill for these obsolete phenomena or the last memories of their working past.

RESURRECTION CREATION OUT OF NOTHING

Much time and money is now devoted to the "remaking of memory" (Jeudy 1986) to create new marketable identities. Thus we restore, regenerate, conserve, and preserve works and events as identities for a touristic society. Things long resigned to decrepitude are resuscitated as heritage or "collectibles."

The obsolescent and the obsolete once more become profitable. We extract the old from fragments of collective memory or, better still, from rare survivals still found in daily life.

Anything can become a tourist product as long as it can be given value. We invent new deposits to be mined: forgotten folklore, buildings in ruin, the sites of ancient cities. We move monuments from one place to another, change their meanings, and make new springs gush. Thus even the "natural" regional distribution of tourist attractions may become obsolete.

NEW CONSECRATION

MacCannell (1976) first analyzed the process of the transformation of things into tourist products. In order to become an attraction, the phenomenon must be "baptized"; it must be named and become associated with a recognizable sign or "marker" bringing it to the attention of the tourist, guaranteeing its "uniqueness," and making it worth seeing.

To display this object, we frame it, elevate it, light it up, mount it like a jewel, and mark it off from ordinary objects. Detached from the ordinary world, it becomes "sacred" within the ritual of tourism. Its old meaning as heritage is stripped, and it is given a new one appropriate to its role within the tourist system. Thus marked, it becomes a signifier of the identity of the society for foreign visitors.

THE NEW SETTING

The requirements of commercialism join with the moral goals of international organizations: to use tourism for the promotion of mutual understanding and to maintain, preserve and respect cultural identities. This accords with modern humanistic ecumenical and universalist ideals whereby each culture is supposed to make a special contribution to "universal culture."

Through the will of these organizations, patrimony and the extant traditions of archaic societies are placed in new relationships and come to constitute a common cultural foundation for all humanity. The chosen markers represent the identity of the place and its rank within the panoply of world heritage. Thus we can see that international tourism acts as a powerful force in the universalization of culture and society.

THE DILEMMA OF TOURISM

The modern concept of tourism as a factor in economic development is pivotal and is the only way to understand the contradiction between the economic and the cultural. Though first aimed at the Developing Nations, this doctrine has recently been adopted by nearly all countries in response to internal challenges.

The key document is Kurt Krapf's paper, presented to the Association Internationale d'Experts Scientifiques du Tourisme (AIEST) in 1961.

TREATED AS AN INFANT

In bringing together developing nations and consumer societies in one global vision, Krapf embraced Rostow's theory of development, by which societies are classified into five stages: (1) traditional; (2) pre-take-off; (3) take-off; (4) push to maturity; and (5) mass consumer. This theory of economic growth has encouraged rich countries to aid poor ones. It imitates child development theory and, though naive, provides criteria for the distribution of aid according to what economists call "the coefficient of capital."

Using this vocabulary, developing nations are "still in their infancy" and need to be pushed to maturity where citizens are assured a "stable consumption economy." The "immature" countries are labeled by their inability and have to accept the paternalistic aid of scientific experts in tourism. They are shown that it is "tourism or nothing." But nothing is not just nothing in this case, it is "the image of death appearing on the horizon".

ECONOMIC DEVELOPMENT

Krapf's argument conceals a paradox: "No one needs imagination to know that a developing country presents the characteristics of an economic take-off." In the terms described above countries have attained stage (2) or (3). As for "traditional society," Rostow's first stage, it is, according to Krapf "doomed to disappear." The economists' death sentence provokes us, for they assert that without tourism a society turns its back on development. In this theory, the gap is accentuated between those developing societies veering toward modernization and isolated traditional societies sliding back into decline.

Yet "traditional society" keeps haunting the imagination. Put aside in the economic order it is stored in the symbolic order, and tomorrow it may reemerge, promoted as a touristic product. Threatened with "imminent death," "traditional society" must be conserved, as a haven of tradition and infancy, in order to sustain the argument for development. Tourism promotion often concentrates on destinations that are virgin, intact, and distant in space.

THE IMAGE OF DEATH

Let us recall some of the debate of the 1960s about the ruinous effects of tourism on culture and environment.

Davydd Greenwood, a U.S. anthropologist studying agriculture in the community of Fuentarrabia in the Spanish Basque country in 1968-69, turned his attention to the Alarde, a lively local festival that drew many tourists. It was a Basque ceremony to celebrate the victory of their ancestors over the French in 1638.

To attract more tourists, the municipality decided to perform the Alarde twice in the same day. The inhabitants not only refused to cooperate with this commercial masquerade but lost their will to participate in the event. For Greenwood "tourism killed the Alarde."

Many similar cases probably exist. Just as the economic benefits emerge, tourism is discredited by the transformation of culture into market value, desecration of ceremonies, debasement of culture and the arts, falsification of traditions, and the loss of identity. The opposition of the economic and the cultural is revealed; here we are faced with the "dilemma of tourism."

In logic, a dilemma is reasoning where the major premise contains an alternative and the minor premises lead to the same conclusion. In practice a dilemma occurs when there are two contradictory possibilities, yet the subject making the choice finds that either way leads to the same consequences. The discourse of tourism decision making and management is rife with this figure of speech. Actors, whose interests should converge but are in fact opposed, face a dilemma: to develop or contain tourism, to restore culture or celebrate it, leads to the same result. To reject tourism is death, but to accept it is also death.

"The touristic dilemma is clear: to freeze or not to freeze, to maintain boundaries or to remove them...the sword cuts both ways".This double-edged sword underlines the break between tourism as seen by outside agents and by the local society, placing visitors and the visited in a reciprocal extermination.

For a developing nation not to choose tourism amounts to eventual death according to economists, but to choose tourism is also death according to anthropologists. To choose in favour of tourism is the outcome of a double bind, the requirement to make a choice between two impossibilities.

The figure of this dilemma is a leitmotif in the discourse on tourism: "blessing or blight," "trick or treat," "boom or doom," "panacea or a new slave trade," "mirage or strategy for the future." There is always the same disjunction between the economic and the cultural which governs the problematics, be they alternative or dominant. This is still the dilemma which underlies the argument for Alternative Tourism, wherein the word "Alternative" gains its force.

Three Examples:

1. The dilemma of tourism pertains to actual situations. The 1989 WTO Seminar on Alternative Tourism in Tamanrasset took place at a symbolically loaded site, which could have been the source of the love of Uranus and Gaia, in the heart of the Sahara Desert. Here at the gates of Ahaggar the difficulties are magnified because of the barrenness of the place. Yet decisions had become urgent; every year the tourists were coming in greater numbers. Algeria, which previously had no tourism policy, had decided on large scale projects, with perhaps 100,000 beds. Ahaggar was targeted as exemplifying the touristic image of the nation.

   But the desert is an extremely fragile environment, with diminishing ancient water sources. Vegetation is sparse but includes unique local species. Garbage is not degradable. The desert people, adapted to the severe environment, have become guides, serving the tourists but anxious about uncontrolled growth. The experts were conscious of the risks and felt the proximity of total destruction. The government was perplexed when some seminar participants prophesied the end Ahaggar within twenty years if mass tourism develops.

2. In Australia's Northern Territory, the management of the National

Parks faced another classic dilemma. This is a special case applied to the Aborigines who at the turn of the century were seen as one of the most "primitive" groups on earth. Survivors of these "totemic societies" are scattered throughout the vast territory. The Australian Government has chosen the National Parks of this region as a "pole of growth," a plan also favored by the White residents of Darwin and the nearby mining camps. The area is highly valued by some for its nature resources and its primitive life. Here we must ask who speaks about the dilemma and whose dilemma it is.

For the Aborigines, the policy gives them the poignant choice of "to be or not to be." Already decimated and chased away by military maneuvers, their numbers are greatly reduced. These lands, ceded to them in the early 1960s, were temporarily retracted by the regional government without extinguishing Aboriginal rights. For the state as well as for the industry, the Aborigines provoke ambivalent attitudes. On the one hand they are inconvenient inhabitants, an obstacle to the development of the parks; on the other, they are a positive presence, certifying the original character of the place and its preservation from the ravages of civilization. From this point of view, Aborigine society is valued precisely because it is near extinction. One can weigh the tensions between international tourism promotion and a "traditional society." It is not just for economic reasons that the Aborigines are valued; they also possess unique skills, especially in hunting and fishing.

Thus we can see the dilemmas of both the parties involved. For the Aborigines to reject tourism is to remain welfare recipients. But to choose tourism and participate in it they would have to learn the industry's skills and become "servants," and thereby be evicted from their welfare status. They might be ready to say, "Anything other than Tourism!" In addition, the state risks making investments from which it would not reap a profit, as the land belongs to the Aborigines who, without spending any capital, might in twenty years become an economic power. Thus each of the participants might be tempted to reject the option of tourism. Do the problematics of the alternative find meaning in this kind of case?

3. The Statement on Responsible Tourism propounded by the 1989 Seminar on Alternative Tourism at Tamanrasset is fraught with paradoxes. It amounts to a paradoxical injunction when it supposes symmetrical behaviour between the partners involved, within the framework of relations defined as complementary. Proponents of Alternative Tourism favour the lodging of tourists in the houses of local people, some of whom respond: "When someone comes to my home because I have invited them, I receive them as a friend. But

when they are imposed on me from the outside, they are an occupier!"

Yes, tourism produces many situations where the imperative of the double bind traps the recipients of the message of development. To escape, it is not enough to reverse the terms of the alternative; one must break away from the frame of reference.

MISLEADING ARGUMENT

In 1970 the American anthropologist P. F. McKean thought about the possible consequences of mass tourism in Bali, where it had not yet developed. The Indonesian government, following the usual plans of the World Bank, included a focus on tourism in Bali in its first Five Year Plan for Economic Development.

The experts invited by the government drew up a Master Plan for Balinese Tourism with a somber prognostication: Bali risked the destruction of its well conserved traditions which would be devastated by the advent of mass tourism; the very attractions of Bali, its artistic creations, were at greatest risk.

To these experts the Balinese were a poor and isolated agricultural population. It was a "traditional society" where temple festivals, shadow puppetry, and sacred dances were integrated with village life. The experts proposed that, for the protection of the Balinese, tourists should be restricted to enclaves on the southern coast, for ordinary seaside tourism.

But the Balinese adopted a contrary policy. They wanted tourists spread throughout the island so that all villages could benefit. They came up with their own idea of "cultural tourism" and wanted to offer the tourists their best. McKean agreed: "Far from destroying, ruining or spoiling the culture of Bali, I am arguing here that the advent and increase of tourists is likely to fortify and foster the arts."

ECONOMIC DEVELOPMENT/CULTURAL INVOLUTION

McKean admits that by opting for cultural tourism as a means to modernization a country consents to transform its culture into a tourist product, its heritage into profit-making capital. Thus such a society undergoes what McKean calls "cultural involution."

In such cases, every society must construct its future by clinging to its past. This implies that the society turn back toward its past in order to construct out of its heritage touristically recognizable symbols of identity. The society has to prove that it is truly unique.

To choose one's heritage as a symbol of identity leads to ambivalence. Should one restore it to the original state in which it was handed down by ancestors? Should one set it apart as an attraction for foreign tourists?

For in this case, its restoration would follow the procedures of cultural engineering rather than of historical methods or subjective memorizing.

Heritage would have to be managed by new criteria in order not only to be profitable but also to be added to the catalogue of world heritage. For this to happen, though, is to pass out of genuine cultural filiation.Here is a potential source of tension.

EVOLUTION OF THE OFFICIAL DISCOURSE

Let us examine how experts and international organizations responded to these criticisms, partially explaining the rise of "alternative" solutions, following this evolution through seminars and meetings because there the ghost of the dilemma mentioned above underlies many of the attempted solutions.

Actually, organizations like the World Bank, the World Tourism Organization (WTO), and UNESCO were from the start attentive to the results of their efforts. From Washington to Tamanrasset by way of Manila, one can see the same guiding thread.

In 1976 the joint World Bank-UNESCO seminar on The Social and Cultural Impact of Tourism responded to concerns about the economic functions of tourism in the Third World and their sociocultural effects. This highlighted the double cleavage between the local host societies and the foreign economic powers, and the growing antinomy between the economic and the cultural.

Analyses since that era have worried about surmounting these dilemmas which permeate the social fact of tourism. How can the local and international join together again; how can we surmount the split between the economic and the cultural? These are key questions in the analysis of the problematics of the alternative.

The World Tourism Organization World Conference on Tourism held in Manila was a major event in changing directions, as can be seen in both the papers and the recommendations.

The latter contained two convergent themes: (1) an insistence on the perpetual advance of tourism through the growth of "national tourism" in the better-off countries and, in contrast to the earlier WTO focus on "international tourism," the promotion of these "national tourisms"; and (2) raising the awareness of nations and organizations of the spiritual values of tourism.

"Tourism...a vital force for peace...a moral and intellectual basis for mutual understanding and the interdependence of nations...suitable for the foundation of a new economic order which will narrow the gap between the developed countries and the underdeveloped...a means to promote the lessening of international tensions and to develop a spirit of friendly cooperation, with respect for human rights...within the equality of societies and nations.

This was a vast ideological movement toward a new conception of tourism, surpassing the still important economic factors by linking nations with the noblest aspects of "tourism in the service of humanity" in the social, educational, political and cultural arenas.

The WTO was attempting to reverse the prior order of causality by asserting that tourism is "primarily a cultural phenomenon." This is highly meaningful if we bear in mind that up to this point international tourism was seen as an economic phenomenon and domestic tourism as a cultural problem.

In light of this change of course, the aims of the Seminar on Alternative Tourism organized nine years later by the WTO in Tamanrasset became clearer.

One can thus understand how the evidence of the social and cultural impacts of tourism from the 1976 Washington seminar led the decision makers and government representatives to first take into account the social and cultural dimensions of tourism (Manila) and convincing all the parties concerned — hosts, guests, tourist industry, and governments — to respect the social and cultural resources on which the sustainable development of tourism was seen to rest (Tamanrasset).

Here the organizers managed to use the mobilizing force of this concept to obtain consensus among the various parties present. The assembly, having been captivated by the words Alternative Tourism, finally chose to endorse "responsible tourism."

The problematics of the alternative were founded on the reversal of the terms opposed in the discourse. But to understand this, one must again pass through the labyrinth of economics. This is critical to the continuing research on the break between Alternative Tourism and International Tourism.

Since the late 1960s, World Bank experts have been sent to evaluate the effects of the introduction of tourism. At first the evaluations were purely economic — foreign exchange generated, jobs created, changes in the standard of living. But increasingly, sociocultural impacts were included alongside and later came to infiltrate the economic model. To the sociologist this is an interesting epistemological jump.

The question of sociocultural impact opens the economics to social analyses. The economist wants to integrate sociocultural data into his evaluation schemes, and therefore turns to the sociologist or anthropologist. One must understand that the goals of the process are to optimize the aims of tourism development.

Economists want to quantify these elusive sociocultural factors into their cost-benefit analyses. This involves choosing "sociocultural indicators" which are then evaluated dualistically as "positive" or "negative" for the purposes of quantification.

Sorting through such analyses of tourism impacts, one generally finds that economic changes are imputed to be positive and sociocultural to be negative, thereby widening the gap between economic and the cultural. This leads to absurdities, whereby the damage caused by economic activities is balanced by economic benefits! It is as though social costs can be compensated by monetary gains in order to produce a unified cost-benefit analysis.

Thus sociocultural effects external to the economic, often judged as negative (i.e., as costs), are, by being neutralized, internalized into the calculations. This distorts the sociocultural data to accord with the norms of International Tourism, as though admitting that culture, society, and identity are not associated with the context that gave rise to them.

This dichotomy is illuminated if we consider that the same economic activity of tourism could be evaluated either as a benefit (+) for the development and preservation it brings or as a cost (-) for the degradation and misappropriation of meanings it entails.

This approach was generally considered an analytical advance, even though it is reductionist in weighing sociocultural data in terms of profit, wherein heritage and everything unique about a society is mummified and exploited as a resource.

The problematics of the alternative stems in part from this operation: the decision maker must catalogue the impacts, clearly defining the positive and the negative, in order to assess tourism.

Measures are thus taken which appear to lead to this result, so that one can build a model for "discerning tourism." Even here the method is still contained within the economic framework.

CHANGE OF COURSE

Since the 1960s the euphoric promises of tourism — return to nature, the noble savage, the peaceful co-existence of peoples — have been called into question by a long list of acts which have aroused indignation:

- Violent expropriation and occupation of territory, pollution and destruction of forests, landscapes, and coasts;
- Dominating financial interests, provoked bankruptcies, real estate speculation, the puffery of "straw men";
- Tourist ghettos, private squads of armed guards, expulsion of locals and marginals, segregated residential ethnic reserves;
- Violation of sacred places, appropriation of arts and crafts, manipulation of collective memories and heritage;
- Indecent behaviour, organized prostitution of women, adolescents, young children.

These aggressive accusations worry the authorities who try to stifle them, but their numbers continue to mount.

The attacks come from many directions: from the tourists who scorn each other, from host populations whose hostility is organized in their own interests, from some sectors of the governments involved, and from experts employed by the World Bank to research the impacts of tourism. By the 1970s these converging critics could not be avoided, and tourism developers realized that the time for impact evaluations had arrived. Rising competition, increasing marginal costs, the burden of tourism and the degradation of the environment shook the faith of the tourism experts: "Tourism can destroy tourism; tourism as a user of resources can be a resource destroyer and, through destroying the resources which give rise to it, make resource-based tourism short-lived".

5

Creating and Delivering Superior Future of Tourism

AN OVERVIEW

Firms create and deliver customer value as a bundle of benefits contained in a core and supplementary product. Since the core of any product is a commodity, the competitive advantage comes from the supplementary product.

Designing and delivering superior customer value is all about adding value to the customer's value chain and doing it better than the competition. Paying careful attention to the details in each and every encounter with the customer ensures a customer-focused delivery of the value created by the firm. Since the customer-focused firm competes on service, it also faces the classic challenge of any service firm—matching demand and supply. In order to maximize the profitability from its value-creating assets, firms have to determine the most profitable mix of segments for its customer portfolio.

How do you design customer-focused solutions that compete on service? Let customer information drive the decision on how best to leverage the productive assets of the firm. Market-based as well as asset-based assessments are necessary to configure value-creating assets into core and supplementary product benefits that provide a sustainable competitive advantage.

How does a small startup bank beat the big boys of the banking industry in their own backyard? Commerce Bancorp in New Jersey is not your standard bank. You will find their branches open at 8:00 AM and at 8:00 PM, and for most of the day on weekends. Vernon Hill, founding CEO of the bank, who also owns Burger King franchises, has embraced retailing practices in successful firms such as Walmart, Home Depot, and Starbuck's. The core product at Commerce Bancorp is the business of banking, of course.

But the total solution includes access and convenience benefits for the customer that most definitely distinguish it from other banks. There are even bathrooms for patrons in each branch at Commerce Bancorp. The total solution for any product includes a core product with supplementary features that in combination present a resultant value to the customer. Product differentiation and superior customer value is not in its core product, but in that total solution. The total solution for Commerce Bancorp is not just banking delivered by human or automated tellers in physical branches, it is banking at the customer's convenience when, where, and how the customer wants it.

Indeed, the difference in a customer-oriented firm is very evident at any Commerce Bancorp branch. Commerce bank has found powerful ways of differentiating itself by being customer focused and then it has been able to execute its customer-focused value creation and delivery.

Firms create and deliver value from their assets. Firms must determine how they might be able to create customer value that is superior to the alternatives available to the customer. With a customer focus, the firm seeks to design a superior solution that will provide the firm with sustainable profits. This chapter covers issues and decisions involved in conceiving, designing, and delivering the customer-focused product offering. What must happen to ensure that the productive assets of the firm, facilities, processes, and people, are set up to create and deliver customer-focused value?

TRANSLATING CUSTOMER NEEDS TO PRODUCT CONCEPT

We have already said that a firm must be able to assess what its customer value is—what its customers perceive as benefits received from the firm, versus what it cost the customers to access and receive those benefits. This assessment must be done both at the aggregate, segment level and at the individual, customer level, where appropriate. The aggregate, segment-level assessment orients the firm's thinking about overall product strategy. When a firm directly interacts with its customer, the individual, customer-level assessment helps the firm configure the product within that strategy to the individual customer.

In keeping with the view that a product is really a bundle of benefits, the core value in any product for any firm is the primary benefit that the firm provides. The supplementary product includes as parts of the solution additional benefits that augment the core product. Typically, a large part of the supplementary product is comprised of services. The example presents in a graphic this view of any product offering. For the most part, the core product is a commodity, as in the example of Commerce Bancorp. All banks offer deposits, withdrawals, and investments and banking products such as checking and savings accounts, and fixed and variable income securities, and today most banks offer mutual funds.

These products comprise the core product for banks. How these products are different from bank to bank is represented in the supplementary components of the total product. Commerce Bancorp offers free checking and money orders and does not compete on its lower interest on its savings accounts and CDs. Thus, Commerce Bancorp differentiates itself on a number of different supplementary benefits to the customer, ranging from the quality of its customer interactions to a number of facilitating services such as bathrooms in its branches. Similarly, most if not all banks have an online presence, but customers at banks like Allfirst Financial can talk with bank personnel via their home personal computer.

The hotel industry is one that grew out of its room-and-board days to a total product offering that today includes a multitude of facilitating services. "Room and board" was the commodity. As all hotels in a certain level, competitors in the same segment, began offering the same set of supplementary services, such as room service, meeting and conference rooms, a swimming pool, a gift shop, personal grooming salon service, business services, cable, or Internet service in each room, these became commodity and part of the core product.

By March 2001, 78 precent of all Ritz-Carlton hotels offered highspeed Internet. While only two hotel chains—Omni and Westin hotels—have laptops available for guests, most hotels in that class offer two phone lines. Thus, over time, as competing firms add supplementary services, these previously differentiating value components become a commodity and lose their differentiating ability.

Consider the recent "advances" in the form of supplem-entary services in the hotel industry. Electronic kiosks can not only check you in with your room key and print your bill at checkout, but can also be an electronic concierge providing a guest with directions or maps to locations of interest. Human butlers are back in the hotel industry. A growing number of hotels at the top end will provide a bath butler to prepare your luxury bath, a technology butler to solve your gadget problems, a private butler to pack your clothes or make your plans.

If you are traveling with a baby or young child, you can find a hotel that offers a room for a nanny and kiddie perks such as baby-sitting, some one to read a bedtime story with live actors, or toys and activities for the child. If you are bringing a pet along, some hotels will even offer you special pet services for a fee! Over time, hotels in the premium category will all be offering some or all of these supplementary features.

These features become part of the standard offering and reduce themselves into a commodity for that category of hotels. You can expect that the "technology butler" service will be adopted by hotels for the business traveller segment, briefly providing a differentiating feature only very quickly to become standard fare. In designing superior customer value, a firm must translate customer needs to the specifications of a solution in terms of core and supplementary benefits.

All hotels need not have the same core product. That statement might seem confusing. Consider the Station Inn, in Pennsylvania, between Pittsburgh, and Harrisburg. It sits 125 feet from the railroad tracks. Railroading buffs sleep at the hotel just to see the freight trains, about 60 of them in a space of 24 hours. Same industry as hotels—but a somewhat different core product. Precise definition of a product can only emerge from deep inspection of the "What business are we in?" analysis.

If product differentiation is derived from the enhancement that the supplementary product provides the core benefit, what constitutes supplementary product? Starting with the familiar: customer service is a common supplementary product (sometimes mistaken as the only element in the supplementary product). There are elements of the supplementary product, such as billing and payment that are also common to all firms. They are required to facilitate the core product. These must also be viewed as part of the supplementary product to the extent that they affect customer value.

A firm can add to the customer value when its billing and payment process is customer focused or can detract from customer value if it is unpleasant in the customer's experience. Thus, there are some supplementary features that are found in all products that may not necessarily be recognized as such. Services marketing scholar Christopher Lovelock visualized this concept as a flower with petals. Think of the supplementary product as composed of elements of the total value bundle that facilitate and enhance (or detract from) the primary benefit sought in a product. Visualize these elements in three broad categories: facilitating services, quality of customer experience, and brand image.

FACILITATING SERVICES

Facilitating services are all those features of the product and activities of the firm that serve to facilitate the consumption of the core product. All firms have to provide some of these services at some level. Large retailers such as Sears, Walmart, and Lowe's will provide assembly and installation services for a fee and sometimes for no charge. Table outlines the four broad categories of facilitating services—complementary services, customer education, customer access, and customer service. Customer-focused firms differentiate themselves by excelling in these facilitating services.

Complementary services are those related to the consumption of the core product. Some are almost necessary, like the waiting area in a physician's clinic or parking facilities at a hotel. Passengers on long international flights enjoy a wide range of inflight entertainment activities such as films, TV channels, and even casino-style gambling or electronic shopping and services such as being able to rent a car or book hotel rooms from the technology at their seats. Some complementary services are product differentiators. For example, recognizing that some of its customers were coming in to the bank to conduct their business bringing little children with them, some Wells Fargo branches have a play area with television cartoons, Nintendo, and the like—

and even sells toys to children. Washington Mutual offers calculators, pens, and piggy banks for a small fee. To compete for advertising within its *Mutual Funds* magazine for instance, the publisher, Time, Inc. offers its advertising customers anything from primary research and use of its subscriber list to assistance in customizing gifts and promotions to readers or sponsorship featured on special cover-wraps.

Only with an intimate understanding of the customer's value chain consumption (and creation) activities can firms begin to see what opportunities there might be to facilitate the consumption of the core product. Sometimes complementary products are outsourced and provided directly to the customer by the supplier, as Wells Fargo did when it invited Starbuck's to open locations at some of its branches. Ultimately, these complementary products ought to be consistent with the positioning strategy for the product. When a complementary feature is offered by all competitors in a particular product category, it becomes a commodity and part of the core product for that category and ceases to be a product differentiator.

Customer education is a form of facilitating service in that it provides information to the customer about the firm or the product in such a way that it facilitates the acquisition and consumption of the product. Instruction manuals and product support via telephone, fax, or the Internet are examples of customer education. Consider what some banks are doing to be more accessible for customers looking for assistance. Tellers and managers are dressed in khakis and casual shirts to appear approachable and friendly. Bank of America has tested concierges in their lobby to help direct customer questions. Home Depot provides free classes on home improvement projects. Once again, the service feature might be a necessary component of the total product, but how it is designed and delivered may be a source of product differentiation.

Customer access has to do with everything that the firm does to make its products available to the customer and to facilitate the acquisition and consumption of the product. The hours of operation and location are a simple example of customer access for a service. The various touch points that are available to the customer to access the services of the firm or to reach someone within the firm would be a measure of the customer access. The methods of billing and payment for the product would relate to access to the product and can be a product differentiator.

For example, the convenience of payment by credit card was once a source of competitive advantage. Convenience and ease of use is a critical component of customer value for any product. Services such as financing options are also related to this idea of customer access. If these are not customer-focused, they will fail the customer and the firm. Customer service is a key facilitating service and includes the commonly understood activity of businesses related to product complaints or failures, product returns, refunds, and such. The accommodation of special requests or adapting to unusual or irregular customer situations would be an example of customer service as well. Poor customer service reduces customer value and risks losing the customer.

Quality of Customer Experience

When the total product provided by all firms contains the same set of facilitating services, the product is not necessarily a commodity. The quality of the service offered remains a source of differentiation and therefore a supplementary feature of the product. Perceived quality enhances, and lack thereof reduces, the value of the core product. For example, even when Internet service is offered by all hotels, the quality of the customer experience with the Internet service is still a differentiator.

One hotel may require you to get into a closet, fish out the cables and force you to shape yourself into a yoga pose to hook up those cables to your laptop, while another hotel may offer wireless Internet access from anywhere on the property. All airlines provide seating and, depending on distance and class, also provide meals and entertainment while transporting you from point A to point B. Differentiation in seating can come in legroom and comfort. First-class services can offer six and a half feet of seat length, single seats, pajamas, and privacy partitions between seats. The quality of the entire customer experience is most definitely a source of differentiation.

Brand image is a supplementary feature of the product in that it adds to customer value. Brand image is the sum total of all the perceptions and attitudes about a brand. The image of the firm in the general media as well as for each individual customer provides a measure of the perceived quality of the product.

The reputation of a firm is usually a result of the firm's product and actions. Where there is very little tangible evidence of the product, as in the case of Web-based services, an entire industry of so-called "reputation managers" has emerged. These reputation managers are Web sites that rate the reputation of others! A firm's image is an implicit source of differentiation in the market. Brand image is the ultimate differentiator. When all else can be seen as equal, the brand image captures the essence of the difference in customer value among the alternatives available to the customer.

Firms have to determine what their total product offering is and what it should be. The value bundle of core and supplementary product needs to be designed based on what the customers expect as standard from all providers of a solution in a product category.

The supplementary product might also contain features that are sources of differentiation among solution providers reflecting the positioning strategy of the firm. Firms must constantly watch the various solutions that are being offered. Sometimes the threat of competition comes from newer business models. For example, online broker ETrade surprised the banking business when it began to open ATMs with new services. A deep and broad analysis of customer needs could reveal value-creating opportunities.

To determine how best to match the total product as the superior solution to fit customer need, the firm must understand the customer's value chain. This is an integral part of the product concept development of the customer-focused firm. A thorough understanding of the customer needs and the customer value chain will help the firm conceive its product from the customer's point of view. Firms that best relate their own value chain to the buyer's value chain, said Michael Porter, will enjoy a sustainable differentiation strategy.

The value chain is essentially a chain of value-creating and value-consuming activities, where the value created as output from one activity becomes the input to another value-creating activity that in turn creates value as input for another activity, and so on. Thus, any activity can be assessed by the value it creates versus the value it consumes. This is why activity-based costing practices make a lot of sense.

As already said the value creating activities *within a firm* are those that contribute to the creation of either the core product or the supplementary product. The value created by these activities is derived by the processing of the productive factors of the firm—its people, facilities, and equipment. There may be assets or value components sourced from external suppliers or intermediaries that contribute towards producing either the core or the supplementary product. Some outsourced services may even be delivered directly to the customer. When any value component of the total product is outsourced, as in the case of a retailer offering customers outsourced financing options for purchases, or airlines outsourcing catering services, there is the obvious issue of quality assurance in the value creation that is outside the control of the firm.

Externally (to the firm) when you relate other firms' value-creation activities into a value chain, you see that the value created by one entity contributes to the value created by the next entity in the value chain. The same idea is referred to by economists, in the context of forecasting, as "derived demand." The demand for a product is dependent on the market for another product, such as aluminum and aircraft sales for example. We know a homeowner who gets a home improvement job done receives (customer) value from the home contractor who in turn is receiving value from the retailer who in turn receives value in the form of products and services from the supplier or manufacturer.

Looking for Customer Value Opportunities

An understanding of the role that the firm's product plays in the customer's value chain could open up value-creating opportunities. A customer-focused firm has a detailed picture of the customer's consumption domain. When a firm views value consumption activities, it can see if there are other value creating opportunities that it can leverage from its assets. The watchmaker Swatch, for example, offers wrist watches with the technology that allows them to function as electronic passes at ski resorts in Switzerland or for public transportation in Finland. Wrist gadgets can now serve not only the function of telling time, but also making phone calls, playing music and videos, browsing the Internet, or sending e-mail.

This example defies categorization of product. What is the product? It is a wallet or a pocketbook, as well as a telephone, a personal stereo, a personal VCR, and an Internet communications device! The exercise of determining what revenue opportunities Swatch's value-creating assets would offer forces a complete redefinition of the product. As we saw the (product) solution is conceived to take advantage of opportunities to meet the needs in the customer's life with the assets that the firm has. Swatch has found a way to provide value to a recreational activity—skiing—and a functional activity—public transportation. It is contributing to the "customer access" components of the ski resort's and public transportation's product. By enabling customer access, information technology provides a whole range of supplementary benefits to a variety of products.

Contrast this with the example of a firm that does not understand the value of complementary product components and the customer's value chain. A customer came out of a movie theater in Kendall Square, Cambridge, and experienced a 40-minute ordeal trying to leave the theater's parking lot. She spent 30 minutes standing in line in frigid weather to pay the $2.50 parking fee and a further 15 minutes to exit the parking lot. When complaining to the management of the movie theater, she asked if she could pay the parking fee as she bought the movie ticket. She was told that the parking lot was owned by a different company and the theater would not take responsibility for the customer's bad experience at the parking lot. In contrast, the airline SAS has been known to provide an annual dinner to taxicab drivers in Stockholm because the SAS management wants the drivers to treat passengers on the way to and from the airport with professional courtesy and respect. Clearly, firms that are customer-focused conceive their product differently from other firms, because of their intimate knowledge of the customer's consumption activities.

Information about the customer's consumption cycle, therefore, is a key prerequisite to exploring the opportunities that might be tapped. An understa-nding of how the customer actually benefits from the solution and the information of how, when, where, and with whom the customer consumes the product should provide some interesting revelations of what the firm is doing and can be doing in the composition of the total product solution for customers. Thus, Procter and Gamble sends its researchers to homes to observe how people actually use laundry detergent. When Samsung was trying to break into the microwave business in the late 1970s and early 1980s, their design engineers observed homemakers shopping for microwaves at the retail store. You can stay ahead of the curve by offering value through supplementary product that your customer information tells you customers will be willing to pay for. Even if the value-producing feature or activity cannot be priced separately, you may be able to command a premium for your superior customer value. Being customer-focused is critical in identifying opportunities for establishing superiority in customer value.

All decisions about the product and, therefore, the value-creating activities of the firm are based on an understanding of the value-consumption activities of its customers. What are the decisions and what are the issues to be considered in determining the total product by a firm? The three major decisions constituting the product strategy are: the product concept, the operations design, and the value creation and delivery process alredy—displayed.

The product concept defines the customer to be served and what value is to be provided. The operations design defines the productive assets of the firm required to create and deliver that value for that customer. Together, the product concept and the operations design define the scope and configuration of the productive assets that can be leveraged to produce the specific customer value that maximizes profits to the firm.

The *value creation and delivery process* executes the product concept with the operations design. In developing the product strategy, the firm makes a fundamental decision in answering the question of how the product will be positioned among all potential solutions to the customer's need. This positioning question poses an asset- and market-based decision that comprises two perspectives.

- The *market-based perspective* looks outward at the market and asks what customer needs can be most profitably served by the firm.
- The *asset-based perspective* looks inward, at the firm's assets, and asks what assets of the firm can be most profitably leveraged by the firm.

The market-based perspective drives the product concept and the asset-based perspective drives the operations design. Thus, the initial step in developing product strategy involves two critical analyses. The product concept requires analyses of the various segments in the marketspace, while the operations design requires analyses of the firm's productive factors. These two sets of analyses are essential to determining what value-creating activities the firm should engage in to generate the maximum revenue from its assets.

A market analysis to determine what would be the most profitable segment mix for a configuration of the productive assets of the firm is the foundation for product strategy. First you need to identify the segments and the solutions that are currently available to the segments. The target market selection or the selected market segments to be served can be based on the profitability and size of each segment that the firm's assets are best positioned to serve. Here, a formal comparison of all the current solutions from the customer's perspective is necessary. Based on this analysis, the firm is able to determine what it can provide better than the alternative available to the appropriate target market, thus framing the firm's competitive advantage. Only after such customer needs analysis is it possible to specify what would be the desired customer value in the product offering.

The intended customer value in the product offering can now be translated into a detailed picture of the product concept—what the core and supplementary product ought to be. Remember that the customer value also reflects the customer's implicit assessment of the firm's solution compared to competitive offerings and, indeed, all solutions that are available to customers in the segment.

To ensure that the product concept can effectively be superior customer value, the core product should combine the imperatives that have become commodities in the product category with the appropriate features in the supplementary product to reflect superiority in customer value. Thus, the product concept embodies the product differentiation and the superiority in customer value.

The operations design decision rests on how best the assets of the firm can be most profitably leveraged and follows a sequence of questions that pertain to the productive assets and capabilities of the firm and how they should be deployed: What people, facilities, equipment assets are needed to create and deliver the product?

Which employees' skills and knowledge would be needed? When and where would specific human capital be needed and for how much time? Similar questions are asked about the facilities and equipment of the firm. Of course, when the asset or resource is not available within the firm, it seeks suppliers or outsources that part of the value creation. Ultimately, the question is what competitive advantage the firm is capable of and how the assets needed should be configured.

The process decisions are about determining the specific activities of the value creation and delivery. The process of making the product and delivering it to the customer must be detailed. The value creation and delivery activities required are set in a specific sequence. The firm must deliberate on the structure, content, and process of creating and delivering the product to the customer.

No product differentiation from supplementary product can be seen in isolation. If the total benefits from the product are not worth the costs that the customer incurs in acquiring and using the product, the product is likely to fail. The more carefully the firm designs the process with the customer in mind, the more likely the process ensures ease, convenience and quality for the customer. Thus, the customer-focused firm designs the creation and delivery process with the customer's percep tion of benefits and costs in the value consumption process.

Firms must also recognize that since customer value is dynamic, they need to continually monitor and improve this customer value. Ignorance of the need to innovate to sustain competitive advantage is a common mistake committed by the complacent firm. The argument is sometimes made that the firm's priority of customer focus minimizes the attention to innovation. Customer focus and innovation are not contradictory, an either/or strategic decision.

Indeed, to be customer-focused would mean that the firm is continually looking for new ways and solutions to meet customer needs—and to be aware that customer needs evolve as well. Now we can know what the firm needs to do to ensure that it is creating and delivering customer-focused value that can be sustained. To sustain superiority in customer value the firm must ensure that management continually assess its market and its assets to ensure that the choice of customer and the value being created and delivered by the firm maximizes the profit goals of the firm. How well is the customer value in the product concept translated to the operations design and the value creation and delivery process? Is the superiority in customer value being executed. The answer lies in the customer's judgment. Customer-focused firms will let the customer decide whether the firm's value creation and delivery is customer-focused.

Continual customer satisfaction assessment information needs to be available for the customer-focused firm to improve by changing the product concept, the operations design, and the value creation and delivery process, or to continually reassess whether its assets and capabilities are being leveraged to realise the maximum profit potential. To ensure customer-focused value creation and delivery, firms must assess customers' perceptions of the benefits they receive as well as the costs incurred by them.

As an ongoing assessment of customer value, firms must continually assess customer needs and customer satisfaction. As customer needs change, the value bundle needs to be reviewed in terms of its product concept, operations design and delivery.

An assessment of customer satisfaction presents an opportunity to improve customer value. The smart firm will continually monitor customer satisfaction to understand what customers perceive as the benefits they are getting from product compared to the costs that they incur. Based on customer satisfaction, does the value bundle need to be modified and redesigned?

Are the assets and capabilities of the firm being leveraged for maximum sustainable profits? If the expected customer value cannot be delivered with the existing value-creating assets, then the firm has two choices. Either it acquires or outsources the required value-creating assets and capabilities, or it determines that the target market decision needs revisiting.

Managing Customer Interactions

The process of delivering value is a tricky and detail-rich exercise; it requires careful planning, using techniques such as blueprinting to visualize the entire customer experience. From the customer perspective, some service encounters are critical incidents requiring more attention than others. All service encounters must be staged for a customer-focused experience just as in the production of theater.

Why does Kimberly-Clark manage the discount retailer Costco's inventory of its diapers? The firm has a salesperson live near the Costco headquarters, and a data analyst responsible for overseeing stock at 155 Costco stores in the western United States. Similarly, Procter and Gamble stations 250 people near Wal-mart's headquarters in Bentonville, Arkansas. Large retailers are asking suppliers to more actively manage the movement of products from factory to retail store shelves.

PandG estimates that stock-outs amount to 11 per cent of an average retailer's annual sales. When firms like Kimberly-Clark pay more attention to how its immediate customers—the retailers—create value to their customers, they demonstrate that they are being customer focused. In fact, the Kimberly-Clark salesperson passed on information on how customers place packages in their shopping cart that played into package design for diapers. Wayne Sanders, chairman and CEO of Kimberly-Clark, attributes this change to the information age.

Prior to the industrial revolution, a service orientation and the individual-to-individual interaction was the predominant mode of competitiveness. Assembly-line production distanced the firm from the customer due to the sheer number of customers and the physical distance between the customers and the firm brought about by the wonders of modern transportation. Manufacturing goods became the engine of individual and collective (national) economic growth.

Mechanization far outpaced services and replaced producer-customer interaction, relying instead on intermediary institutions to provide a specialized set of competencies that the producing firm lacked. Businesses lost sight of the customer. Now, information technology has brought this full circle, back to the customer.

We call it the information age because what has changed in our time is that new technology has revolutionized the way information is handled. Another equally significant revolution is the change in the customer's domain. Customers not only have access to more information on products and service offerings, they also have the ability to interact with the providers of products and services in ways not previously possible. Providers can also present enhancements to customer experiences from the functionalities presented by technology. Service providers must, however, also manage customer participation when they utilize technology.

When firms take advantage of online marketplaces, it might be necessary to make changes in organizational structure so that value creation and delivery processes are adjusted to the addition of the online delivery. Two key technologies underlie this information age technology phenomenon: the Internet and wireless communications. What customer access to these technologies has done is to bring customer interactions to a new level and to the front and centre in how a firm deals with the customer. These interactions are essentially service encounters with the customer.

Much has been said about the service encounter—customer interactions with the firm. In a way, all customer relationship management (CRM) solutions are basically technology support to ensure that the firm maximizes returns from customers by enabling customer-focused interactions. The service encounter is truly "where the rubber hits the road"—where the prospects of customer loyalty are materialized or lost. It is where promises made in advertising are honoured or reneged on, and where expectations of customers are disappointed or met. It is where all the assets of the firm need to be brought to bear. Service encounters with the customers are also laden with the challenges of a product that is produced and consumed in real time, where failures are bound to happen. When the firm designs the value creation process with the customer in mind, it will be prepared for all predictable eventualities. When the service fails, smart firms have smart processes, that recover and learn from the failure. They have service recovery and knowledge management processes in place.

As firms compete more and more on services, the management of the customer interaction becomes critical to ensure superiority in customer value. As the core product is a commodity, and most facilitating services approach the commodity state, the competitiveness comes from how the customer is treated by the firm at each and every encounter. This chapter discusses a method for designing the value delivery process with special attention paid to the service encounter and the critical incidents in the value creation and delivery process. A framework for designing the service encounter based on the theatrical metaphor is offered as a way to examine the customer focus of value creation and delivery.

Analyzing customer interactions can be very rewarding. Amazon constantly tracks the reasons for every customer contact. It has made numerous changes to its value creation and delivery process based on customer input. The customer service function at Amazon is considered a research lab for ways to improve the Amazon customer experience.

We can turn to the unique characteristics of services to obtain a clear understanding of what is involved in a customer interaction. Something intangible is always exchanged in the interaction (intangibility). Without a customer, there is no interaction and the separation of production and consumption is irrelevant (inseparability).

To conduct the interaction, the firm has the resources and infrastructure in place that "perish" when not utilized (perishability). Each interaction is unique (variability). From these characteristics, emerge situations that are challenges and opportunities typical to the service firm.

We need to keep these in mind as we design the process of creating and delivering customer value. At the most general level, all customer interactions occur in a certain place (or space), at a certain time, for a certain duration, between certain entities, in a certain manner for a certain purpose. Consider these as ingredients in a customer interaction and categorize them into elements of structure, content, and process.

When the customer interaction is mapped onto the consumption activity cycle, the objective of the interaction becomes the driving force behind the design of the interaction in terms of its structure, content, and process.

- Structure relates to who or what entities are involved in the interaction.
- Content relates to the subject, the task, and its significance in the interaction.
- Process relates to the sequence of steps in the interaction.

The primary decisions that would configure the structure of the interaction involve the nature of the interaction—what entity should represent the firm, should the interaction be face-to-face or not, what technology can be utilized, where should it occur, and so forth. As a complementary question about the customer: What entities from the customer's domain are involved in the interaction?

Similarly, decisions determining the content of the interaction should centre around the task and include what information should be required in the interaction, what should transpire between the parties, and what value should be created and consumed in the interaction. Decisions about process would include a script of the interaction and the roles of both parties in the interaction.

Any of these decisions must be based on the information that the firm has about the customer's consumption cycle and on preferences regarding these dimensions of the interaction. For example, technology may provide the firm with scale economies, but the customer may want to disengage from the script and interact with a person instead. Ultimately, the important question is what value is being created in the interaction.

As we saw earlier the execution of the product concept as the delivery of the product involves a process, a sequence of activities. Therefore, designing the product must necessarily include a design of the delivery process. Lynn Shostack proposed a technique called "blueprinting" to detail the process design in the delivery of services. The service blueprint is a map or flowchart as a visual representation of the process of service delivery. Essentially, the blueprint design is diagramed in three steps. In the first step, all types of customer interactions with the firm are listed. Next, these interactions are arranged in sequence of occurrence. In the final step, processes within the firm that are required to create and provide each customer interaction are mapped. How and what information, materials, facilities and equipment, and people are processed must be included in the service blueprint.

The customer-focused blueprint is one that is designed with the customer in mind. With the activities in the customer's consumption cycle in mind, processes within the firm need to be designed in such a way that the desired value added in the solution is reflected at each and every encounter with the customer. Commerce Bancorp, for example, encourages its employees to make suggestions in streamlining the service delivery process. Commerce Bancorp employees receive a fifty-dollar reward for finding something about a process that does not contribute to customer value and instead is an impediment to serving the customer; the bank immediately adjusts its operations.

Even as a simple representation of the value creation and delivery process, the service blueprint has a variety of important strategic, analytical, and diagnostic uses. In designing the delivery of the product, it can be used to determine the uniqueness of the service process. When compared with competitive blueprints, where and at which points in the process the firm derives its competitive advantage and superiority in customer value become evident.

Thus, the service blueprint can be used in a strategic analysis of the differentiating features and benefits of the service delivered by the firm. Only with such comparative analysis of the service blueprint is it possible to ensure that the value creation and delivery processes are commensurate with the superior customer value planned in the product concept and operations design.

The service blueprint has two major dimensions that characterize the nature and scope of the service delivery process: complexity and divergence. The complexity dimension reflects the number of steps or activities in the process. A highly complex service process has a great variety of activities during the series of customer interactions. Some of these activities occur in the front stage and some in the back stage, away from the customer's view.

A so-called line of visibility determines what the customer sees or does not see. The customer-focused firm will need to examine everything that the customer sees and experiences to determine whether the service delivery at the service encounter is contributing to or detracting from customer value. The divergence dimension reflects the degree of flexibility at each customer interaction.

The greater the divergence, the greater the customization built into the service—the greater the number of options the customer is given to choose from at each interaction. Therefore, supplementary product benefits such as customization must be mapped into the service delivery process. Complexity and divergence decisions will determine the position of the firm's offering compared to competitive offerings. Competitive blueprints can be compared to determine how competitive value bundles differ from each other. It becomes clear that the positioning of each competitive offering is reflected in the service blueprints.

The patient experience is very carefully orchestrated to support the entire concept of the "Shouldice Method." The surgical procedure itself is probably the least sophisticated element of the whole process. The recovery process is more important than the surgery. Every step in the blueprint is designed for a speedy recovery and an overall "enjoyable" experience—despite the anxiety and pain of the surgery. The method is known for a very low recurrence rate and high customer satisfaction. The hospital even has patient reunion parties each year that are sometimes attended by as many as a thousand former patients. For this service, its critical steps are not in the surgical procedure but in in the recovery process and the total customer experience. All customer interactions depicted in the blueprint are not of equal importance in terms of criticality towards customer value—some are more important to the customer than others. It is imperative that the firm employ its knowledge of customer expectations so that the critical interactions are highlighted for priority when allocating resources of the firm. This is the primary application of the blueprint technique.

Jan Carlson, CEO of the SAS airline, popularized the notion of the "moment of truth" in services. While each customer interaction is a moment of truth, those product features and customer encounters with the firm that are considered critical to the satisfaction of the customer are considered *critical incidents.* The critical incident technique has been applied in the managing of services to understand what can make or break the customer's experience. The method was initially developed for the U.S. Air Force in simulations to help in cockpit design and pilot training.

A simple question to the customer soliciting a verbal description of a typically satisfying and a typically dissatisfying experience with the product and firm would yield valuable information on what might constitute a critical incident. The incidents to which the customer attributes a satisfying or dissatisfying experience are those that are critical to customer satisfaction. When a particular point in the service delivery process keeps recurring in customer descriptions of satisfying and dissatisfying experiences, it becomes clear that it is a critical incident. These incidents can also uncover "failpoints"—points in the process that are especially likely to fail to perform as desired.

Some are internal to the firm and cannot be obvious to the customer, while others occur during direct interactions with the customer. For each of these, the design of the process should ensure "fail-safe" methods and have a system recovery process in place. Fail-safe processes require a metric that triggers the recovery processes. Thus, benchmarking the performance at the failpoints is critical to the successful implementation of the product concept and operations design to deliver the desired customer value. For firms that rely on intermediaries to bring the product to the customer, critical incidents may lie outside the firm's control. Consider, for example, what Handspring, Inc. does to make sure the customers of its products are served well at the retailer. The firm sends its employees from channel marketing posing as customers to retailers such as CompUSA and ensures that its product is stocked and well displayed and that the floor salespeople are presenting the product to the customer in the way Handspring had instructed them to do. Microsoft hands out a free Casio pocketPC to every sales rep who completes its training. These examples show an awareness that customer interactions at these intermediaries are failpoints and need to be monitored.

Critical incidents help in assigning the appropriate level of resources within the firm. Thus, the service blueprint is useful from a quality control perspective. Customer evaluations of a firm's service can be linked to specific customer encounters in the blueprints and all processes directly affecting or affected by the critical incidents must be monitored for quality. Customer-focused quality control efforts can be focused on critical variables that can be controlled. Service recovery procedures must be designed into the process at these points.

Interactive technologies provided by the information age revolution are now an integral part of the design of the value creation and delivery process. These technologies work through the three primary productive components of customer value—the people, the infrastructure in facilities and equipment, and processes and systems of value creation and delivery. Consider all the ways in which the customer can interact with a firm. Each touch-point can be made by the converging technologies of today. For example, in some interactions the location of either buyer or seller becomes irrelevant. Customers can interact by wireless or wired means, which can be by voice, video, or text, initiated by either party; they are constantly getting cheaper and better in features and functionality. The basic difficulty with any of this newer interactive technology is that the objective and role of the technology can be lost sight of and the technology itself become the focus. The final measure is whether the technology is contributing towards sustainable profits for the firm by improving customer value.

The benefits of interactive technology come in the form of efficiency and efficacy. Efficiency is reflected in increasing productivity and efficacy is reflected in improved customer value. Both of these outcomes contribute to the bottom line of the firm. For a firm competing on service, interactive technology is critical to sustain profits because of what it can do to customer value. Maximize the return from interactive technologies by deploying it at the critical points; prioritized by its customer value-creating power. For example, a common source of dissatisfaction and irritation to the customer is the length of waiting time before being served. Any point in the process where there is likely to be a wait is a potential critical incident requiring the firm's express attention. If there are interactive technologies that can be used to effectively manage the customer in these situations, customer value is not threatened.

All the service components in the total product, being susceptible to the inherent characteristic of being produced and consumed in real time, force customers to the experience of "wait." Demand and supply need to be matched as closely as possible.

To avoid idle capacity, services adopt the queuing (and scheduling) approach to processing customers, resulting in a certain amount of wait before the process begins. In multi-stage processes, which many services are, in-process waits are common as well. The problem of course is that no one wants to wait. Customers will wait for a certain amount of time that is reasonable to them as per their expectations. What is reasonable is a very subjective judgment, of course—one that requires analysis of the factors that determine the perception of waits.

Maister's work on the psychological cause and effects of wait suggests a way to reduce the negative consequences where wait is a given.

- Preprocess waits feel longer than in-process waits. Allow the customer to begin the process by completing the first step in the value delivery process.
- Unoccupied waits feel longer. Keep the customer in wait occupied with activities, preferably related to the product or service.
- Uncertain waits feel longer. Keep the customer informed about how long the expected wait is to likely to be.
- Unexplained waits feel longer. Keep the customer informed about why they are having to wait.
- Inequitable waits feel longer. Serve customer based on priority, determined by what is considered just in the ambient society.
- Value of the service. Ensure that the customer value you are providing is clearly superior to any alternative.

The most important common thread through all of these suggestions is that they all have to do with managing the customer perceptions. The firm is better placed if the customer perceptions can be influenced favourably by managing customer role and expectations in the value creation and delivery.To varying degrees, customers play a role in the production of products and not just in the consumption. Firms that realise this have paid serious attention to how the customer fits in the organization. In services, the role of the customer is abundantly evident. Customers engage in a coproduction role. In services or in the service component of the product, customers are coproducers in self-service configurations.

All services as we saw earlier involve some kind of customer participation, as in the case of providing required information to the tax preparer, for example. Even when placing the order with the provider, the customer is essentially contributing to the production of the product by providing input into product specifications. When the customer is interacting with the firm and this interaction has some relevance to the production of the product, by definition we have the customer engaging in coproducing the product. Service firms instinctively manage the role of the customers in their participation in the service. Restaurants have menus, professors have syllabi, airlines have their method of emplaning passengers according to a certain priority, etc. Sometimes managing customer roles may be in the form of a complementary service.

For example, Universal is experimenting with a calming zone adjunct to its roller-coaster rides, for people who need help with coaster-phobia before they get on the ride. UPS and other package delivery firms instinctively accommodate special customer requests as to where their packages should be deposited if the customer is not at the location of delivery.

It is a matter of perspective. If we take the notion of value creation a step further, we could argue that even in the case of packaged goods, the value hasn't really been created to the customer until the customer actually begins to use the product. Value creation and value consumption are both inextricably interwoven into a continuous and overlapping set of activities. This is an important issue in a service orientation.

In the case of services, customer interaction is a given. And the firm must include the customer in the design of its operations. The customer-focused firm by always keeping the customer in central view manages the role of the customer in the value creation and the value consumption activities. For example, providing excellent product assembly instructions improves the value created for the customer in an "easy to assemble yourself" product.

Conversely, even with a well-engineered product, poor instructions reduce customer value. Recent product innovation studies have shown that some firms are equipping customers with the tools to design and develop their own products, ranging from minor modifications to major new innovations. PTC (formerly Parametric Technology) is a world leader in computer-assisted-design (CAD) technology, whose software solutions bring suppliers and customers together so that a client can use the software during product development to virtually interface with upstream and downstream players. Ultimately, anything that the firm can do to manage the customer's role in the value creation as well as value consumption process is an imperative for the customer-focused firm. As mentioned earlier, Procter and Gamble is recruiting families to allow a team of their ethnographer-filmmakers to observe their daily routines to get a better sense for how their customers use household products.

The actual use situation says a lot about how a product should be designed. It would also be a way to learn how the customers should be instructed in the appropriate use of the product.

How does a firm take a systematic approach to managing the customer? First, the firm identifies all the activities that the customer enacts in the value creation as well as value consumption blueprint. Next, the firm scripts the role for the customer at each activity. Firms then have to determine how best to communicate and educate the customer in playing the appropriate role.

Customers' performance of their roles will depend on their ability and inclination to perform those roles. The consumer's ability will depend on consumption skills that the customer's past experience may have provided. The customer's inclination will depend on the personal characteristics of the customer. Familiarity with the service and service provider could affect the ability and the inclination of the customer in the role performance.

In the case of services and the service components of a product, customer role is managed by the service provider. The service provider's production skills and motivation could affect the way in which the service provider manages the customer's role. The service provider's familiarity with the segment and the specific customer will influence the service provider's skills and motivation in managing the customer's role performance. The service provider's production skills are reflected in its operations and customer interaction skills. The personal characteristics of the service provider can affect the service provider's motivation. When designing the service delivery process, it is important that the firm incorporate these factors on the customer's role performance.

CUSTOMER INTERACTION

The essence of customer-focused design of the value delivery process is in the design of the customer interactions that make up the blueprint.

Customer interactions have gone by various names in research on services—service encounters and moments of truth, for example. Designing the customer interaction requires analysis and decisions regarding three of the structural dimensions of the value delivery process: the process itself, the participants, and the physical facilities and equipment. Customer roles have to be defined so that customer participation can be designed into the delivery process as appropriate.

One useful framework that has utility in managing customer interactions is to view service encounters metaphorically as "drama." When firms and customers interact, firms try to put on the best performance—like theater. The firm's *actors* perform their roles for the *audience*, the customer. In any service, there are actors and audiences involved in producing *performances* in a *setting*. For example, restaurant customers are audiences with hosts and waitstaff as actors in the physical setting of the restaurant.

Just as in theatrical production, there is a stage (the dining area) and a backstage (the kitchen); there are acts (welcome and seating, appetizers, main course, and dessert), scripts (menu and specials), props, and costumes. Each element is carefully choreographed to produce the intended impression on the audience. Any service provider can examine each of these elements and determine the exact impression that would be appropriate for each customer segment. The "drive-thru" or take-out type of fast-food restaurant confronts different impression management challenges compared to the sit-down type of restaurant.

Different types of services would require a different combination of these theatrical elements for the desired impression. Services rendered at arm's length over the telephone or by mail, such as in investment brokerage services or credit card services, would see these elements differently from the face-to-face setting of hotels or airlines. Internet "clicks" retailers would find a different set of issues compared to the "bricks" retailers. Hybrid retailers have to approach the issues differently for the two different settings.

In some cases, the performance is shared by a number of customers, as in a restaurant or a hotel or airline where customers share many aspects of the firm's productive factors—employees, facilities, and equipment. The setting dictates a shared product, and some aspects of the setting are visible (onstage) to the customer and some are invisible (backstage). Performers or actors (frontline employees) utilize scripts, costumes, and props in their performances. Every feature or theatrical element is carefully choreographed for the intended impression. Therefore, just as in theater, managers can focus on impression management for customer-focused business activities. World-class service firms like Disney employ a service orientation profile (personality and skills) in their hiring; they call their employees the cast and carefully train them in both operations and customer interaction skills. Disney's "guests" are treated in a customer-focused manner evident in the culture, in the way the cast is empowered and motivated to provide customer-focused performances.

What is the type of setting where the customer value is delivered? There could be no interaction necessary with the value provider at certain phases in the consumption cycle, and there could be phases of physical, face-to-face interaction, or electronics-mediated interactions. At each interaction, the value provider must determine the line of visibility between onstage and backstage, what is or should be visible to the customer. What is the process and duration of the various steps in the interaction, and what kinds of orientation must there be for the participants? What is the customer role in each setting, and are there other customers in shared experience?

Ultimately, all of the theatrical elements need to be carefully directed and choreographed to provide the appropriate impression. *Servicescape* is a term that refers to the immediate physical and social environments containing a service experience, transaction, or event. The servicescape plays a number of different roles such as packaging the value bundle, facilitating the value delivery activities, socializing the employee and the customer, and differentiating the product. Managers must understand which servicescape elements can be controlled for the desired behaviours from both employees and customers.

What is the role of each process in the value creation and delivery as seen by a firm with a customer focus? What should the structure and content of the process include by way of design? What are the critical points in the process for its meeting customer needs and preferences? The firm should have in place metrics and customer-determined benchmarks that will trigger recovery procedures, anticipating that the firm will sometimes fail the customer. Using the theatrical metaphor, any impression that the actor, the audience, the setting, or the performance imparts must be examined and managed by the firm. The focus is on the effect each customer interaction or service encounter has on customer value from the customer's point of view. Customer-focused firms design the value creation and delivery process with the customer in mind.

Value-creating assets are perishable in that when idle they incur costs without generating revenues. Demand and supply management is an imperative for any firm, especially those that produce services or whose products have a significant proportion of service components. Analysis of demand patterns and capacity utilization should drive yield management in a customer-focused firm.

Following the dot-com crash, four-star hotels and other premium services in the hospitality industry found themselves losing business as corporate expense accounts became slim. By mid-2001, in some locations, you could get a room at the Biltmore, the Ritz, and others like the Waldorf-Astoria and the Plaza in New York for less than at such budget hotels as Holiday Inn, Comfort Inn, or Best Western. In the previous year, hotel overbuilding had prompted analysts to warn of lowered revenue from lower prices. The dot-com boom had hotels already committed to expansion. Similarly, key players in the cruise industry, also "over-built" following an ambitious expansion spree, found themselves in a quandary.

The number of berths among cruise ships worldwide was scheduled to increase by about 12 per cent over a couple of years from the year 2000. Vacations on cruise ships could be had for bargain basement prices. Why are firms better off selling their product for such low prices? If your assets are idle, you are still incurring fixed costs. As long as the variable costs are covered, every additional revenue dollar contributes to the fixed costs and profits as contribution margin. This situation is especially common to service firms and to firms whose assets are being used to provide services directly to the customer. Every firm must continually assess whether its value-creating assets are producing maximum value at minimum costs. Most firms instinctively reduce capacity during low demand periods and increase capacity during peak periods. The airline industry uses sophisticated methods to get customers committed early so that a certain level of demand is ensured for any given period.

The 21-day and 14-day airfares ensure that airlines have a certain amount of capacity filled before prices are raised. Idle capacity is too expensive to carry. Hotels will charge you if you are a no-show and some will charge you a fee for a late checkout. Upscale restaurants, too, will charge for no-shows and require cancellations to be made 24 hours in advance, just as hotels do. Underutilized capacity could be disastrous for any firm, especially for assets that produce services.

The hospitality industry is a perfect example of capacity-constrained services that have to address the challenge of perishable revenue opportunity from their productive assets. An important consequence of the inherent characteristics of services and of service components in products is that the product cannot be produced without customer interaction—production and delivery processes of services are idle unless a customer is being served.

For a number of reasons, fluctuating demand is an inevitable fact of life for businesses. There are times when demand exceeds supply and at other times supply exceeds demand. For firms that produce services, the demand-supply mismatch results in situations where revenues and profits are not maximized. Every firm seeks to generate the maximum profits from its assets; this goal requires yield management for long-term profit maximization. The firm needs to manage demand and supply such that it attracts and serves the segment mix that provides the maximum total profitability.

This chapter is about managing demand and supply so as to maximize the returns from value-creating assets. Patronage and capacity of productive assets must be managed for maximum profitability. The pattern of the flow of customers dictates the utilization of the productive factors of the services. Thus, the firm should attempt to smooth peaks and fill valleys of fluctuating demand patterns. The first section is about how to understand the demand patterns and to study the capacity of the value-creating assets. Next, a method for assessment of the revenue-generating utilization of the firm's assets is presented. Finally, ways in which the firm can improve the profitability of its value-creating assets are suggested.

The task for the firm with perishable assets is not just increasing demand, but increasing demand during low-demand periods. The key is in the timing of demand as much as in volume. The task may be more one of shifting rather than building demand. This is a daunting task, especially when the causes for demand patterns may be uncontrollable, such as weather or the school year and other institutionally imposed events such as filing taxes or reporting quarterly earnings. When the demand is predictable and some behaviour can be modified, firms must find a way to shift demand when and where possible. Before you attempt that, you need to have a sense for the profit implications of shifting demand, because the quality of demand is just as, if not more, important than its quantity. Quality of demand refers to how desirable the customers are. A firm should be relentless in making sure that the profitability of the mix of segments making up demand is maximized. Segments are selected to be served based on the long-term profitability of the customer. Therefore, demand management should consider the timing of the demand as well as the profitability of the demand being served at all times.

A measure of how well a firm is doing is the profits generated from its assets. In service firms, this is yield management, plain and simple. Yield management is practiced extensively by airlines and hotels in the service sector, for example, as they seek to maximize the returns from assets by maximizing the utilization of capacity at maximum margins. Customer-focused firms base their yield management techniques of demand and capacity management on their knowledge of the customer behaviour without losing sight of creating and delivering superior customer value and sustaining profits for the long term.

Demand management should aim to manage volume and revenues generated by the firm for maximum long-term profits. Capacity management, at the same time, should aim to minimize the costs of production along with maximizing utilization for maximum profits. When competing through service, the analysis required for customer-focused yield management is discussed. Customer-focused firms will seek to understand customer behaviour to manage customer demand. They will also seek to cost-effectively adapt capacity to the demand level without affecting the customer experience. The objective of yield management is to manage customer behaviour and the capacity utiization of the firm such that returns from assets are maximized.

DEMAND ANALYSIS

Demand analysis is a critical review of the profitability of customers being served at any given time so that demand management methods. Creative financing skills and practices by the firm can provide cost efficiencies in raising capital and purchase conveniences.

Demand analysis begins with detecting and identifying the demand patterns. Are there discernible nonrandom fluctuations in demand? Firms must first establish the cycles of demand in terms of the time frame across which demand fluctuations occur. Take the example of customer call centres. Utilization patterns may reveal that there are peaks and valleys during the day as well as across the days of the week, weeks of the month, and months of the year. By mapping customer interactions over a demand period, firms can identify all of these peaks and valleys in customer demand patterns. Since each time frame has a different pattern of fluctuation, firms must identify when they occur in each time frame. What is the extent of the fluctuation—how high are the peaks and how low are the valleys? Firms might want to focus on those peaks and valleys that display the highest variance from the desired levels of capacity utilization.

As the timing and patterns of the fluctuations are determined, it is also important to establish at which points in the firm customers interact and to identify the utilization patterns at each point of customer interaction. Managers must look at their blueprints and determine the demand patterns, particularly at the failpoints, for all of the appropriate time frames. The variation in significance of the failpoints makes it imperative to prioritize capacity allocation decisions according to their significance in affecting customer value.

It is necessary to identify the customers or the segments that interact at the different times and to determine their prospects for profitability. Different segment-mixes are likely to patronize the services at different times. Further, the proportion of each segment within the total number of customers served at any given time could be different. To enable prioritizing capacity allocation, the size and profitability of each segment need to be examined. The size relates to the volume of revenues received from the customer, whereas profitability includes the revenues as well as the costs associated with serving that customer.

Yield management objectives cannot be met unless the firm understands customer behaviour in interaction patterns over the relevant time frames. Firms must use their understanding of customers to determine what causes the fluctuation in their demand patterns. Why do these patterns occur? What factors affect not just the customers' purchasing patterns but also their consumption patterns? When customers' consumption activities require interaction with the firm, it would require identifying the demand patterns in each interaction activity and its effect on the firm's capacity. This is where customer knowledge is critical. Without an understanding of the customer's purchasing and consumption decisions, it would be impossible to attempt effective demand management. Why do customers in each segment interact with the firm at the times that they do? Can that behaviour be changed and if so, what will change that behaviour? Once that is determined, it becomes apparent that the next question is: Are the costs of changing that behaviour worth the incremental effect it has on total profits? The answers to these questions lead to possible avenues for the firm to explore in its attempt to change customer behaviour.

Capacity analysis complements demand analysis and begins with identifying the processes in the blueprint that relate to each customer interaction. Very simply, the capacity in terms of servable customers for each value-creating process supporting each point of customer interaction needs to be calculated. The firm must identify what productive factors can be profitably adjusted to demand patterns by increasing or reducing capacity without affecting the quality of the customer experience. The alignment of the firm's assets and resources to demand fluctuations will require an analysis of the capacity of the productive factors of the firm.

The productive factors of employees, equipment, and facilities, allocated over a period of time, determine the capacity of a firm. The amount of time that the productive factors are available divided by the average time it takes to serve a customer gives the number of customers that could be served. Since the capacity for a service depends on the various steps in the process, the weakest link in the process, or the bottleneck, determines the capacity of the whole process.

Capacity for a multistep process is said to be balanced if all the steps in the process are about equal in the number of customers they can serve in the same amount of time. Not all customer interactions with the firm are likely to be of critical importance in the customer experience. In order to prioritize the attention of capacity management practices, it is important to focus on those customer interactions that are likely to be critical incidents—the failpoints. Next, the cost of the productive factors for the value-creating processes for those critical incidents needs to be ascertained. The key question is: What is the feasibility of stretching or shrinking the productive factors? For each capacity-determining productive factor, an important input into capacity management decisions is how costs and customer value are affected by its shrinking or stretching.

There are several implementation considerations in determining which capacity management practice is appropriate in a situation. For example, what is the minimum capacity at which the firm must operate? The minimum capacity at which a firm must operate takes into account the volume of customers required to cover fixed costs (assuming variable costs are already covered in the pricing).

The maximum capacity is, of course, the maximum number of customers that can be served. The optimum level of operation is not at the maximum capacity. Within this minimum-to-maximum range of capacity, there is an optimum capacity level at which both profits and customer satisfaction are maximized. Handling more customers than that could result in deteriorating quality. For example, there is a maximum tolerable waiting time at each interaction for most customers. When wait is inevitable, as we saw in the preceding chapter, there are considerations to be made. The main consideration is how these waits affect customer value. For example, in-process waiting is a less significant contributor to customer dissatisfaction than preprocess waiting. Adjusting capacity requires an analysis of wait time and its effect on customer experience.

Service firms must determine their optimum capacity based on frontline employee-customer ratio, such that quality is not compromised. For example, in airlines, the ratio of airport agents to passengers ranged from 15 to 1 at

Continental to 68 to 1 at Southwest. Of course, the ratio should make sense based on the service design. As Southwest does not issue traditional boarding passes, they require fewer ticket agents at the airport. Similarly, frontline-to-customer ratios are commonly used as benchmarks in industries such as health care, education, and the hospitality among others. At every customer interaction point in the value creation and delivery process, firms must judge the desirable ratio of frontline capacity to customers.

Many operations optimization techniques seeking to minimize costs allow firms to ignore customer satisfaction unless specifically built into the algorithm. These yield management techniques ought to be designed and implemented with the primary

The objective for any firm is to maximize the return from its assets. To accomplish this, firms are naturally inclined to garner the most profitable segment of the market for which they are best suited. Firms need also to analyse the profitability of segments being served with the timing of their interactions with the firm. Which type of customer makes the interactions at what point in the demand period/cycle? The firm can then allocate its resources according to that profitability analysis.

It is possible to calculate a yield index to indicate how well a firm is doing in the realization of its profit potential—not revenues, but profits. The difference between the average price actually charged and the cost to serve the customer is the average profit per customer. Multiplying average profit per customer by number of customers should approximate the total profit of the service firm, which can also be seen as, simply, total revenues minus total costs. From an efficiency point of view, actual realised profits should be compared to the maximum potential profit.

Equation A depicts this total profitability index as *revenue efficiency* (actual versus maximum possible revenues) minus *cost efficiency* (actual costs versus targeted costs). Since revenue is price times volume, Equation B translates the total revenue efficiency into price efficiency and volume efficiency. *Price efficiency* is the average price charged divided by the maximum price that could have been charged. *Volume efficiency* is the number of customers served compared to the number of customers that could have been served at full (optimum) capacity. The total cost efficiency can be similarly translated in the equation. Target costing, a technique used to determine the lifecycle cost at which a company must produce the product for a customer, would be very useful in ensuring that the profitability of the value produced by the assets is feasible.

If profit efficiency can be seen as price efficiency minus cost efficiency, Equation C reveals that the *yield index* for the firm is the profit efficiency multiplied by the volume efficiency. Equation D suggests that you could calculate these efficiencies for each segment to arrive at the yield index of each segment. Segments with the highest yield are served so that the total lifetime profitability of the segment mix is maximized. Calculating the profitability efficiencies for different segments would reveal that not all customers cost the same to serve, just as not all customers bring the same revenues.

Thus all segments are not equally profitable. Some cost less to serve and some bring more revenues than others. But, there maybe cyclical periods when you need the relatively less profitable customers to help generate revenue from idle capacity, as long as price charged can cover the variable costs and have some profit left over to help cover fixed costs. Firms need to examine the size and profitability of all of the customers/segments that are being served by the firm. Only then can firms pick the segment mix with maximum total profitability across a demand cycle.

They must also get the specific customers to interact with the firm at specific points in the demand cycle according to their profit contribution to the firm. In a hypothetical case: the proportion of the segments in the segment-mix must be such that the firm is maximizing the sale of its most profitable value bundles as well as maximizing serving the most profitable customers. The most profitable customers are gauged by their lifetime value.Thus, if value bundle I is the most profitable product for the firm, the firm should attempt to increase the percentage of this value bundle sold during any given time period. Further, assume that there are two segments A and B in this example. For each value bundle during a given demand period, the firm should maximize the proportion of the high-profitability segment being served.

Any yield management approach seeks to improve price efficiencies or cost efficiencies and at the same time attempts to maintain the demand at optimum levels. This is a challenge because of the inherent trade-off between price and quantity demanded. If you lower price, you could increase volume, but that does not automatically convert to profits because you may have sacrificed revenues and you could be spending more to attract and serve these customers. In other words, when you lower the price, you may improve volume efficiencies but lose price efficiencies and cost efficiencies as well. Therefore, a systematic approach to determine the most effective way to match demand and supply requires simultaneously measuring price, cost, and volume efficiencies.

Productive factors of the process are represented by capacity in the number of customers that can be served by the people, equipment, and facility. With activity-based costing methods, their costs can be assessed against their contribution to customer value. Firms attempt to keep costs down based solely on financial criteria. Indeed, any adjustments to capacity that must be made to keep costs down must be based on their impact on customer value. Consider how some common practices to adjust capacity might effect customer value. Firms attempt to shrink capacity during low periods of demand. Practically speaking there is a limit to this—hotels cannot shrink or expand the number of rooms, for example. But it can close off rooms and other physical facilities and equipment for maintenance and reduce the staff during low periods. Customer-focused managers will consider the impact of these actions on customer value for patrons being served during that period.

During peak periods, firms increase staff and bring all equipment and physical facilities into the operation. When other opportunities to increase capacity are utilized, such as outsourcing, then quality control is the issue that has to be traded off with the cost and volume benefits. Firms may also investigate other customer value opportunities if it can put its value-creating assets to a different use.

When the margins are attractive and the value-creating assets during low periods can be reconfigured to produce a different solution, firms might consider acquiring more capacity. In general, capacity management is about expanding capacity during peak times and decreasing it during periods of low demand so that cost and volume efficiencies can be maximized. Demand management involves smoothing the peaks and valleys so that revenue and volume efficiencies are maximized; the most common techniques are pricing and promotions tactics. An important question in this whole exercise is to determine whether the service lends itself to the various capacity management techniques. Ultimately, the customer-focused firm will maintain a caveat in adjusting capacity: how will it affect customer value?

When different segments must inevitably be handled at different times of the demand cycle, an important consideration to be made is availability of alternate segments. For example, Bermuda began targeting younger travellers, under the age of 49, to boost its offseason visitor revenues. With a resident population only one-tenth the size of the number of annual visitors, Bermuda's local economy depends on tourism. About a third of Bermuda's visitors are passengers on cruise ships. These cruise ship arrivals being seasonal, Bermuda is looking to attract younger vacationers year round instead of just the spring and summer high season.

Bermuda used a guarantee to support perceptions of off-season weather—at least 68 degrees or a 10 per cent discount in any hotel, dining, shopping, or ground transportation service! Segments can be mixed by their time of use or time of purchase. As a demand management tool, the timing of various consumption process activities such as purchase and use are levers that the firm can use to make its demand more predictable and to manage the utilization of its assets.

For example, the time of purchase, use, and cancellation in travel, entertainment, hotels, and conferences, must all be considered in managing demand in service firms and in firms where assets are being used to produce services. Group business is a savior for the hospitality business. It ensures a large volume of committed demand from one customer—but groups are usually booked far in advance and the price is discounted. The firm has to leave itself the appropriate amount of capacity for the anticipated "full-rated" customers for the same time period to be purchased closer to the time of use. When the anticipated demand is low, firms are forced to look for segments such as trade shows, business conferences, and executive seminars and the like. The Royal Caribbean Cruises positioned one of its new ships as "the first million dollar conference centre at sea." Segments to be served at any given time can be selected based on their lifetime value and their responsiveness or sensitivity to customer value changes.

Managing segments for maximum profitability by shifting demand involves understanding the sensitivity of the segments to the product bundle. Adjustments to the product can change customer value and shift demand. The productive factors can be aligned by the sensitivity of the segments to changes in customer value in such a way as to shift segments to other points in the demand cycle. But first, the firm must understand: What are the service preferences (value), sensitivity to price, and promotion specials? Will changing the customer value by changing either the benefits or costs of the value bundle change customer behaviour or shift demand to low-demand periods?

MODIFYING CUSTOMER BEHAVIOUR

Why do customers perform those interactions when they do? What will it take to change their behaviour to perform those interactions during other times? In other words, what is their behaviour sensitive to? Essentially, this analysis is reflected in a change in customer value. Segments differ in price sensitivity; different segments will switch their interaction times at different price levels.

Insofar as customer value is affected by price, pricing is a powerful tool to modify customer behaviour. Firms can do this with adjustments to the value bundle, by manipulating elements in the supplementary product. Adjustments to benefits and costs as reflected in customer value can be analysed for its effect on customer behaviour. In how it affects customer value, the amount of customer participation sometimes allows flexible pricing. Automation versus personalized service can be used to provide varying degrees of levels of service to the customer.

Customers may choose the technology during peak periods such as in the case of the self-service checkout counters in many stores. Standardized versus tailored versions can be used to shift demand. Different versions of the product with different combinations of features using product bundling are effective demandshifting mechanisms. Firms in some industries do this instinctively without much sophistication while others such as airlines and hotels use very sophisticated methods. Firms that have a good customer understanding are better equipped to adjust customer value without losing superiority among its competitors. Price promotions are powerful demand-shifting tactics. There are numerous examples of price promotions, from early bird specials to discounts during low periods. The problem with most price promotions is that they are not aligned with demand fluctuations, so that the effect on the customer is random—where the firm is simply hoping to build demand without a sense of timing and how it would affect demand fluctuation patterns. Unless the firm's assets always operate at the same level of capacity, every firm should be offering price promotions to bring in customers during periods when the assets are idle. Anything from customer convenience in payment such as interest-free deferred payment schedules to outright price bargains are common uses of pricing for this purpose.

Customer behaviour can be modified to the benefit of both the customer and firm with customer education on how demand fluctuations can affect their own customer experience. Different industries have different norms in the attempt to inform the customer about peak times so that those customers who would not want to be subjected to long lines and wait times can choose to interact with the firm during lowdemand periods. Most customer service phone lines will inform you of the expected wait times after you are greeted and logged in to their system. When there is an exaggerated peak and valley pattern, firms must find ways to educate customers to move their patronage to a different time or access point to help with the strain on capacity while reducing the risk of a poor customer experience that could be detrimental to customer loyalty and sustainable profits.

Customer lifetime value and customer preferences and priorities can and must be kept in mind when attempting to manage demand by changing customer value. Any type of membership benefits and loyalty programmes can be designed to essentially manage demand. The terms of the membership programme need to ensure that the firm is managing the use of its productive resources according to the lifetime value of the mix of customers being served. Any change in customer value with demand and supply management technique should be monitored for its impact on brand loyalty and customers' lifetime value to the firm.

Managers of firms competing on service will find that demand fluctuations are a definite predominant challenge. Demand must be managed by smoothing the demand fluctuations and making capacity adjustments in value-creating assets. The smoothing of demand requires building demand during low and shoulder periods and moving excess demand from the peak times to the low or shoulder demand periods.

When and why do the customers' consumption activities and demand fluctuate as they do? Demand analysis must include an understanding of customer behaviour and the profitability of the various customers and segments being served at different times during a demand period. Thus, their sensitivity to various customer value changes would determine the appropriate demand-shifting actions that the firm might attempt. Capacity management requires a cost-revenue analysis of the productive factors or the value-creating assets. That analysis should focus on capacity utilization. What is the profitability of the value bundle created by capacity (assets) that was being utilized? Are the value-creating assets being used to serve the maximum profitable customer mix at any given time?

MANAGING CUSTOMER RELATIONSHIPS

The task of creating and delivering superior customer value must be complemented with the selection of the appropriate customers and the effective management of relationships with those customers. Managing customer relationships should be guided by an understanding of what the customer's equity is to the firm. Customer equity, the value of customer to the firm, improves as superiority in customer value improves. Since customer equity is perhaps the firm's most valuable asset, the firm must continually seek to improve customer value for it best customers. A firm's potential return on customer equity should determine the investment it makes in customers. For its most valuable customers, the firm must guarantee superior service quality and customer service, with special attention to recovering from inevitable product failures when they occur.

Maximizing long-term profitability comes from maximizing customer equity—firms must maximize the lifetime value of the customer, including revenues, referrals as well as costs of serving the customer. Customer acquisition and retention efforts must be guided by the worth of the customer to the firm.

Maytag provides premium service to its premium customers—those who purchase the Neptune line of laundry machines. Neptune customers get a dedicated staff, a separate toll-free number and fast response on service calls. This is an example of the common business practice where firms allocate resources by the profitability and value of the customer. They utilize the opportunity in directly interacting with individual customers to determine customer profitability and allocate assets accordingly. And what are the benefits of the practice of differentiating among your customers?

Broadly referring to the practice as CRM can sometimes defeat its purpose by losing sight of the basic meaning of the term: managing customer relationships. Managing customer relationships would mean actively planning, organizing, directing, and controlling a firm's business relationships with its customers. The term might be "new" in its current usage, but the business practice of managing relationships with customers is certainly not new. What has prompted the increased attention to CRM is new technology: how well firms can practice CRM has been advanced by information technology in the new economy.

Technology brings with it the risk of missing the benefits of huge investment costs if used inappropriately, however. The benefits can seem so attractive that the costs are rationalized until the technology fails to deliver.

The American Customer Satisfaction Index, a measure of customer attitudes towards about 200 companies from over 30 different industries, has actually shown a decline, while at the same time CRM technology investments had grown about five times. When used with a fundamental understanding of CRM's purpose, the benefits of CRM technology enabling the business practice of managing customer relationships are clearly powerful. Siebel, Peoplesoft, Oracle, and other CRM technologies are really customer information management or customer knowledge management systems. These systems gather data and convert it to knowledge that will help firms in their customer relationship management activities.

The most significant contribution of CRM technology to the practice of business is not the technology itself, of course. It is in what the technology does to the practice of managing customer relationships. Because technology has now made it easy to do all the tasks of gathering and analyzing customer information, firms have been able to discover and realise the incredible benefits in proactively managing customer relationships. For example, Continental Airlines' customer information system allows its staff to mine data on passenger profitability and is also able to suggest remedies and perks for special requests or complaining customers.

Customer benefits from relationships with firms have been conceptualized under three categories: social, psycholo-gical, and customization benefits, in a two-part study using interviews and surveys. Financial services such as brokerage and banking are heavy users of CRM technology. Deregulation and information technology have effectively blurred the boundaries between those two once-different financial institutions.

They have had a heavy reliance on information because these are primarily knowledge businesses. "Signature"-level customers at Charles Schwab wait no longer than fifteen seconds to reach a customer service person, whereas other customers can wait ten minutes or more. Some banks have coded their customers so that customer service reps can decide on rates and fees depending on the customer's profitability code. Centura Banks rates its customers on a profitability scale of 1 to 5. The most profitable customers get service calls from staff and an annual call from the CEO.

Attrition rate at the bank is down 50 per cent in four years, and—more interesting—the percentage of unprofitable customers has gone down from 27 per cent to 21 per cent. The hospitality industry was able to slash 50 per cent of its promotion programmes and increase response rates by 20 per cent with a good database of response behaviour from its mailing list. CRM systems have provided firms with the data they need to determine the revenues and costs to serve at the individual customer level, allowing firms to prioritize their allocations of value-creating assets and resources to the more profitable customers. According to AMR research, the CRM market grew from $200 milllion to $1.1 billion between 1994 and 1997, and is expected to reach as much as $16 billion—an indication of how much firms want this technology to manage customer relationships. A firm's knowledge about its customers has allowed it to adjust customer value based on the profitability of the individual customer.

Just as with power, information technology has to be used judiciously. Discriminating against less profitable customers can seem unreasonable to all paying customers and could backfire with publicity. AT&T withdrew its minimum usage charges for its basic-plan customers who were unprofitable. GE Capital tried to charge credit-card users who were not accruing a minimum level of interest charges and ended up having to sell its credit card business. When used appropriately at the individual level, information technology can be very rewarding. Capital One's senior vice-president for domestic card operations, Marge Connelly, says, "We look at every single customer contact as an opportunity to make an unprofitable customer more profitable."

CRM systems are not just about profiling customers and loyalty programmes. To derive maximum benefits, one must broaden the thinking about CRM technology. The technology should be viewed as knowledge-based systems that seek to prioritize commitment of a firm's assets and resources to the more profitable customers while enhancing the relationships with ALL (right) customers. Pricing may not be the appropriate means to deal with the unprofitable customer. CRM systems give the firm access to information that may reveal other ways to manage the unprofitable customer. *Enabling* the managing of customer relationships is the goal of the CRM system. Managing customer relationships is about selecting, acquiring, retaining, and enhancing relationships with customers by using an intimate knowledge of the customer's consumption domain to maximize the return on the firm's assets. With CRM systems, firms have the knowledge and the technological capability to identify, retain and enhance more desirable customer relationships.

This chapter covers issues regarding which customers to acquire and retain for maximum sustainable profits. How do you assign value to customers and what is involved in that evaluation? Who is the right customer? Who should be in your customer portfolio? Firms look at customers as investments. How do you value these investments? Or, What is the equity of your customers?

Selecting the Right Customer

Markets consist of customers with diverse needs and differences in customer profitability. When serving multiple groups of customers, the goal must be to maximize the profitability of the combination of segments. When different segments are targeted, the firm essentially has a portfolio of customer segments just as investors have an investment portfolio that maximizes returns at a certain level of risk, firms manage customer portfolios for maximum profits. In other words, this is the selection of customers at any point in time, compared to other segments, from which the firm can generate maximum profits. Firms must attract these most profitable customers and then must establish systems and procedures to retain them.

Most firms serve different segments depending on how the definition of segment is aggregated. The "segment-of-one" used in common business parlance to refer to customization at the individual level is really a maximum disaggregation of a market segment. As we saw in the preceding chapter, most firms facing fluctuating demand and experiencing peak, shoulder and low periods of demand find it inevitable that, at different times, different segments must be served. Of course, each of these segments must have a compatible fit with the overall corporate image as well as a compatible fit with the products, services, employees and other customers. The question is, are they selected based on their combined long term value to the firm?

Most firms forecast the volume and revenues from various segments at certain price points at different times in the purchase cycle. In the typical firm, sales and communications efforts follow these underlying assumptions in pricing and in messages targeting sales prospects. The typical firm then attempts to formalize advertising campaigns to reach as many people as possible in the case of packaged goods. In the case of business-to-business services, the salespeople focus on making a sale. Most firms then struggle to orchestrate all these messages for acquisition of the customer in a coordinated fashion.

Much less attention is paid to the retention of the customer. Barring the well-run operation, common business practice for many firms is short-term oriented. On the contrary, a customer-focused firm begins by approaching sales as acquiring the right customer. The customer-focused firm also approaches the acquisition of customers as only the first step in managing the relationships with its customers. Once acquired, the customer must be retained. But, not always retained at any cost—a necessary condition is that the benefits outweigh the costs of acquiring *and* retaining that customer.

Customer-focused firms align all their activities and processes in acquiring and retaining the right customer. They see their value-creating assets as most profitably leveraged by focusing on the most valuable customers. In principle, the value of the customer is determined by contribution to the firm's objectives over the lifetime of the customer. The right customer is that customer whose inclusion in the firm's target market helps maximize returns on the firm's assets.

FIRM'S PRECIOUS ASSET CUSTOMER EQUITY

Ask a manager, "What is your firm's most valuable asset?" Chances are that you will not get the response, "my customers." You will find even fewer firms that actually make an assessment of this value in any real sense. The valuation of the customer is implicit in sales figures—essentially, the revenues generated by customers of the firm. What is the flaw in using sales as a proxy in valuing a firm's customers? Consider this.

Two customers with the same cash value of purchases may not be of the same value to the firm. There may be differences in the cost of serving these two customers. The true value of the customer to the firm, or the equity that the firm has in that customer, must include all revenues and also all costs related to that customer, as in financial investments.

A recent framework by a team of researchers defines customer equity as the "total of the discounted lifetime value of all the firm's customers." They articulate three drivers of customer equity: value equity, brand equity, and relationship equity. They define value equity as the objective assessment of the utility of the brand, and value equity is driven by quality, price, and convenience; brand equity as the subjective assessment of the brand above and beyond the perceived value, and brand equity is driven by brand awareness, attitude towards the brand, and corporate ethics; and relationship equity as the tendency of the customer to stick with the brand, and relationship equity is driven by loyalty programmes, special recognition and treatment, affinity programmes, community-building programmes, and knowledge-building programmes. Their framework—the customer equity diagnostic—is offered as a way to determine which customers to acquire as well as what will enable their retention.

If we define customer value as the value of the firm or a product as perceived by the customer, customer equity is the converse and refers to the value of the customer to the firm. If the objective is to maximize the returns from your investments—the customer portfolio—you must maximize customer equity. This makes sense because you can maximize sustainable return on assets by maximizing customer equity for the long term. To maximize customer equity, we must be able to measure it. If customer equity is simply the value of a customer to the firm, we can articulate that value in the same way that customers articulate our value to them.

Just as customer value is the difference between benefits and costs to the customer, conversely, customer equity is the difference between the benefits and costs to the firm in serving a customer. One team of researchers describes their method of measuring customer equity as follows: "[we] first measure each customer's expected contributions towards offsetting the company's fixed costs over the expected life of that customer. Then we discount the expected contributions to a net present value at the company's target rate of return for marketing investments. Finally, we add together the discounted expected contributions of all current customers."

Evident in their metric are the following important points about customer equity:

- It is the sum of the equity of all of a firm's customers.
- It summates the gross contribution of each customer, taking into account benefits as well as costs of serving a customer.

- It includes consideration of future revenues and variable costs from each customer.
- It is a time-discounted present value of future benefits to the firm.

It becomes evident that the customer equity concept when disaggregated to the individual customer level allows us to look at the revenues and costs of serving an individual customer. It helps answer the question, which customer should we serve? The ideal customer to the firm is the one that gives it the maximum long-term customer equity, which theoretically you want as a brand-loyal customer. However, as we will see in the next section, the converse is not true, because not all brandloyal customers provide maximum customer equity.

The concept of brand loyalty is a well-researched topic. The notion of a customer having a lifetime value and the prominence of database systems in managing customers have spawned a renewed interest in relationship marketing. Just making repurchases doesn't make a customer brand loyal. There must be some commitment by the customer to the firm for relational continuity reflecting a positive patronage bias. Not all brand-loyal customers have a positive disposition to the provider—some relationships may be forced because of a lack of choice. Brand loyalty reflects a financial, social, or structural bonding with the customer. Relationship marketing seeks to enhance the mutual benefits from the relationship with the right customer—seeking brand loyalty from the right customer. To determine who the right customer is, we need to understand what benefits the firm expects from an ideal customer.

At the outset, it is clear that the stream of purchases from the brandloyal customer is the primary benefit. In truth, the value of a brand-loyal customer to the firm must go beyond the purchases made over the lifetime of the relationship with that customer. As we know, revenues can be direct and indirect. Direct revenues are all of the customer's purchases, and indirect revenues are the cash value of all of the other benefits the customer accrues to the firm, in the form of direct revenues from referred customers. Costs to serve are drastically reduced, as brand-loyal customers are generally easier to serve. The argument is that as customers get familiar with the firm, its processes and products, customers will require less costly assistance from the firm in purchasing and using the product.

Loyal customers may even be able to open up ways in which to reduce the costs of serving the customer. Other benefits of brand loyalty would include product improvement contributions, new product opportunities, ideal sources for market information, and favourable word of mouth. At an overall level, all these benefits add up to a degree of stability and potential growth for the firms. Those brand-loyal customers who are committed in their patronage recognize their benefits from the firm and show commitment in the provider firm.

To select the right customer, the firm must be able to measure the value of the loyal customer from all these benefits as well as the costs of acquiring and retaining that customer. It is not easy to quantify all of these benefits. But it is possible to calculate the direct and indirect revenues from each customer. It is also possible to calculate the acquisition costs and relationship maintenance costs. Information technology has allowed us to obtain that data and made it easy to calculate the lifetime value of a customer.

A commonly used practice inherited from the direct marketing industry experience is called RFM (referring to "recency, frequency, and monetary data")—a method to determine whom to send promotions from among your customers. It takes into account the value of a customer's purchases, how recent they were, and how often they were purchased. As with the danger of any one approach, RFM has been used without much consideration for other important dimensions of the most valuable customer, such as how profitable the customer really is.

RFM is therefore not a proxy measure for the lifetime value of a customer. Indeed, if the costs of serving different customers show a variance, then the RFM method could attract the wrong customer. As we know, there are three main factors in calculating the lifetime value of a customer. It is not just a simple product of the value of each purchase and the number of times the customer will purchase the product over that customer's lifetime. The lifetime value of a customer should also include referral value. And, it should include the lifetime costs as well. CRM technology has made it possible to do this, but, how many firms actually use this understanding in how they design and implement their CRM solutions?

Lifetime revenues is the sum of all purchases that the customer will make. An assessment of the progression of purchases over the lifecycle of the customer is a key point to be made here. For instance, consider what a college student's financial lifecycle would mean to a bank. First, it is a savings or checking account with a debit card and perhaps even a credit card. The college student may also be a good candidate for an education loan. Once graduated, this ex-student is now in the market for a car loan, and quite soon a home mortgage. Once other life events such as marriage and children occur, there are more car loans, mortgages, home equity loans, trusts, custody accounts, education loans for children, and associated financial products that a typical family would need.

USAA, the life insurance and financial services company, follows marriages, births, and other life events so that it can advise customers on changing needs. Every firm should attempt to develop such a long-term consumption profile for the typical customer in each segment, charting their potential purchases over a lifetime to take into account the life events of the customer—a customer lifecycle analysis. A similar case may be made for business customers based on an assessment of growth potential, so that any

B2B firm has to project the growth of its customers and factor that into a lifetime value calculation.

Not all customers become brand loyal. We have seen that superior customer value is a prerequisite for brand loyalty. What percentage of new customers find the firm's customer value to be superior? The lifetime value of a customer must also factor the probability of the acquired customer becoming brand loyal. The probability consideration takes into account that a customer may not be a good fit, that a competitor may have been able to provide a better fit, or that the need situation changed for the customer, such as in the case of relocation of the consuming unit.

Lifetime Costs

An activity-based costing approach allows a firm to account for direct costs that the firm incurs in the relationship with a specific customer. Once again, with information technology it is possible, where it makes sense, to attribute marketing and operating costs to individual customers. To obtain the full benefit from CRM investments, it is important to track costs at the individual customer level as well. Costs include acquiring and remarketing to the customer over the lifetime of the customer. Costs also include value creation and delivery costs of serving the customer. Thus, the costs after acquisition include not only the costs of serving the customer, but also relationship maintenance and development costs such as the costs of cross-selling or upselling, called remarketing costs. Once again, as in Equation B, the costs related to the first purchase are separated from that of lifetime purchases so that the probability of repeat purchase is taken into account when calculating lifetime costs.

The indirect revenue of referrals from a loyal customer is an often overlooked aspect of customer equity. The typical CRM solution and database marketing approaches ignore the referral power of a customer in calculating the lifetime value of a customer. Most firms do not even capture this data, partly because it is difficult to obtain information when knowledge systems in a firm are not configured to obtain it. The other reason may be that firms are not proactively looking for referrals from their loyal customers in any systematic way.

How is the value of referrals from a customer calculated? To answer this question requires looking at the process and mechanics of how referrals work. Who provides a referral? Customers who are satisfied and who have a certain degree of loyalty are the ones who are likely to convey favourable messages about a firm and its products and services. A key piece of information needed here is what level of satisfaction a brand-loyal customer needs to have before being likely to refer a customer. The next obvious question is, who receives the referral? Customers are likely to convey this information to family, friends, and colleagues. However, not all who receive the referrals are appropriate customers for the firm. What proportion of the customers who received the referral are good candidates for the firm? Out of the ones that are appropriate for the firm, not all are likely to be suitably influenced by the referral to make the first purchase. Finally, if a purchase is actually made, what proportion of referred customers makes repeat purchases? Those that are moved to try the product may not all turn into loyal customers, but if they do, then their lifetime purchases add to the value of the customer making the initial referral. Equation C reflects these fractional outcomes in the mechanics of calculating referral value.

Maximizing the collective lifetime value of its customers should be the goal in managing customer relations. By increasing the number of customers *and* by increasing the lifetime value of each customer, firms can maximize their long-term profitability.

From earlier study it becomes clear that to maximize the lifetime value of customers, you need to:

- Maximize lifetime revenues
- Maximize lifetime referrals
- Minimize lifetime costs

Potential customers in a target market are by definition not yet customers. They may or may not be aware of or inclined to purchase from the firm. Firms have to nurture customers' dispositions to the firm through a number of stages before they can benefit from the loyalty of those customers. The acquisition process of customers could begin at any of the different stages on the road to loyalty. Customers may or not be aware or have an understanding of the features and benefits of the product. If the knowledge of the product is favourable, customers may have a liking or preference for the product. Some customers may even have purchased the product but may not be repeat purchasers, may not be loyal to the product, or may have switched to a competitor. The right customers from any stage need to be moved towards a state of loyalty to the firm and its products. Can CRM technology be configured to capture information about the customer's stage in this process?

Once the appropriate customers are acquired, firms must look for increased usage and frequency, cross-selling opportunities, and trading up to premium versions. Retaining customers requires proactive customer management. If not, as indicated earlier customers are likely to be indifferent to the firm, and a heavy user may become impatient and switch to the competition. Proactive customer management seeks to increase interest in the light user and treat the heavy user with appreciation and respect. Thus, in keeping with equation A the goal of maximizing lifetime revenues is achieved by maximizing the average purchase per year as well as the duration of the customer's relationship with the firm.

Referral customers have very low acquisition costs, since your brandloyal customers did the marketing for you. Following the mechanics of the process of word of mouth, it is clear from equation C that maximizing lifetime referral value requires maximizing the number of referrals from each customer and maximizing the lifetime value of each referred customer. To maximize the number of referrals, one must maximize the drivers of referrals from a customer. In other words, firms must attempt to increase the probability of a customer making a referral of profitable customers. Firms must move loyal customers to become advocates of the firm.

When word of mouth is seen as a powerful customer acquisition tool, firms will find a way to stimulate referrals. Many firms are not proactive in stimulating referrals, assuming simply that "good word of mouth will happen if we do a good job." What must firms do to increase the value from referrals?

First, firms must identify the current and potential advocates of the firm. Firms must proactively look for individuals and organizations that are likely sources of referrals and stimulate and reward them for the right kind of referrals. Satisfied and loyal customers are not the only ones who can stimulate positive word of mouth. There are opinion leaders: such individuals and organizations as consumer reports, firms such as Gartner and Forrester, who might be considered experts in the field, and most important, the general and trade media. Other ambassadors for the firm include players in often overlooked sources such as suppliers, resellers, employees, and other stakeholders such as investors. Community chat rooms on the Web are rich sources of information for the firm about what word of mouth is transpiring among its stakeholders.

Second, firms must attempt to stimulate referrals. Any new customer acquisition activity should record information on how the customer was moved to deal with the firm. When the firm obtains and records this information in the consumption profile of any customer, it is able to use it to calculate the average number of customer referrals made by each current customer of the firm. Customers and advocates with similar profiles need to be approached about playing a referral role. Since some customers may be amenable and others not, firms must explore what it would take to move suitable customers to play an advocate role.

Finally, from Equation C it is also clear that the better the fit between the referred customer and the firm's products, the greater the lifetime referral value. Research has also shown that the customers referred to by satisfied customers tend to be a particularly good fit with the firm and its products and services. The fit is better than with those customers attracted and acquired through marketing messages such as advertisements and coupon mailers. Brand-loyal advocates bring in like-minded customers. To get referrals to actually make a purchase or try the firm's offerings, it is necessary to get some incentives into the hands of the referred customers.

Reducing the costs of acquisition, costs of serving, and the cost of remarketing per customer can increase the lifetime value of a customer.

Reducing costs to serve means that you need to be more efficient in the yield from your value-creating assets. To reduce costs of acquisition and remarketing you need to be more effective in your marketing, both to new and to current customers. CRM technology can be used to continually learn from experience and utilize knowledge to reduce operating and marketing costs at the individual level.

ATTRACTING CUSTOMERS

To maximize the total lifetime value of their customers, firms must proactively manage customer relationships. As seen proactive customer relationship management should seek customer appreciation from the heavy user and attract more interest from light users with better value bundles if they can contribute more in their lifetime value to the firm. This is in contrast to the firm that may have good customer service, for example, but in its reactive mode will leave the light user relatively indifferent to the firm and the heavy user susceptible to a competitor.

Most loyalty programmes involve some kind of reward for the continued patronage of their customers. Referred to as frequency marketing, continuity programmes, awards or points programmes, or simply loyalty programmes, the goal of these programmes is to market and manage relationships with customers. First instituted by American Airlines in the 1970s to get around government regulation that prevented price competition, now many firms' programmes attempt to solidify their relationships with its customers. The rewards or awards, as they are called, may come in the form of free products and services at the firm, or sometimes even free products from other firms.

The smart firms impose restrictions on the use of these rewards, so that they are used to increase demand when and where needed. For example, the hospitality industry blocks out certain dates so that the promotions are targeted at different segments to entice customer utilization at low demand periods.

The problem is that many of these programmes are misguided in design and implementation. One obvious omission is evident when the lifetime calculus is compared to the criteria for the rewards.

The rewards focus on revenues for the most part. That costs are taken into account is not clear at all. That would be a surprise for managers who have not considered costs of serving the customer. Brand-loyal customers are not necessarily profitable customers. In their knowledge of their own value and indispensability to the firm, the brand-loyal customer could make costly demands of the firm. The firm, in doling out the goodies along with the product and other business favours, may actually be spending more than it recognizes as costs of serving that customer. The only criterion for these (brand) loyalty programmes should be that they should maximize the customer equity for each customer, based on the calculus of lifetime value that we have discussed.

To be meaningful and powerful in managing relationships with the right customers, these customer acquisition and loyalty programmes must specify the following:

- Objectives of the programme
- Market and customer scope of the programme
- Value for customer scope of the programme
- Impact scope (costs, timing, impact on people, process, physical assets, other customers, publicity opportunities, etc.)

The objectives of the programme need to be stated in the context of customer relationship management. What is the expected value of the programme to the firm? What specifically must the programme accomplish? Perhaps it is to shift demand from peak to low periods, to attract new segments, to get light users to become heavy users, to promote a new product offering, or some other specific objective. Without a known objective, no programme can be assessed on merit.

The next specific decision for customer relationship programmes is to specify the customer that the programme is intended for. Often, frequency programmes are so loosely formulated that the rewards are earned by the wrong customer. Consider this example of the unfortunate consequence of a poorly guided programme. One Mr. Phillips logged 1.25 million frequent flier miles—about $25,000 worth of airline travel—with an investment of 50 hours of his time and $3,140. Mr. Phillips took advantage of an offer he found on the package of a Healthy Choice frozen entrée: 500 American Airlines miles for every 10 UPCs, with early birds receiving a double count of miles! A Mr. Fisher participated in the same programme and got 12,000 Northwest Airlines Miles.

Even if the airlines got an awfully good financial deal with Healthy Choice, one must ask who the loyalty programme attracts—whether the airlines are in the grocery business or in the airline business. How do their returns from this investment compare with the returns that they would have achieved with programmes that targeted the frequent flier instead of the frequent grocery shopper? The objectives of the programme should determine the appropriate segment or customer for the programme. The problem with most programmes is that they don't take into account the profitability of the customer.

Who should be the target of the programme? Not every customer is right for the firm, as we have seen, nor is every customer right for every programme. The best programme is one that tailors the award to the target customer. Thus, giant supermarket retailer UK-based Tesco mails 100,000 variations of promotions to its loyal customers. Further, some customers may be more costly to retain, while others may be increasing their profitability to the firm. As it is evident that firms need to look at the acquisition costs and retention costs of its customer base when determining the focus of their retention efforts.

The calculus of the lifetime value of a customer is clear in its indication of what needs to be factored into deciding to which customer to target the promotion. Low acquisition costs and low retention costs are realised from your most profitable customers. At the other end are your customers who were costly to acquire and cost you a lot to serve. Given the acquisition costs, the firm must keep a close eye on the customer's cost of retention. If the firm misjudged a customer's lifetime value or committed more resources to the acquisition of the customer than the revenue stream would justify, the firm has to either reduce retention costs or stop serving the customer if possible.

For the chosen customers, the firm needs to decide what they would do to motivate the customer to act. Customer knowledge should indicate what the customer is sensitive to, so that the value of the promotion can be appropriate for the specific customer or segment. The value of the promotion may be in the form of additional product, a complementary service, a straightforward price-break, or a discount for future purchases or a gift, among other things. Software firms are able to use lead customers in beta-tests and other benefits about new and innovative offerings before the rest of the market will find out, giving these B2B customers early mover advantage in their value chains in their industry.

Of course, a projected cost/benefit analysis is a must what additional revenues have been realised and at what cost? For service firms, and where the programme is about service components, it is imperative that the promotion take into account what it would do to the demand patterns of customers. The last thing you want is for customers to strain your operation if your programme ends up drawing more customers during peak times when you are already at optimum levels of served customers.

Any programme must consider the impact on other customers, on the staff, physical assets, and the delivery system or process. For example, a shortage of airline seats infuriates frequent fliers who, as brand-loyal customers, having diligently set aside miles for use on family vacations, find they are not able to use the miles because use of awards is limited to a certain proportion of the volume on each flight and are restricted to certain times and dates. Estimates are that about 10 per cent of all miles flown on a carrier can be from people cashing in on these rewards. Does it make sense for frequent flier awards to range from personal digital assistants to designer watches? Are the costs and impact of these awards assessed? Another less obvious criterion is the potential for publicity in a promotion. A promotion that is newsworthy could attract the attention of a large number of potential customers and other stakeholders.

Firms must prioritize the management of customer relationships as a firm-wide imperative. Dell Computer, for example, has a "customer experience council" consisting of senior executives from each division or business line and major function that reports to a corporate vice chairman, no less. The council oversees measurement of several aspects of customer behaviour, including the effectiveness of its loyalty programmes. Dell even measures all the costs its customers incur in purchasing and using their products, including such things as shopping, ordering, installing, operating, servicing, and disposing of products. The real value of tracking these revenues and costs over the lifetime value of the customer is that it allows firms to understand their brandloyal customers and anticipate their future needs. Such management practices will be able to deliver benefits to the heavy user to maximize their lifetime value.

The lifetime value of the customer must be calculated for each customer an assessment of revenues and costs over the lifetime of the customer's relationship with the firm. The investment in acquiring and retaining a customer must be made based on the customer's lifetime value to the firm. A continuous monitoring of up-sell and cross-sell opportunities could increase the lifetime value of the customer. The potential customer equity from each segment or customer should determine the extent of value-creating adjustments to be made in terms of delivery process or product outcome customization in terms of value or other benefits to the customer or in terms of adjusting the price and other costs to the customer. These changes in promotion offerings to acquire a new customer or remarket to a current or inactive customer will impact both costs and revenues and their effect on the lifetime value of the customer will determine subsequent investments in acquiring and retaining customers.

Maximizing customer equity requires maximizing customer satisfaction by providing superior customer value. Ensuring product quality as the key driver of customer satisfaction requires checking the links between the firm's assessment of customer expectations and its ability to translate that assessment into product concept, operations design, and execution. The doorman greeted the guest as the taxi pulled up to the Windsor Court Hotel, a 324-room hotel in downtown New Orleans, one of 120 independent luxury hotels of Preferred Hotels and Resorts Worldwide.

Later, the waiter at the restaurant in the hotel accommodated off-the-menu orders but the waiters did not make eye-contact with the diners. The guest room did not have the current edition of the Yellow Pages. This guest was one of Richey International's hotel spies, who had just conducted the Preferred test for the hotel. He has determined based on his experience as a customer that this hotel had met 88.5 per cent of the Preferred standards, passing the 80 per cent minimum. Firms such as Preferred want an unbiased assessment of the quality of their product and hire independent quality assessment firms such as Richey International to do the benchmarking of its hotels.

6

A New Class: Trendies on the Trail

As Crick argues, 'human beings', the tourists themselves, are only infrequently the object of consideration in much tourism research. And yet it is upon tourists that the industry is founded. In part this has resulted from academic prejudices of analysing production rather than consumption and the tendency to focus upon the impacts (economic, environmental, cultural) of tourism where tourists are at best a homogeneous and undifferentiated group and at worst are deemed immaterial.

It has been suggested at various points in earlier that tourists need to be taken more seriously, and recent campaigns on the ethical forms of travel and tourism from development agencies (such as VSO and the Tear Fund) seem to suggest that they are. To this point in the book, a number of key factors have been stressed.

First, sought to demonstrate the significant economic changes that have resulted in post-Fordist modes of both producing and consuming goods and services. In part, these changes can be traced through to the emergence of new and varied forms of tourism in the Third World.

It was also argued that these changes have tended to invest more power in us, the consumers, or the tourists: we have more choice. Second, it has been suggested that the influence of the new middle classes can be linked to the emergence of what may be referred to as postmodern cultural forms.

The importance of these social groups in both producing new forms of tourism in the Third World and forming a significant role in taking such holidays was highlighted.

Both points stress the increasing significance of tourists, with the second factor highlighting the importance of social class. Of course this is not to say that class is the only factor in studying tourism; far from it. But it is a significant factor and is especially important in the analysis of new forms of tourism, in that the 'world of tourism is rife with the class distinction in our everyday world'.

Yet an analysis of the significance of class and tourism is only weakly developed. It was argued that analysis of tourists has centred around either classifying tourists or carrying out motivation and attitude surveys. Although such approaches are of interest, they have tended to limit the scope of tourism analysis. This chapter explores what use an analysis of class offers in developing a critique of Third World tourism. As elsewhere in the book, this is not a definitive statement of how tourists should be analysed and understood, but an attempt to broaden our thinking and approach to the field of tourism.

Initially, the chapter discusses the importance of social class as a concept and how it is reflected in travel and tourism. In particular, the relationships of contemporary global change to the way classes are formed will be considered.

The second half of the chapter identifies a number of crucial factors evident in the formation of new middle-class tourism, and it is argued that travel and tourism have an increasingly important symbolic role to play as social classes seek to define and distinguish themselves from other social classes. The final sections of the chapter indicate why social class analysis is of importance in considering the impacts of Third World tourism.

CLASS, CAPITAL AND TRAVEL

Of all social science concepts, arguably, it is class that has been subjected to the most thoroughgoing marginalisation since the 1980s. Politicians began to talk in terms of classless societies, academics became preoccupied with the fragmentation of traditional class lines (working class/middle class/upper class) and more and more people have begun to think in terms of their individual, as opposed to class, status. This is a lure of individualism that led Crompton to conclude that the 'retreat from class ... is becoming the sociological equivalent of the new individualism'.

However, a recognition of the role of social class in contemporary capitalism has begun to re-emerge. A number of authors have begun to illustrate the relationships between cultural changes and the development of new middle classes. In common, these authors agree that these significant and numerically expanding class fractions have an instrumental part to play in new cultural forms.

Indeed, Lash and Urry refer to postmodernism as a 'hegemonising mission' for the new middle classes, and elsewhere they are considered as both producers and consumers of postmodernism - *par excellence*. We identified a number of key characteristics of postmodernism and highlighted their relevance to the analysis of Third World tourism.

Briefly these involved: the emergence of specialist agents and tour operators (and its adjunct, more individually centred and flexible holidays); the de-differentiation of tourism as it becomes associated with other activities, and the growth of interest in *Other* cultures, environments and their association with the emergence of new social movements. Nevertheless, the different ways in which different social classes consume tourism is vastly under-researched. This is significant in that we have argued above that much new tourism is based on the notion of individual travel. A culture of travel (as opposed to tourism) that is shamelessly hedonistic has emerged: chill out, the world's a breeze, so experience it. But most of the existing commentary amounts to little more than the rhetorical and polemical ranting of middle-class writers bemoaning the scale, effects and popularity of mass tourism.

The analogy of tourism to pollution is commonplace and is often expressed in socio-cultural terms where it is the swarms or tidal waves of tourists that constitute a problem that must be contained. It is a view that appears to be prevalent across the arts, academia, the media and the industry.

The renowned French photographer, Henri Cartier Bresson, contends: 'I'm an adventurer ... The Africa I experienced was literally that of the "Voyage au Bout de la Nuit". It was a time when people were travellers, not tourists ... I travelled on a shoestring. Regimented tourism is a contagious form of pollution'.

Rosenthal admits that perhaps it is timely to 'accept that some areas will remain "sacrificial resorts" which continue to attract tourists who do not seek an experience of "deeper" quality'. And as an operator contends: 'With the days of the package holiday ... drawing to a close, we are about to discover very special holidays for very special people: like you'.

Equally limiting is the fact that the role of geography, the spatial dimension, is all but ignored, despite its fundamental role both to understanding tourism as a process and how social classes are constituted as part of that process. As Thurot and Thurot note, the ability of the middle classes to maintain their 'social distance' from others has become more difficult because 'great distance no longer offers substitutable destinations'.

The circulation of tourist areas has tended to focus either on the deterministic cyclical nature of tourist development or the cyclical character of tourists themselves. In the former approach, tourist areas are modelled as moving from discovery to overcrowding. In the latter approach, a taxonomy of visitor characteristics are noted. Although this approach offers greater scope for thinking about the relationships between social class and tourism, the links remain weakly developed.

By acknowledging the importance of cultural consumption in the study of social classes, the French sociologist, Pierre Bourdieu (1984), has provided a productive way for thinking about the relationships of class and tourism. A number of authors have noted the applicability of his influential work to tourism.

Briefly, Bourdieu (1984) argues that social classes wage 'classificatory struggles' seeking to distinguish themselves from each other by education, occupation, residence and so on, and, of course, through commodities, which is taken to include both objects (cars, furniture and so on) and experiences, such as holidays. They achieve this, Bourdieu suggests, by constructing 'lifestyles'. We have already alluded to this notion of lifestyle as a useful way of considering the individuals' uses of a range of objects, experiences, hobbies and beliefs to, sociologically speaking, 'mark their territories'.

These lifestyles, Bourdieu concludes, are the products of what he terms *habitus*, and it is worth spending a few moments considering the significance of this concept. Habitus represents the ability and disposition of individuals and social classes to appropriate objects and practices, to act in certain ways, that differentiate them from others.

A knowledge of 'foreign' food, good wine, classic literature or Latin American film, for example, may all assist in differentiating from others without such knowledge or appreciation. Habitus is, therefore, a 'cognitive structure' which 'gives people a sense of their place in the world'.

Or as Painter suggests, 'Habitus gives individuals a sense of how to act in specific situations, without continually having to make fully conscious decisions. It is this "practical sense", often described as a "feel for the game", that Bourdieu's theory of practice seeks to understand'. And for Bourdieu it is the necessary starting point for a theory of *strategies* that 'aims to account for the logic according to which groups, or classes, form and break up'.

Two important points emerge from Bourdieu's work. First, social classes are in constant struggle to ensure that differentiation from class fractions above and below are maintained. Travel has always had an important role to play in this process of differentiation, and as tourism has become more widespread the struggle has intensified.

It is difficult to deny that Marbella, Kos, Phuket and 18-30 provide a very different set of meanings and representations from Tikal, Chiang Mai, Kilimanjaro and Explore. So different places, the different experiences to be had, and even different operators, add up to what we could describe as a 'symbolic system'; it is the way in which we represent objects and experiences and then communicate this to others. And we can also argue that these different components 'each embody particular class "tastes"'.

Habitus, therefore, represents a certain 'class culture and milieu' and provides the basis for class reproduction and differentiation. The traveller/tourist distinction, although highly stereotyped, is reflective of a wider debate over social class differentiation.

These battles are an example of everyday hegemony in practice. Of course, this also suggests that social classes are themselves constantly formed and hence the term class fractions to distinguish from the 'once-and-for-all' idea of *the* working class, or *the* middle class.

Social class formation is, therefore, a dynamic process, 'a flame whose edges are in constant movement, oscillating around a line or surface', and of conceptual importance in helping to understand the dynamic nature of tourist consumption: today's cool spot is tomorrow's classificatory dinosaur.

Second, a discussion of class also suggests the importance that exploitation (of one class by another) should play in the analysis; in 'order for a social collectivity to be regarded as a social class it has to have its roots in a process of exploitation'.

Moreover, an exploitation-centred analysis of class provides for a more coherent strategy for considering the characteristics of the middle classes in contemporary capitalism; hence, the straightforward observation 'one person's welfare is obtained at the expense of another' (1985:65). Traditionally, class analysis has been undertaken with a production-side bias with the focus of the exploitation of the workforce by capitalists, and a principal focus on economic measures (occupation, income, and so on) as indicators of class position.

The critical part of Bourdieu's work is that 'domination remains, but it must be reconceptualised in a world of consumption. Domination is now mediated by taste'. Reflecting this power, Eagleton refers to habitus as a 'practical ideology', or what we might call an 'everyday hegemony', whereby the need to dominate is translated into routine social behaviour.

The importance for our discussion of tourism is that the struggles inherent in social classes have both a social element (ecotourism is better than package tourism) and spatial element (the Brazilian rainforest has more kudos than a Gambian beach). In other words, tourism can be used to differentiate and exploit both socially and spatially.

So exactly how are these struggles waged and differentiation achieved? An important part of the answer lies in the accumulation of capital. But in this case it is not the finance capital necessary to sustain profits or individual financial assets, but cultural and symbolic capital linked to certain kinds of tourism.

CULTURAL AND SYMBOLIC CAPITAL

As a number of authors have contended, consumption has become more skilful in recent years. Not only do consumers ask more questions of the commodities they buy (the least polluting car to buy or holiday to take?), they are also more sensitive to the symbols they are consuming.

The consumption of holidays has assumed an increasingly significant role in the cultural differentiation characteristic of other forms of consumption and the Third World has an important role within this and represents a sizeable cultural asset. It is a way of investing in and accumulating what Bourdieu refers to as cultural capital.

Unlike economic capital, cultural capital is not something that can be strictly bought, but instead relies on the ability of individuals to join the game of being able to 'know' and 'appreciate' what to eat, drink, wear, watch and what types of holiday to take. In other words, it requires the skill of reading the cultural significance of certain types of consumption; for example, the significance of 'original features' in the process of gentrification or the cultural significance of certain types of holidays, whether ecotourism in Kenya or backpacking in South-East Asia. In the former case, 'it is not simply that a desire to see ecological attractions in far-off destinations conveys a sense of superior status; rather it is the actual ability to appreciate ecology which indicates cultural competence'. In the latter case, it will be argued that cultural capital is also accumulated through journeys to remote and hazardous regions.

It is these young travellers who often emerge as 'figures of admiration'. As Bob Samuel, information manager at Trailfinders, observes: 'There is a lot of kudos in coming back and telling your friends you have travelled overland in Cambodia. It gives you a certain cachet' .

If tourism has increasingly taken on a symbolic meaning (in part due to the dramatic increase in tourism), it has also meant that tourism as a commodity embodies 'sign-value', an important means of stocking up on cultural capital. It is symbolic in the way in which travel and tourism embody certain attributes: personal qualities in the individual, such as strength of character, adaptability, resourcefulness, sensitivity or even 'worldliness'. In a somewhat traditional sense, travel is widely regarded as 'character building'.

In this way tourism is not only something to be enjoyed but represents a strategy for building a reputation that can be converted into economic capital. In other words, it transforms travel into a commodity with exchange-value and can be traded in, so to speak, for material benefits; and hence the phrase 'curriculum vitae builders'. Trailfinders' 'long haul travel consultants' must be aged 22-30 and 'have travelled extensively'. But of course it is not only the travel industry that recognises the 'benefits' of travelling and there is a number of occupations where overseas travel is an increasingly significant component or, indeed, pre-requisite.

Curriculum vitae building starts young, as Sansom contends, with universities and employers agreeing 'that a constructive year out embellishes your CV', and myriad agencies offering opportunities for a 'year out' - in the UK, this includes Raleigh International, Group Activity Projects, Frontier, The Year Out Group and VSO's Youth Volunteering.

How are the sign and exchange values of these travel commodities maintained or enhanced? Before we try to answer this question, consideration will be given to how class fractions may be conceived in relation to tourism. This is not to suggest that class fractions are fixed and immutable as described below; rather, it suggests a heuristic approach - a style of analysis - that may help our understanding of tourism and class.

ECOTOURISTS

The first principal grouping Bourdieu terms the new bourgeoisie. They are located firmly within the service sector with jobs involving finance, marketing and purchasing, for example. They are also class fractions that earn a lot and are correspondingly high in terms of economic capital (finance). They can afford expensive holidays that are exclusive in terms of price affordability and the numbers of tourists permitted: private game reserves with luxury accommodation and limited capacity, for example.

They are class fractions, therefore, which can take holidays in environments which, by virtue of price, are exclusive. For shorthand, we shall refer to this group as ecotourists, older and professionally successful tourists or as Wood refers to them, the 'cream of Manhattan and the City'. 'Ecotourist' has a double meaning, however, for not only does it signal an interest and focus of this type of tourist on the 'environment' (*eco*logy), it also indicates the ability to pay the high prices that such holidays command (*eco*nomic capital).

It is not a coincidence that the 'taste' of which Bourdieu speaks is actually translated into culinary metaphors for the holidays aimed at this social class, for luxurious eating is another of this fraction's cultural characteristics. Thomson Holidays' 'Travel à la Carte' urges you to 'choose from the menu or dream up a dish of your own' and Barrett (1989) refers to 'delicatessen' travel agents. It embraces the delicate, discriminating and generally luxurious holidays to an off-the-beaten-track, out-of-the-way place.

And there are apparently no expenses spared on the level of service and culinary provision. As Africa Exclusive, a tour company specialising in East African safaris, put it, 'gastronomy is taken as seriously as zoology'. It carries a level of cultural capital as well.

It is a way of buying into a shared meaning that the environment has an acknowledged value: 'ECO-TOURISM ... It's not in any dictionary yet, but if you want to impress at your next dinner party, it's a dead cert'. So, not only are the new bourgeoisie high on economic capital, they are also high in terms of their ability to accumulate cultural capital.

EGO-TOURISTS

The second important class fraction that Bourdieu identifies, and one that is potentially more important, is the 'new petit bourgeoisie'. This social class is characterised by the increasing numbers working in employment involving 'presentation and representation' such as media and advertising, but it also encompasses a wide range of service jobs (such as the guides working for small tour operators) and the growth in the number of people working for charities, for example.

You may recall that some commentators have emphasised the significance of this social class in interpretation and representation. This not only includes opinion-forming in terms of the latest film to see, clothes to wear or designer alcohol to drink, but also how we should perceive issues such as homelessness or overseas development: in other words, a guide to the things we should be 'into'.

Made reference to this group variously as taste-makers, trend-setters, new cultural intermediaries or cultural brokers, labels which seek to capture the structural significance of such groups in postmodern culture. Unlike the new bourgeoisie who are high on both economic and cultural capital, however, the new petit bourgeoisie are not so economically well endowed and must seek out cultural capital in order to establish their social class identity. In this way the burden of class differentiation weighs most heavily on this social class who must differentiate themselves from the working classes below (mass packaged tourists) and the high spending bourgeois middle classes above (ecotourists).

Part of the reaction has been for the new petit bourgeoisie to deem themselves unclassifiable, 'excluded', 'dropped out' or perhaps, in popular tourism discourse, 'alternative'; anything other than categorisation and assignment to a class.

And yet, as Bourdieu concludes, the A to Z of their practices, from 'aikido' to 'Zen' (or from alternative tourism to wildlife tourism) exudes classification, being nothing other than, 'An inventory of thinly disguised expressions of a sort of dream of social flying, a desperate effort to defy the gravity of the social field'.

This slide into individualism is an expression of what Smith (1987) refers to as a new ideology founded upon the 'pursuit of difference, diversity and distinction'. Indeed, the pursuit of difference is of critical significance in understanding the expansion of tourism in the Third World. Contradictorily, while the assertion of individualism becomes a frame of action of the new middle classes, it also reaffirms their class status and position. And, as already argued, the struggle and, by inference, exploitation, are 'quasi-inevitable'.

The idea of 'classlessness' or 'individualism' is an indelible mark among these class fractions, resulting, some argue, in the arrival of ego-tourists suggests, 'curriculum vitae builders'. Ego-tourism is more characteristic of less formalised forms of travel, such as backpacking, overland trucking (Truck Africa refer to their customers as 'would be backpackers') or small group travel, which often involve longer holidays overseas, especially in Third World regions.

'Going-round-the-world' or 'taking a year off to travel' has become a latter-day equivalent of the Grand Tour and an important component of the culture of travel. Ego-tourists must search for a style of travel which is both reflective of an 'alternative' lifestyle and which is capable of maintaining and enhancing their cultural capital.

Furthermore, it is a class fraction that attempts to compensate for insufficient economic capital, with an obsessional quest for the authentication of experience.

MacCannell (1976) portrayed the middle classes as systematically scavenging the Earth in search of new experiences and Errington and Gewertz note, 'For travellers, the encounter with what was seen as "primitive" - the exotic, the whole, the fundamentally human - contributed to their own individuality, integration and authenticity' (1989:42). Stressing the link of ego-tourists to environmental issues, Gordon (1990) associates tourists he observed in Namibia to 'an emergent, urban-based, alienated petit bourgeoisie'.

Ultimately it is a competition for uniqueness with which ego-tourists engage. This is bound with the knowledge, difference and distinction that certain forms of tourism imply - a struggle, so to speak, to stamp the hallmark of individualism in the traveller's passport.

While individualism has always been a key characteristic of bourgeois culture, which regards travel as an 'activity for the stimulation and development of character', the rate at which individualism is sought now has significant consequences and impacts for places, especially in the Third World.

Individualism also underscores why ego-tourists feel they are exempt from the criticism levelled at much Third World tourism. First, as Sherpa Expeditions contends of its customers, 'They are involved and interested in the world around them, and in their turn are interesting people.' And, second, individualism provides the foundation for claiming the moral high ground in the battle over 'what kind of tourism?'

These are people travelling on a shoestring, and as individuals their practices are not harmful to environment or society. Ego-tourists conveniently disaggregate their actions - they are individuals and their actions therefore have no significant impact. In other words, they refuse to acknowledge their part in a larger entity or mass. By contrast, some argue their travels are actually beneficial, supporting local, indigenous businesses, or forging new cultural understandings with Third World communities.

Hutnyk's study of travellers working in Kolkata refers to the 'hegemonic understandings of how those mostly middle-class children of privilege who are able to travel - even, or especially, as "alternative travellers" giving "aid" as people who "care" - see their relation to the ... "Third World"'.

As we shall see below, however, moral claims are by no means sufficient to secure victory in this battle. The new middle classes have adopted strategies to remedy this by, for example, creating jobs and professionalising not just occupations, but consumption practices as well.

In effect, the boundaries between these new middle classes - between ecotourists and ego-tourists - are blurred: they share their ability to make relatively expensive journeys overseas and their willingness to wage hegemonic struggles to define and differentiate their forms of tourism. In this way, tourism has become part of that critical assemblage of goods, practices and experiences that are taken up as social 'bridges and doors', so important in bonding some and excluding others.

A new class of tourist? Tourism cannot be understood as just a means of having some enjoyment and a break from the routine of everyday, an entirely innocent affair where there are some unfortunate, incidental impacts or some fortunate incremental benefits to 'host' communities. To recap, so far we have argued that we need a deeper understanding of tourism to appreciate fully its content and expression and, of course, its potential impact.

There are two principal components to this argument. First, tourism must be understood as a commodity with both a symbolic or sign value and an exchange value. Second, much so-called new tourism is an expression of the new middle classes' hegemonic struggle for cultural and class superiority.

Travel, of course, has always been an expression of taste and a way of establishing class status. But, with the rapid growth in the numbers of people taking holidays, it has never been so widely used as at present. Put simply, the democratisation of tourism has created a social headache when it comes to classes attempting to differentiate themselves from one another.

Two fundamental questions arise from the discussion. How are the sign and exchange values of these travel commodities maintained and enhanced? And how do social classes pursue differentiation and to what effect? In answering the first question, we shall concentrate on three key methods that are used to define and legitimise contemporary tourism: the appeal to intellectualism and professionalism, together with the discourse that has arisen to describe travel today.

In addressing the second question we will identify what we have labelled 'hegemonic spatial struggles' pursued by the new middle classes. Underlying this discussion is the acknowledgement that much new tourism focuses on the Third World.

THE NEW INTELLECTUALS

It has been argued that the new petit bourgeoisie have sought to intellectualise new areas of activity and expertise (Bourdieu, 1984; Featherstone, 1987). These 'new intellectuals' attempt to ape and popularise intellectual lifestyles and transmit intellectuals' ideas to a wider audience - arguably the ultimate in a cultivated, even scholastic and 'romantic flight from the social world'. Tourism is a particularly important component in this respect.

The 'de-differentiated' characteristic of much contemporary Third World tourism was noted, in which academic prefixes are increasingly apparent. Holidays have moved beyond sheer relaxation towards the opportunity to study and learn, to experience the world through a pseudo-intellectual frame.

With the acknowledgement of tourism as an environmentally, socially and culturally problematic activity among certain fractions of the new middle classes, tourism and tour companies catering for the intellectual demands of these class fractions are of increasing importance in the legitimation of travel.

Thus we find companies such as Academic Travel (part of STA, an ostensibly student-oriented travel agency), Adult Education Study tours (established in 1982), who offer 'special interest travel for thinking people', and Temple World, offering 'exclusive journeys into wildlife, archaeology, natural history and ecology', whose guest leaders are academics such as the geographer, Andrew Goudie.

Moreover, the intellectualisation of travel has been enhanced by interlinkage between academia and tour companies. It is convenient for companies such as Himalayan Kingdoms (1992-3) to prioritise places on their Bhutan visit (a country that has imposed severe restrictions on the number of tourists admitted each year) to Fellows of the Royal Geographical Society, and for Temple World to run a series of 'Royal Geographical Society African Tours'.

At the height of what we might term 'intellectual mimicry', the travel operator Voyages Jules Verne offers tour leaflets (or information sheets) that are indistinguishable from weekend broadsheet newspaper supplements and are appropriately entitled *Travel Reviews*. Intellectual legitimation is sought in this instance by interspersing descriptions of holidays and itineraries with other considered features: 'Islam', 'The Turkish Inner Man' and the 'Shepherds of Shanghai', for example.

Among the younger new petit bourgeois tourists, with less economic capital, intellectualisation is sought in other ways. Most frequently this involves the claim of cultural superiority, of true and real contact with indigenous peoples, pursued through organised tours, such as 'overlanding', or 'individual' travel informed by travel guides such as the *Rough Guide* or *Lonely Planet Guide* series.

As Guerba put it, this means more than 'scratch[ing] the surface', it requires getting participants 'personally involved in the country, its people and its wildlife'. In addition, as noted earlier, longer periods of travel overseas have in themselves evoked the spirit of intellectualism and are increasingly referred to as sabbaticals among the new middle classes. But intellectualising is insufficient in itself, and has necessitated the use of other forms of classification and legitimation.

TRAVEL PROFESSIONALS

In the context of socio-economic and cultural change discussed earlier coupled with the associated growth of the new middle classes, there have been two notable processes at work. First, professions have become relatively more open following the educational 'revolution' of the 1960s, and the aura (medicine, law, the City and so on) with which they had been traditionally conceived has, at least in part, been dismantled.

Second, however, with still relatively limited access to the established professions, the new middle classes have been busy legitimising new licences and certificates: a classic process of establishing new professions (with professional education and qualification periods, codes of ethics and accrediting bodies or institutes), or professionalisation as Bourdieu notes (1984).

This dual process may indicate that the infallibility of professional distinction is beginning to falter and surprisingly little analytical consideration appears to have been focused on a logical extension (or migration) of the struggle for distinction through professionalisation, into consumption practices.

Professionalism is a key characteristic assigned to company tour leaders, who in many cases are introduced personally: 'dedicated professionalism' as one brochure says indicating that a tour manager not only has a 'deep love of and insight into the areas visited', but also has 'academic credentials and expertise in a specialised field'.

This citation of 'experience' and academic qualifications is commonplace. The following pages cite and quote many tour company brochures dating from 1992 to 2000. In many cases the quoted passages are repeated from year to year.

In tour companies specialising in overland trucking and travelling for ego-tourists, this also means that tour leaders are 'experienced international travellers in their own right'. At Journey Latin America even the reservation staff are 'South American experts' and have 'travelled extensively in Latin America'; the tour leaders are all graduates (some in Latin American Studies), a portfolio similar to Trailfinders. Tour leaders in these companies also embody, and are ambassadors of, new middle-class lifestyles, testify.

In addition, the spirit of professional dedication is also widely cited, where work in this part of the tourism industry is more akin to a vocation. Encounter Overland refer to their trips as 'projects' and talk of their leaders in glowing terms: 'ordinary men and women - often previous trip members - who have elected to put promising careers on hold and devote half a dozen years or more to what they like doing best'.

And, of course, with greater flexibility in the service sector a higher proportion of new middle-class employees are able to take longer periods off between jobs or contracts, or are able to negotiate relatively long periods of absence. All in all a more dedicated, professional, and avaricious tourist class has emerged.

The point we anticipated earlier is that 'travelling' has emerged as an important informal qualification, with the number and range of stamps in a passport acting, so to speak, as a professional certificate; a record of achievement and experience. Not only is travel a professional pre-requisite for employment in parts of the tourism industry, but it is an important attribute in many new professions, such as overseas development work; it has become a rite of passage into certain occupations.

There are also indications that professionals working in other disciplines have begun to diversify into travel. Many of the occasional tour leaders, for instance, are professionals in other fields. For example, the two directors of Papyrus Tours, a company established in 1984 with an aim to provide tours to East Africa, who were supportive of conservation efforts are also a senior officer in a large local authority and a self-employed professional landscape architect, respectively.

Of course, we should also note that Third World tourism has created a huge range of job opportunities for the new middle classes in the First World. It is not just operators in the industry but consultants, journalists, tourism commentators, academics and charities focusing on tourism issues; take The International Ecotourism Society (TIES), for example, whose founder and president, Megan Epler Wood, explains that: 'It was decided that The Ecotourism Society should be an organisation for professionals.

It was clear in 1991 that a broad array of professionals from a variety of disciplines was needed to make ecotourism a genuine tool for conservation and sustainable development'. And more recently, TIES website describes the organisation as 'Representing a worldwide network of 1,700 members from 55 professions and 65 countries ... We'd like to invite you to the growing ranks of ecotourism professionals who are working with TIES'.

It is these professionals who are the opinion formers, the teachers, the advisers, even the ones who take decisions, and a number of publications have sought to prescribe 'technical information on how to do ecotourism "right"'. But the degree to which these 'benevolent' organisations are somehow value free is questionable. It is clear who these professionals are: in the TIES's case, middle-class Americans, many of whom represent other powerful NGO interests (WWF, Conservation International, IUCN and so on - see listing of board of directors and advisers). We must ask what vision of the world they are pursuing and the degree to which such visions are imposed from the First World on the Third World, a question considered in the context of the activities of these organisations.

The commencement of professionalisation processes in consumption is also detectable. As noted earlier, consumption has become more skilled. First, there are clear signals that the distinctions between occupational professionalism, and consumption and leisure, are beginning to blur. Illustrative of this is the growth of outdoor management and 'team' building exercises, especially popular among the new middle classes.

High Places, for example, which offer mountain holidays in a number of Third World countries, also offer 'another type of HOLIDAY! ... training programmes for people at work in industry, commerce and the public sector'. This is an operation appropriately called 'HIGH PROFILE', an experience for people like 'YOU, the sort of people who come on our holidays', described elsewhere as 'intelligent and discerning people who wish to retain a taste of independent travel'.

Second, and more significant, tourists themselves are attempting to professionalise travel, a process encouraged, it would appear, by tour operators and environmental organisations. While the emergence of a formal travel qualification, such as the need to support an application for a Himalayan

Kingdom expedition 'with your climbing CV', remains the exception rather than the rule for the time being, the number of tourist codes addressing the ethics and conduct of travel have exploded.

A tourist 'Code of Conduct' established by the ECTWT, has been reproduced in many places, especially by the network of organisations concerned with the effects of tourism, but also, for example, among travel agency associations and tour operators who have formulated their own versions. Area-specific codes with emphasis on ecological and cultural issues such as the 'Himalayan Tourist Code' formulated by Tourism Concern (in the UK) have also appeared.

Organisations such as these have attracted increasing support from members of the new middle classes and from new independent tour operators like High Places, which reproduces the Himalayan Code in full and which claims to strive to 'adhere to the ethics' of Tourism Concern. It is the emergence of an ethical, if not professional, approach to tourism reminiscent of Kutay's observed 'Peace Corps-type travellers looking for a more meaningful vacation'.

These codes of ethics form the backbone of a hegemony of travel (or ecotravel as it is now known in North America), which is advanced by the new middle classes, the small independent tour operators and the vanguard of this hegemony, tourism organisations.

Together they begin to represent a new tourism social movement with organisations such as Tourism Concern, the Campaign for Environmentally Responsible Tourism (CERT) and the US-based International Ecotourism Society, emerging as symbolic 'institutes of travel'.

These institutes now provide ethical yardsticks against which the activities of operators and tourists can be measured and classified. With an overwhelming concern for environmental ethics (such as the US National Audubon Society's 'Travel Ethic for Environmentally Responsible Travel'), it is in the ecological and indigenous heartlands of the Third World that these hegemonic struggles are most readily detected and played out.

THE DISCOURSE OF 'NEW WAVE TOURISM'

'Out goes the "'ere we go, 'ere we go" Spanish Costa-style, in comes a more thoughtful middle class approach'. This was how Frank Barrett of the *Independent* newspaper, the UK's champion of new middle-class values, describes the shift to 'new wave tourism'.

There can be little disputing that the attributes and qualities of the supposedly more alternative, individualised and sensitive forms of travel are generally unspoken but appear to be deep within the new middle-class psyche.

As The Travel Alternative, a specialist company offering craft and textile holidays, comments: 'On a recent tour a passenger said "You can either be a tourist or a traveller." We would like to think that our tours allow everyone the opportunity to be travellers'.

Of course, it is not only through the classificatory distinction between tourist and traveller that differentiation is pursued via discourse. But it is illustrative of the battle being waged to put into words exactly what kind of holidaymaker we are and what we stand for; and, conversely, state exactly what we are not for; as Barrett argues, 'tourist' is the 'worst kind of insult'.

Some observers have momentarily reflected on the highbrow nature of traveller and the intellectual snobbishness within which the whole debate is framed, and have attempted to rescue 'tourist' from middle-class derision. Tourist has become prefixed by benevolent adjectives such as the 'The Good Tourist' or 'The Reluctant Tourist', title to a series run by the UK broadsheet *Independent* which culminated in *The Reluctant Tourist's Handbook*. There are also references to ethical tourists, alternative tourists and so on.

Arguably though, this is further confirmation that contemporary tourism is charged with the classificatory struggles in and between class fractions. As Culler observes: 'Once one recognises that wanting to be less touristy than other tourists is part of being a tourist, one can recognise the superficiality of most discussions of tourism, especially those that stress the superficiality of tourists'.

By contrast, the term 'traveller' assumes that it is no longer a process of tourism with which the individual is engaged, but a considerably more de-differentiated, esoteric and individualised form of activity; travel is to tourism, as individual is to class. It is a strategy for seeking differentiation or a 'paper-chase aimed at ensuring constant distinctive gaps'.

Most importantly, the discourse adopted by these class fractions is a further reminder that consideration of the way in which power is expressed and imposed must lie at the heart of the analysis of tourism.

Many small tour companies and individual travellers have attempted to maximise the distinction. As already argued, the practices of travellers are perhaps best conceived as part of the 'cult of individualism', though it is deeply ironic that they are largely indistinguishable from each other by virtue of their discourse, dress codes and the informal 'packages' they follow through travel guides.

Whole regions have become travel circuits (in popular travel discourse 'doing' South-East Asia, Central America and so on). Errington and Gewertz (1989) reproduce excerpts from a Papua New Guinea guest house visitor book to illustrate the fundamental traveller distinction, with two US travellers advising: 'Explain difference between tourist and traveller ... Be a traveller, not a tourist. It makes a big difference'. Travellers, therefore, attempt to create their own aura, while attempting to prevent the encroachment of 'tourists' in their quest for authentication:

Momentarily alone in one of the wildest places on earth, you feel exhilarated, exhausted and scared. Unfortunately the feeling is unlikely to last more than a few moments. If you are lucky, all that will happen is another traveller will appear on the ridge to exchange pleasantries and wonderment. If you are unlucky ... your reverie will be interrupted by half a dozen Londoners swearing and shouting.

Mass tourism and tourists have also become the target of independent tour operators. Intellectualism oozes through, with package tourists 'invading' backpackers' discoveries and the celebration of areas where the invasion has been forestalled: at the height of aestheticisation, Cambodia is lucky for its 'fascinating culture bruised by war' and even luckier with a culture 'unscathed by tourism'. Companies refer to the 'anonymity and inflexibility' (J. & C. Voyageurs), of 'run of the mill', 'conventional' (Explore) and 'impersonalised' (Africa Exclusive) mass packaged tours, and celebrate their demise (Magic of the Orient). Ultimately, it is an appeal to the idea that travel is 'individual enough to be a sustainable alternative to the juggernaut of mass tourism' (Explore).

In its place, and by contrast, we have the emergence of Zimbabwe, where 'nothing is packaged' (Africa Exclusive), and the 'Unpackaged Caribbean' (Kestours). For luxury tour operators and their new bourgeois clientele (ecotourists) exclusiveness is sufficient enough a distinction, with Cox and Kings taking 'a select few to Africa', and operators speaking of 'a small and select clientele' (Abercrombie & Kent) and 'limited edition holidays' (EcoSafari).

For tour operators catering more for the young and adventurous ego-tourists where economic capital is clearly insufficient to confer taste, it is the invidious distinction of participant travellers from tourists that has become critical. It advances the distinctions beyond a mere reference (or 'charge') to packaging and instead focuses on the qualities and practices of travel and contrasts these to tourism.

This is particularly notable of overlanding operators such as Dragoman specialising in trucking for young travellers, a world 'shunned by the masses who prefer the resorts and beaches', or, as Explore put it, travel for 'people who want more out of their holiday than buckets of cheap wine and a suntan', a stereotype also used by Exodus Adventure. In similar vein Journey Latin America contrast their ('Small Group Escorted Tours') participants to those who prefer 'two weeks in Torremolinos' and where preference is for a 'cold beer after a three hour walk in the jungle, not nightly booze-ups'. As Tours to Remember warn, if you are looking for 'two weeks in the eastern equivalent of Benidorm', look elsewhere.

Logically, tour companies also promise 'tourist-free' zones (Naturetrek), 'few lager and litter louts' (Cara Spencer) and avoidance of 'Tourist haunts' (High Places). In a more positive sense, Encounter Overland celebrates the traveller-cum-wayfarer: 'today's custodian of the ancient relationship between traveller and native which throughout the world has been the historic basis of peaceful contact'.

So what of the qualities and practices that are claimed to constitute the distinction and embody the traveller? The simple listing of adjectives applied to travellers in travel brochures begins to map the key coordinates. By implication, if not explicitly as noted above, the counter-distinctions constitute tourists. If, for any reason, the citation of these *qualities* proves insufficient, however, there are other pre-requisites which help define travellers.

High Places tours of India, for example, demand 'patience, stamina, humour and adaptability', and Journey Latin America cite 'essential qualifications for all trips' as 'emotional balance, maturity, a spirit of adventure, and a desire for good companionship'.

There are two other notable features of travelling and travellers. First, with an overwhelming emphasis on a mixture of often physical activities, especially among ego-tourists, bodily fitness is important.

High Places offers the symbolically new middle-class holiday: mountain biking. Second, and most important, there is need for the fellowship of other like-minded travellers, whether it be small intimate group tours (with generally between six and twenty participants) or individual backpackers meeting at predestined travel guide-recommended hotels, restaurants or sites. In both cases, albeit in rather different ways, the emphasis is on participation, on 'action and involvement' (High Places) and, ultimately, on accomplishment (a recurrent theme in tour brochures).

It is not that travellers are unreflective; just the opposite, as Hutnyk observes of back-packers in Kolkata (India) where a 'popular alternative critique of travel' emerges from their reflections, and manifests itself in:

- The search for 'authentic' experiences; b) dismay at the effect of tourism; and c) condemnation of other tourists and sometimes themselves. The correlates of these three moments are a) claims to the 'once-in-a-lifetime' experience; b) nostalgia for the days when such and such-a-place was not so well known; and c) 'of course I'm doing it differently' stories.

As Hutnyk (1996) concludes, not only is there an intense struggle in classifying and legitimising this notional traveller-tourist distinction, but ego-tourists vie among themselves over what actually constitutes a traveller in the first place. Borzello considers that 'Truck travellers are not travellers but a very peculiar sort of tourist.' And it is an intense classificatory struggle that has pronounced spatial reflections, a point to which we turn below.

TALES OF THE UNEXPECTED

Both explorers and dragomen journeyed through far-flung lands in search of long-forgotten civilisations and empires. They explored hostile deserts to find nomadic tribes and ancient cities. They went in search of legendary mountains deep in the heart of jungles and brought back stories of fabulous wildlife.

These fabulous stories or 'travellers' tales' have a deep history. There are noted discussions and a resurgence of interest in ethnographic travelogues and travel writings. But debates around the contemporary nature of tales, myths, or rumour-mongering and 'traveller lore', have remained sketchy. This is of particular significance for, as Massey argues, tales are a culmination of the ongoing process of travel which fill out our geographical imaginations, and that story-telling is the archetypal 'traveller's medium'; 'rumour-mongering is the architect. Rumour is the stuff of the social'. Travellers' tales are a modern (or perhaps postmodern) continuation of the stories of colonial encounters.

They are a useful way of demonstrating how discourse is used to represent or recreate a reality and impose meaning, in much the same way as the fantastic tales retold by colonialists in the nineteenth century. As Hutnyk shows, 'word of mouth, the say-so of a friend of a friend, and rumour and gossip, operate to orientate and produce experience for travellers. This discourse must be read as a text'. In this way discourse can be conceived as part of that everyday hegemony.

Latter-day travellers' tales are a powerful way of sustaining the aura and mystique of the Third World (reminiscent of Said's *Orientalism*) and in turn sustaining the value of travel as a commodity. Their construction is often complex and draws upon a range of images and representations, including film, travel writing and colonial explorations.

Tales also have an important part to play in the reproduction of social class. It has already been suggested that tales have an important symbolic currency as a form of cultural capital; the example used suggested that travelling on a 'shoestring' simultaneously denies the existence and need for substantial lumps of economic capital and confers status, uniqueness, worldliness and resourcefulness.

As Calder records of travelling in rebel-held Nicaraguan territory, by the time you reached the 'safety' of neighbouring Costa Rica 'all that backpacking bravado returns and you have a couple of cracking stories with which to trump fellow travellers' tales'. Travel and the construction of tales, therefore, represent an informal credentialism.

The construction of tales is also intimately bound with the quest for authenticity. It is a way of creating an aura in an effort to remove this experience from the tourist's world. These are feelings that cannot be 'snapped'. Take this example from High Places:

The trip begins with a short drive from Nairobi down into the Great Rift Valley, to our camp set among the trees, overlooking grassy plains where zebra and giraffe graze. The only sound is the breeze and a kettle boiling on the stove. Time to relax as the trip unfolds ... Walking through the Loita Hills, in Maasai territory, following little-used trails and using local warriors as guides ... watching a majestic herd of elephants cross the Mara plains, or a cheetah stalk its prey; sitting round the fire, swapping stories with Maasai warriors; relaxing, as the sunset turns the empty plains red.

Of all modes of travel, it is trekking in areas of solitude that most gives rise to a romantic gaze and the construction of tales almost spiritual in their content. The phenomenal growth of trekking in South-East Asia, Latin America and Africa underlines its importance in new middle-class travel. It is the authenticity of this form of alternative tourism that lies at the heart of trekking, and the accumulation of tales relies upon authenticity to verify its uniqueness and currency: as High Places promote, 'Our trips are unpretentious, authentic and adventurous', and Trailfinders contrast 'staged tourist "shows"' with the experience of 'untouched' and 'traditional' villages in the highlands of Thailand.

In this case authenticity is expressed in a somewhat different manner, conveyed through an emotional response that is either unique or intensely difficult to achieve. It is an exclusionary experience, that even if the struggle to dominate and control a spatially discrete area is lost, tourists are still unable to share the aura. Frank McCready (Sherpa Expeditions Managing Director) comments on the realisation of dreams: 'When the ordinary person reaches a place like Annapurna Base Camp it changes their whole view of life ... Some of the places we take people are so fantastic I've seen grown men entirely overcome with emotion.' It is this experience of exhilaration and exhaustion that culminates in the eulogising of trekking. Himalayan Kingdoms comments: 'The blend of grandeur and timelessness defeats all superlatives and such a place should be visited at least once every lifetime'.

To return briefly to the theme of aestheticisation: in order to legitimise and authenticate the travel experience, tales must be aestheticised in two important respects. In the first place, there is the dual requirement to make trips both purposeful and distinguishable from those of the average tourist or, indeed, traveller.

Travel is purposeful, tourism is not. For example, one travel writer notes of a visit to Nepal, 'We had tea and increasingly battered chocolate to deliver to a friend of a friend working in a health clinic there'. Sabbaticals, 'research' work, the presence of friends, colleagues and relatives, the emergence of work brigades and the visits promoted by overseas development charities - a range of work - and activity-centred holidays, are all used by the new middle classes to signal that *this is more than just a holiday*.

It must be sufficient in distancing itself from supposedly inactive or inert forms of tourism. Exodus ('Overland Newsletter', summer 1994, 'What the customers say' section) notes, 'I think that was the best trip I've ever done, partly because of, rather than despite the difficulties and challenges we faced.'

Second, there has always been a nagging inadequacy around the assertions that 'one cannot sell poverty, but one can sell paradise'. The quest for authenticity, like travel itself, has had to seek out new experiences. No longer can it rest upon the cultural preservation and discovery of highland tribes and deep forest natives.

It has migrated to the quest for danger and risk and the emergence of contemporary travelogues and diaries: '"I'm keeping a journal; maybe I can make it into a book," says one traveller to me as we sit in a bar in a small village'.

Tales legitimise travel by sensationalising it, making it appear daring and risky, while at the same time peripheralising danger. Of Vang Tau (Vietnam) the *STA Travel Guide* notes: 'a two hour boat ride from Ho Chi Minh City and a million miles away from conflict'. Similarly, Encounter Overland's philosophy remains: 'With true adventure there is always an element of chance and of risk. This fact is not regrettable. It is often the fact upon which the best travel experiences are based.' Suffering can often enrich the travel experience, as extracts of Morrison's *Tales of the Unexpected* suggest:

A glass of fiery rice liquor was thrust into my hands, and I sat down with them and joined in their infectious laughter, without a single word of common language between us ... Seven years on I'm none the wiser about the purpose or origins of that strange harvest festival in northern Thailand ... As it was I could find no mention of the festival or town in anything I read, which probably accounted for the fact that I was the only westerner on the scene.

But it wasn't this smug one-upmanship that made it so special, but rather the very act of discovery. For one impetuous moment I dared to stray from the charted territory ... and it was bliss ... To me, surprise is the primary reason to travel. All those other time-worn clichés about broadening the mind and stimulating an appreciation of the world are merely justifications, not motivations ... Think about those special moments from your last few trips, the ones that you bore your friends rigid with at parties.

Are they accurate reports of the splendour of the temples or the excellent cuisine? I hope not. No, it's those unexpected events when your plans are interrupted by that out-of-the-blue experience ... To my mind, if there's one thing worse than a holiday that fails to meet your expectations it's one that *does* ... And let's be brutally honest here, if in the second week of your big adventure you haven't had at least one near-death experience you're going to want your money back. Right? ... do we really want a boil-in-the-bag cultural experience? No we bloody well don't - we want an unpolished, unbleached wholegrain adventure with bits of stone and finger-nail in the bottom!!!

Most invidious, however, is to utilise tales to aestheticise risk and boost the cultural capital accumulated in travel. As suggested earlier, while the hazards of travelling in particular regions may act as a warning, it simultaneously signals the degree of legitimacy or coolness to be attributed to particular destinations.

As Gordon-Walker notes of Peru, 'travellers who are disappointed not to have captured a Sendero Luminoso flag raise their spirits ... and swap stories about friends of friends who have been robbed'. Similar experiences were recounted by Warde and in 'Weekending in El Salvador'.

Travelling in potentially dangerous regions, being hoisted from a bus and frisked at midnight or braving certain urban areas are experiences to be enjoyed and admired by other travellers. Risk titillates, even eroticises, adventures in the Third World. And it is this genre of tale-telling that has come to the fore in discussion among fellow ego-tourists, in travel guides and reviews and within television coverage. In short, it is now widely adopted discourse focused toward social differentiation and the insurance, or hope, that certain places will stay unexplored by other groups of tourists.

THE SCRAMBLE FOR THIRD WORLD DESTINATIONS

We have argued that a pseudo-ethical and moral infrastructure underpins the growth of Third World tourism (Lea, 1993), with new middle-class tourists (or travellers) contrasting their morally justifiable means of travel with the morally reprehensible practices of tourists.

There is a temptation to conclude from this, as Gordon-Walker does, that you 'cannot help suspecting that the campaign for "sustainable tourism" is little more than a rationalised desire to keep the Third World a cheap place to visit' (1993:19).

But such a conclusion would result in underselling the importance of how First World tourists impose their desires on Third World destinations.

If the new middle classes are forced to wage this hegemonic classificatory struggle founded on taste, then it might be reasonable to expect that such struggles will also be reflected spatially. So at the very heart of this campaign lies, not just the preservation of a nice cheap place to visit, but the playing out of the battle of social class differentiation.

The professionalisation and intellectualisation of travel, together with its associated discourse, have been insufficient in themselves to ensure social differentiation and, more importantly, the creation of physical distance between mass tourists and travellers.

The new middle-classes must adopt strategies of exclusion, to seek and protect the new travel commodities. Extracts from veteran correspondent Martha Gellhorn's piece, 'Too good for tourists', illustrate the process by which this is achieved. It is an attempt to persuade and to impose the idea that this First World view is correct:

The airport terminal at Belize City is very encouraging. It is an overgrown shack ... After each passport has been examined as if passports were new-fangled inventions, you enter a square, wooden room where the baggage has been dumped in the middle of the floor. A free-for-all follows ... My heart rose like a lark. This is how it used to be before the Caribbean was homogenised by tourism. Tourism, even ... minor, modest tourism, corrupts. I cannot exaggerate the pure physical pleasure of underpopulation and empty space ... Half a century ago I thought this ghastliness of packed humanity was the peculiar doom of China: now much of the world I knew and loved is ruined because there are too many of us and we move everywhere. For my taste, Belize is ideal.

A young American in the shortest possible frayed shorts was questioning the American Rum Point owners about the effects of tourism on the population and the environment, his thesis for the University of California at Berkeley. We agreed that tourism is a destroyer and Belize is far too good for it. None of the inn owners I had met, English, French, American, Belizean, Irish, want to expand, though, between them, they could take care of less than a hundred perceptive guests. They love the country as it is. How much better if oil is found in viable quantities in the north, and tourists go somewhere else. It is astonishing at my age to stumble on a new country. I feel astonished.

As some authors contend, the near-absence of other tourists to which Gellhorn alludes is most efficiently achieved by the consumption of 'positional' goods (Hirsch, 1976), with dominant class fractions attempting to impose scarcity (Featherstone, 1987; Leiss, 1983). At the simplest level this involves claiming certain areas 'receive very few tourists' (Detours, 1992), are 'tourist free' (such as national parks visited by Naturetrek), or that even whole countries are for the 'traveller rather than the tourist', as Meon describes Ecuador (1992).

But this amounts to little more than marketing, and alternative strategies and claims must be pursued, such as active searches for 'off-the-beaten-track' (or, as Asian Affairs claims 'even further off-the-beaten-track') and 'lesser visited areas', areas 'rarely visited' (Himalayan Kingdom) or just 'secrets' (Okavango Tours and Safaris). Exclusiveness, uniqueness, romanticism and relative solitude are central to the philosophy of these tour operators.

This philosophy both embodies the contradictions in contemporary travel to the Third World and reveals the protracted and increasing difficulties which companies and travellers have in spatially defining separated practices from other like-minded travellers.

As tourism spreads to more and more destinations in the Third World, the distinction of a mass packaged tourist from the individual character of travel is spurious. Ego-tourists crowd into cheap guesthouses, basic bus stations and out-of-the-way beach resorts, while ecotourists crowd into game reserves and national parks. So how far is travel little more than a figment of wishful middle-class thinking? It is worth considering the views of Budi (aged 28), an Indonesian guide from Bali, interviewed by Tourism Concern's Sue Wheat:

Q. Do you think there is a difference between a 'tourist' and a 'traveller?'

A. The traveller thinks they know everything about the local people and the country. But it's usually because some other traveller told them before. But they do whatever they like - some travellers are good, but 90 per cent are not, they can be very impolite. With the tourist, everything is organised, so they don't destroy as much.

The traveller wants to see something new, and wants it to be cheap and then tells others about it. I prefer tourists ... they go to specific places, it is more professional. But the traveller is uncontrolled - they won't go to the places already prepared for them; they want to go to other places and then they spoil it - and don't spend any money! Travellers always talk the same and say: 'Don't go to Kuta because it's spoiled.' Then they go to a new place.

The example of the island of Bali is taken further, which alludes to this blurring of tourist distinctions, and with an examination of the effects of tourism policy on the island.

It is a context, therefore, within which new tourism must not only do battle with mass tourism and tourists, but contend within itself both spatially and qualitatively for the most virtuous practice. This is particularly notable in safaris. For example, Papyrus Tours ensure that they spare you 'any involvement in safari bus "rat runs"', referred to by Africa Exclusive as the 'herds of landrovers that ... plague some other parts of Africa' (but which do not afflict, of course, this tour operator's safaris in Zimbabwe).

Even vehicles themselves are a point of differentiation among safari operators and overland trucking companies, with Into Africa claiming that 'landrovers do less damage' than larger trucks and are more sensitive to both wildlife and local people.

Similarly, trekkers face increasing difficulties in spatially legitimating their experiences, as Edwards's (1992) lamentations have already indicated. With the sharp increase of trekking in northern Thailand, for example, it is more difficult to find a trek which visits 'untouched' or 'traditional' villages, we are warned by Trail-finders, a company with which it is possible to visit 'more remote villages less exposed to western influences', where 'Groups are welcomed as a refreshing diversion to normal

Tourism is no recent phenomenon on the Indonesian island of Bali. Colonised by the Dutch, the Balinese held on to a unique blend of Hindu, Buddhist and animist religions that imbued their cultural and social life. Tales of this exotic society living in tune with art and nature attracted foreigners as long as a century ago, and since independence, Bali has been the jewel in the crown of government tourism policy, hosting ever larger numbers of visitors.

Contemporary tourists to Bali display a wide mixture of motivations. The island accommodates seriously wealthy hedonists and conventional package tourists (many on long-haul stopovers or multi-centre holidays), alongside large numbers of young Australians who arrive on charter flights and regard the island as a cheap and cheerful holiday spot and a surfing mecca. There is a huge pool of homestays and guesthouses, known locally as *losmens*, catering for this budget market.

Bali's enduring image as a cultural paradise still draws independent travellers who also patronise the *losmens*, and it features frequently in the brochures of companies appealing to the new tourist as a land where it is possible to get off the beaten track while never straying far from creature comforts: 'the industry has been controlled so that hotels are primarily located in the southern peninsula, leaving the rest of the island essentially unchanged and uniquely Balinese'.

The village of Kuta, close to Bali's international airport, has been a favourite haunt of budget tourists since the 1970s, when its residents woke up to the lucrative possibilities of turning their homes into *losmens* and offering other services from bike hire and restaurants to massages on the huge crescent-shaped beach, which soon became a haven for novice surfers.

Losmens began appearing in nearby Sanur, and on the north and west coasts too - for example at Lovina Beach patronised by the backpacking fraternity as a restful retreat from an overdose of culture or socialising in southern Bali: 'It's a good place to meet other travellers, and there's quite an active social scene' (Wheeler and Lyon, 1994).

The inland village of Ubud, renowned for its artists and lush beauty, has also grown rapidly. From a scattering of *losmens*, restaurants and artists' studios attracting back-packers and longstay visitors, Ubud has mushroomed into the alternative inland base for anyone not locked into a standard beach hotel package deal. Nowadays, new tourists wishing to escape the mass market experience still favour Ubud, but may well avoid the commercialised southern coastal resorts, opting instead for accommodation in less developed spots.

However, if the entrepreneurs of outposts such as Candidasa and Lovina Beach are counting on increased custom from this source, they may be disappointed. Like the first visitors to the island, new tourists are specifically interested in Bali's unique harmony of culture and landscape and they still tend to visit the prime sites on every tourist's itinerary.

As many commentators have remarked, Bali's cultural life has so far been remarkably resilient. But as tourist sites become increasingly crowded and as its distinctive art forms become increasingly commercialised, new tourists may well decide not to bother with Bali at all, taking up instead the Indonesian Tourist Board's invitation to explore the rest of the republic's giant archipelago and leaving this particular 'paradise' to the surfers and conventional package tourists.

This analysis of Bali's tourism industry was prepared especially for this book by Alison Stancliffe before the October 2002 bombing of Kuta in Bali. We believe that the effects of the bombing will be felt largely in the short term and the long-term analysis made here will continue to be relevant. *Village life.*' At possibly its most advanced, spatial legitimation involves promises of carefully researched itineraries which avoid the 'overcrowded trek routes, often exploring untravelled or Restricted Areas, or visiting cultural festivals unknown to most westerners'. Ultimately, legitimation for this company is sought through the pages of the *Geographical Magazine* with the co-director writing of their trek to Mustang:

An understanding and appreciation of both cultural values and ecological balance is essential when visiting such remote and unspoilt regions. This expedition was the first in a series which it is hoped will help turn the tide of 'tourist pollution' to remote areas of the world.

This form of tourism therefore means the need to ensure the absence of other tourists. Some areas are considered especially attractive by virtue of the exclusionary nature of state policies which limit the number of tourists, and the political scientist, Linda Richter, identifies a key issue in tourism planning as *class versus mass tourism*.

The small, land-locked, Himalayan mountain kingdom of Bhutan, to the north of India, is undoubtedly the most unequivocal example of this phenomenon. Bhutan has chosen to concentrate its tourism on high-spending, 'classy' tourists. The country allowed entry to its first tourists in 1974, but only at the rate of 1,000 per year. The rate has increased in recent years so that up to 5,000 may now enter per year, although in 1988 the government closed some monasteries to foreigners because of 'growing materialism' among monks who accepted trinkets such as sweets and pencils together with money from visitors.

A glance through several of the trekking brochures shows that Bhutan is an expensive destination as a result of the weekly charge levied on all foreign tourists. This restrictive entry has been utilised by some 'alternative' travel companies to demonstrate the exclusivity of their holiday destinations (Naturetrek; Himalayan Kingdoms; Coromandel). In 1986, a study made by the WTO/OMT praised the Bhutanese system. WTO/OMT planner, Edward Inskeep, agreed that 'selection' can be achieved: 'the limited tourism approach can be applied, through selective marketing techniques, to attract tourists from any socio-economic groups who respect and do not abuse the local environment and culture' (Inskeep, 1987).

Trekking companies thus enter an intense competition for the most authentic locations, and that means destinations with the least tourists and, by implication, the most difficult to enter. Take the following sample of statements from the UK-based Himalayan Kingdoms, for example:

As yet undiscovered by mass tourism, our 'Hindu Kush Trail' provides an unspoilt route to the base of Tirich Mir.

Special permission is needed to enter Chitral ... so already there will be a noticeable lack of tourists. This is a trek with plenty of time to interact with local people ... The inhabitants have rarely seen Europeans and are friendly and hospitable. [We] will not see human habitation for two weeks.

In March 1992 the first trekkers were allowed access to the former Kingdom of Lo, and it is now the Government of Nepal's policy to restrict numbers ... Our first trek ... came back with wildly enthusiastic descriptions. Our own expedition to Ramdung ... was the first British group to gain entry for twelve years . [Tibet] has always been a difficult country to enter. This is little frequented by western trekkers. ... but few follow the routes we use ....

But it is with environmental conservation that tour companies and tourists have discovered perhaps the most effective method of exclusion, or 'inclusiveness'. Many tour companies are now supportive of conservation measures and cite membership of both global (WWF, CARE, FOE and so on) and the more localised (such as Elefriends and Mountain Gorilla Project) environmental organisations. Such projects are essential to both ecotourists and ego-tourists in restricting the number of visitors to such areas and in so doing securing some form of exclusiveness, however circumscribed in practice.

Beyond this, some companies have actively pursued conservation policy. Examples are Papyrus Tours, where the director is a founding trustee of the Kenya Wildlife Trust (a UK-based trust seeking to support conservation initiatives in Kenya), or Worldwide Journeys and Expeditions (1992), which claims management involvement in the only formerly privately managed national park in Africa, Kasanka (Zambia). Similarly, the certificated purchase of an acre of rainforest has also been encouraged by multinational environmental organisations such as Programme for Belize and the Nature Conservancy; these areas are often reserved for the consumption of discerning First World ecotourists.

Sustainability has proved the perfect ally of the new middle classes, with the social construction and application of ecological concepts such as carrying capacity proving the ultimate justification for natural exclusiveness.

As already argued, notions of sustainability are hegemonic in their own right and are readily translated spatially. The inflated ranks of academia have been quick to seize upon this, using 'research holidays' to impose their own ethnocentric analysis and recommendations.

Of Thailand, Brockelman and Dearden (the latter a former President of TIES) argue that the number of trekkers be kept relatively low, concluding that 'nature trekking should ... be promoted for special tours and not among general tourists' (1990:146).

The social exclusiveness of their proposals, the class-laden nature of this debate, and the cultural capital that is to be accumulated and invested, are plain to see:

It should be designed for serious naturalists or Nature enthusiasts and others wishing to experience genuine local cultures. Most such persons are reasonably affluent and educated and read a variety of Nature, conservation, and botanical or zoological society publications ... Such clientele is likely to get the most out of the experience, and probably also leave behind the best impressions.

In this chapter we have attempted to show how the contemporary socio-cultural changes outlined are reflected through the growth and popularity of travel in many parts of the Third World. While the discussion does not imply a determinism that social class lies at the heart of all tourism, it has sought to show that it is an important and frequently overlooked factor in attempts to explain why tourism spreads and seeks out new frontiers.

In this respect, it is a further demonstration of why the boom-to-bust cycles of tourism, which are most frequently used to demonstrate the circulation of destinations, amount to descriptions rather than explanations.

The chapter has argued that a sizeable proportion of new forms of tourism in the Third World can be related directly to the burgeoning new middle classes of the First World. This group is being joined increasingly by new middle-class tourists from the Third World, most particularly from South-East Asia. This growth was also related to the increased interest in otherness, with a particular concern for ecology and ethnicity, both of which are found in plentiful quantities in the Third World.

In addition, it was argued that central to the swelling ranks of the new middle classes is the necessity to differentiate socially from other social classes. This is most readily achieved through the construction of lifestyles, of which holidays are undeniably an important part.

The chapter explored how both ecotourists and ego-tourists are able to accumulate what has been identified as cultural capital and the strategies - professional, intellectual and discursive - that are employed to ensure that the accumulation of such capital is sustained and enhanced. In particular, we have argued that this provides a rather different understanding of the current debate over sustainability.

This debate can be recast, in part, as the drive towards sustaining the opportunity and ability to consume authenticity and exciting experiences, which simultaneously necessitates the exclusion of other types of tourists. Ultimately, this represents a cultural and social reaction of the new middle classes to the crassness with which they perceive tourism and a craving for social and geographical distance from tourists.

7

Employment Characteristics, Trends Tourism and Career Prospects

The World Tourism Organization forecasts that international tourism will continue growing at the average annual rate of 4 per cent. By 2020 Europe will remain the most popular destination, but its share will drop from 60 per cent in 1995 to 46 per cent. Long-haul will grow slightly faster than intraregional travel and by 2020 its share will increase from 18 per cent in 1995 to 24 per cent.

Since e-commerce has taken off on the internet, tourism products have become one of the most traded items on the net. Tourism products and services have been made available on the net at bargain prices through intermediaries. In recent time, tourism providers (hotels, airlines, etc.) have started to sell their services through the internet.

This has put pressure on intermediaries from both the virtual and the traditional brick and mortar stores. Space tourism is expected to "take off" in the first quarter of the 21st century, although compared with traditional destinations the number of tourists in orbit will remain low until technlogies such as a space elevator make space travel cheap.

Technological improvement is likely to make possible air-ship hotels, based either on solar-powered airplanes or large dirigibles. Underwater hotels, such as Hydropolis, expected to open in Dubai in 2006, will be built. On the ocean tourists will be welcomed by ever larger cruise ships and perhaps floating cities. Some futurists expect that movable hotel "pods" will be created that could be temporarily erected anywhere on the planet, where building a permanent resort would be unacceptable politically, economically or environmentally.

BENEFITS OF TOURISM

Tourism is now the world's largest industry. The World Tourism Council estimates that travel and tourism provides employment for more than 100 million people world wide (that's one in sixteen workers) and is responsible for over 7% of world wide capital investment. In the year ended June 2003, there were 1,261,818 visitors to the Fraser Coast. Of these 67% were intrastate visitors (849,000), 17% were interstate visitors (214,000) and 16% were international visitors (198,818). In the same period 5,223,187 visitor nights were spent in the region. Domestic and International tourism contributed in net terms approximately $6 billion to the Queensland economy. Tourism generates $2.4 billion annually as an export earner, accounting for 11% of total Queensland exports overseas, second only to coal exports.

MULTIPLIER EFFECT

A tourist dollar is a new dollar injected into the local economy. A percentage of this new dollar is spent in the community by the recipient and this dollar is spent and re-spent creating a multiplier effect. The more new tourist dollars entering a local economy and the longer the percentage is retained locally, the greater the economic benefit.

EMPLOYMENT OPPORTUNITIES

Tourism is a labour intensive industry and creates many job opportunities, especially for young people and part-time and full-time workers. In the tourism hospitality and recreation industries alone there are 50 categories of employment and approximately 200 classifications of occupations.

DIVERSIFICATION

Tourism can provide diversification, making the local economy less reliant on a traditional base e.g. agriculture and mining. This is particularly significant for regional rural communities.

OPPORTUNITIES FOR BUSINESS

Tourism creates opportunities for the establishment of new products, facilities and services and expansion of existing businesses which would not otherwise be justified solely on the resident population.

PRESERVATION OF THE ENVIRONMENT AND HERITAGE

Tourism highlights the need for proper management and, through effective policies and planning, can ensure that the environment, heritage and inherent character of an area is preserved.

THE CATALYST FOR RESIDENTIAL DEVELOPMENT

In many places visitors who initially travelled to particular areas as tourists, have relocated to those areas to become residents and acquire a better quality of life.

IMPROVED TRANSPORT SERVICES

Tourism can stimulate the establishment of new and improved transport services to and within a regional area.

A BROADER SOCIAL OUTLOOK

Tourism provides the opportunity for residents to interact with other people and cultures and brings new ideas into the community.

Tourism Costs and Benefits

Costs

Social Costs

- May attract visitors whose lifestyles and ideas conflict with the community's. An example may be the visitors' use of drugs and alcohol.
- May change individual behaviour and family relationships.
- May lead to an increase in sexually transmitted diseases.
- Loss of traditional values and culture through imitation of visitor behaviour or cultural diffusion resulting from normal, everyday interaction.
- May create crowding and congestion.
- May compete with residents for available services, facilities, and existing recreation opportunities.
- May result in harassment of visitors perceived to be wealthy and an increase in crime.

Can involve violations of human rights. People have been displaced from their land and beaches have been reserved for hotel guests while access is barred to local people.

Benefits

Social Benefits

- Brings in outside dollars to support community facilities and services that otherwise might not be developed.
- Encourages civic involvement and pride.
- Provides cultural exchange between hosts and guests.
- Encourages the preservation and celebration of local festivals and cultural events.
- Facilities and infrastructure developed for tourism can also benefit residents.
- Encourages the learning of new languages and skills.
- Tourism related funds have contributed towards schools being built in some areas.

Environmental Benefits

- Fosters conservation and preservation of natural, cultural and historical resources.

- Encourages community beautification and revitalization.
- Could be considered a clean industry.

Environmental Costs

- May threaten specific natural resources such as beaches and coral reefs or historical sites.
- May increase litter, noise, and pollution.
- Brings increased competition for limited resources such as water and land, resulting in land degradation, loss of wildlife habitats and deterioration of scenery.
- Directly contributes to sewage and solid waste pollution.
- Emissions generated by forms of transport are one of the main environmental problems of tourism.

Economic Benefits

- Helps diversify and stabilize the local economy.
- Provides governments with extra tax revenues each year through accommodation and restaurant taxes, airport taxes, sales taxes, park entrance fees, employee income tax etc..
- Creates local jobs and business opportunities. These include those jobs directly related to tourism (hotel and tour services) and those that indirectly support tourism (such as food production and housing construction).
- The multiplier effect:
  - Brings new money into the economy. Tourist money is returned to the local economy as it is spent over and over again.
  - Helps attract additional businesses and services to support the tourist industry.
- Is labour-intensive.
- Earns valuable foreign exchange.

Economic Costs

- Tourism development of infrastructure (airports, roads, etc.) can cost the local government a great deal of money.
- May inflate property values and prices of goods and services.
- Leakages:
  - If outside interests own the tourism development, most of the economic benefits will leave the community.
  - Considerable amount of foreign exchange revenues leaks back out of the destination countries for tourism-related imports.

- Employment tends to be seasonal. Workers may be laid off in the winter season.
- Many jobs in the tourism industry are poorly paid. This is a particular problem in LEDCs where the local workforce lacks the skills to fill the better paid management positions.
- Tourist numbers can be adversely affected by events beyond the control of the destination e.g. terrorism, economic recession. This is a big problem in LEDC countries dependent on tourism.
- Tourism follows a "product life cycle", with a final stage of decline, where the destination no longer offers new attractions for the tourist, and the quality has diminished with the rise of competition and tourist saturation.

BENEFITS COMMUNITIES

Tourism is one of the most effective ways of redistributing wealth, by moving money into local economies from other parts of the country and overseas. It brings income into a community that would otherwise not be earned.

Economic Benefits

Economic benefits resulting from tourism can take a number of forms including:

- *Jobs*: Employment may be associated directly, such as tour guide or managerial positions; or in supporting industries like food production or retail suppliers.
- *Increased spending*: Increased spending in the community generated from visitors or tourism businesses can directly and indirectly promote the viability of local businesses.
- *Economic diversification*: Tourism operators can play a role in highlighting the broad prosperity that tourism can bring to a community and will contribute to a greater understanding and respect for the value of tourism.

Economic diversification is, for many communities, an insurance policy against hard times. By offering an additional means of income, tourism can support a community when a traditional industry is under financial pressure, particularly where that community relies heavily on a single industry.

Case Study: Farmers markets

The popularity of farmers' markets is increasing becoming a key driver of economic development in regional areas. Activities such as visits to farms and farmers' markets, fruit picking and agricultural farm accommodation may provide important supplemental activities to struggling rural areas.

Some of the benefits of Farmers' Markets seen include:

- Showcases local produce and local products
- Encourage visitors from other areas
- Showcase the local and regional areas
- Allows for community events to be incorporated
- Provides distribution opportunities for small businesses
- Valuable contribution to the economic development of the area as money is spent locally
- Infrastructure

Infrastructure including roads, parks, and other public spaces can be developed and improved both for visitors and local residents through increased tourism activity in a region.

SOCIAL BENEFITS

Community identity and pride can be generated through tourism. A positive sense of community identity can be reinforced and tourism can encourage local communities to maintain their traditions and identity.

ENVIRONMENTAL BENEFITS

Providing financial or in-kind support for the conservation of the local environment and natural resources will enhance the reputation of any tourism business.

Tourism, particularly ecotourism, can place a greater focus on the conservation of natural resources through the recognition of their importance to visitor experiences and their economic value to the local community.

CAREER IN TOURISM OPERATORS

Maximum benefit from community involvement for the tourism operator occurs when a tourism venture operates in harmony with the social and cultural aspirations of the local community. Involving the community in the development and subsequent operation of tourism projects will not only create greater local support for the operation, it also has the potential to:

- Increase business profits through improved word of mouth referral;
- Grow repeat business from improved experiences with the community; and
- Increase visitation through recognition of best practice standards.

Communities form the backdrop of any tourism product. They provide the support that tourism needs to survive and are often part of the reason visitors are attracted to a destination. Sustainable and responsible tourism is about ensuring a win-win for the community, economy and environment. The attitude, resources and strategic thinking of tourism operators is essential.

OUTLINE OF ADVANTAGES AND DISADVANTAGES

Advantage (depending upon implementation some of these can turn into disadvantages):

- Employment (1 emp/1000 tourist) (labour intensive, few administrative positions, little upward mobility.)
- Infrastructure development (roads, water, electricity, telecom and cybercom, but not necessarily local priorities.)
- Cultural preservation (economic incentives to preserve food, fashion, festivals and physical history, but these tend to be superficial elements of a culture.)
- Environmental protection (econ incentives to preserve nature, wildlife and urban cleanliness)
- Foreign exchange (generates resources to import food, pharmaceuticals, technology, consumer goods.)
- Development of health care services (those these aren't always available to local people.)

Disadvantages (depending upon implementation some of these can turn into advantages):

- Cultural destruction, (modernization (world mono-culture), freezes culture as performers, loss: language, religion, rituals, material culture.)
- Primary products (sun, sand, surf, safari, suds, ski, sex) (little value added, neo-colonialism)
- Environmental destruction (game drives, resorts: golf, ski, beach, desert, world as play ground, SUV.)
- Marginal employment (low skill, low wage, menial services, prostitution, drug trade, gambling, hustlers.)
- Low benefits (no job security, no health care, no organizing, no work safety rules or enviro standards.)
- Development of illegal and/or destructive economic activities (markets for drugs, endangered species, etc.)
- Outside hiring (skilled middle and senior management recruited out of the area and transferred in.)
- Concentration employment (walled resort enclaves.)
- Seasonal employment
- Outside decision making (decisions made outside of the area, corporate dollars corrupt government.)
- Unrealistic expectations (divert young people from school and brighter futures.)
- Anti-democratic collusion (industry support of repressive governments)

- Land controlled by the elite (people relocated, agriculture eliminated, prohibited from N.P.)
- Negative lifestyle's (STD's, substance abuse, begging, hustling)
- Diverted and concentrated development (airport, roads, water, electricity to tourist destinations, development not accessible to locals),
- Little forex stays in country (airplanes, vehicles, booze, hot air balloons, generally have foreign owners),
- Package programs
- Cruises (eat and sleep on board so the economic benefits to the ports-of-call is very thin and limited.)
- Unstable market (fickle, affected by local and world events, generally highly elastic)
- Health tourism (traveling to get medical procedure at lower cost) has it own set of unique challenges, which include: Determining the credential, skills and quality of the facility and personnel. Language communication challenges on topics requiring a lot of details, sometimes even when both parties seemingly speak the same language. Different cultural issues and expectations around health care and the body. Post-treatment complications, after the "tourist" has left the facility.

Solutions (for visitor):

- Act to support cultural diversity
- Engage in activities that add value to the community
- Don't do activities that deteriorate the environment
- Don't engage in illegal activities
- Act to disperse the benefits
- Patronize locally (community) owned enterprises.

Solutions (for the host):

- Support the traditional cultural legacy
- Training and education in local culture, history, natural science, etc.
- Select development and activities that draw from local traditions and add value to the community
- Don't promote activities that deteriorate the environment
- Don't engage in illegal activities
- Adopt a programme to disperse the benefits
- Patronize locally produced products and locally (community) owned enterprises.
- Make business and foreign exchange transactions transparent and efficient.

ECOTOURISM, RESPONSIBLE TOURISM AND E^3 TRAVEL PROGRAMS

IBF has long been uncomfortable with the terms eco-tour and ecotourism because there is no accountability and they have been used to embrace ANY travel that includes "nature" — getting out of a city — even when getting there is by a gas guzzling SUV (sport-utility vehicle or four-wheel drive); ripping up the savannah in the process, and regardless of its impact — that is not us. Other not uncommon characteristics of "eco-tourism" can be; energy-intensive accommodations, encouraging gluttonous amounts of eating (with no reference to dining room waste, how food was produced, or where — a reliance of imported foodstuff and drinks,) prodigious amounts of promotional materials that are paper intensive, and other wasteful and/or energy intensive practices, and little client education on impact of cultural behaviour on the environment.

Consequentially we rarely use the term ecotourism in any of our publicity. "Responsible travel" is facing the same deterioration. It should be "(original) eco-tourism plus" . Too often it is defined and practiced with a diluted focuses on cultural responsibility and economic benefit, and a general neglect energy intensiveness (i.e. motorization) and other sustainability issues.

As an alternative we measure programs by a "E^3 Travel" standard (environment, economics and education). This is very similar to the triple bottom line concept of sustainable business (environment, social justice and fiscal), but we like to think of it as the top line for travel programs.

- Environmentally friendly (using primarily non-motorized transport, but reflecting all aspects of the projects including reducing printing and paper consumption, selection of energy efficient lodging, consuming local produced food and goods, and minimizing waste at all levels),
- Economic/equity benefits (supporting the decentralized, indigenous economy, including local produced food, goods and services, and local employment generator) and
- Educational/enriching/engaging (training guides and helping participants to explore the diversity and complexity of the local natural and human ecology.)

If you draw these as a triangle, each element reinforces the others:

- The use of non-motorized transports virtually mandates patronizing local business. In many parts of the world it is often impossible to bicycle from tourist enclave to tourist enclave in a day. The increased exposure to the local culture, local cuisine, local economy, local interaction, and environment inherently leads to enhanced education and more enriching experiences. But environmental issues go beyond choosing the mode of travel. It is worth bringing your environmental consciousness/audit to every aspect of your travel project: If you use a travel provider, is the advertising and back office side of the "eco-tour" company as environmentally friendly as they would have you thing that their programme is? Can you steer away from energy intensive and import intensive hotels and over-sized everything and steer toward local produced services and goods? Vacation is a time to pamper yourself, and you can still indulge yourself in quality, but you may want to pass on providers of lavish (and wasteful) quantity.

- Aiming for an enriching and well rounded educational experience, is a natural to get more into the community and supporting local business. This argues for eliminating the barriers of glass, steel and speed that go with motor vehicles. Walking and bicycling are great modes for picking up information, engaging with the community and environment around you and supporting the most-local economy.
- Including as a goal equity and supporting local suppliers of goods and service dictates increased interaction with the cultural and enriching experiences. The use of non-motorized transport virtually assures that the benefits will be decentralized and widely beneficial. Sort through you choices is not always easy: There are foreign owned businesses with excellent environments practices and who provide their employees and the surrounding community with excellent compensation and benefits. And, there are local owned business that exploit their employees, do very little to share there good fortune with the surrounding community, are energy and resource intensive, and materially wasteful (make no attempt to reduce, reuse or recycle.) It is hard to make hard and fast rules here, but the small businessperson in the community is usually pretty equitable and a contributing member of the community. The also likely to be fairly well interwoven in the culture and environmentally responsible.

Incidentally, in tourism E^3 product doesn't seem to be a gender thing: We have seen both male and female own travel specialist who were both good and bad. We have seen foreign owned, male and female, boutique hotel operators who were good and bad. And, we have seen locally owned, male and female service providers who were both good and bad on a E^3 audit.

Within the E^3 structure, an urban bike ride with a lecture on a historic district, a work project in a village and forest walk learning about ethno-botany and looking for primates all can come out on top, as we think they should. Traditional "S"-tourism" (sun, sand, sea, skiing, sailing, sitting, swimming, scuba, snorkel, safari, sitting, sleeping, sight-seeing) can be done in a E^3 way. It is not necessarily the location, the activity or the personnel, but it is how it fits together, the benefits and the costs. Help heal the world when you travel.

Do the E^3 of defined activity guarantee sustainability? No, not if integral to getting to the activity is airplane travel by the participants.

Given current technology, even with carbon offsets, you are at best at a "second-best solution". The theory is that second-best solutions are never as good first-best, which in this case would forgoing the flying. A reasonable expectation of how people are going to get to the E^3 activity must be incorporated into the equation. The triple bottom line of responsible tourism is 3 E's: environmental sustainability, engaging in the local economic, and enriching your life from the culture. Actually, it is about the same for all life.

Tourism is the act of travel for the purpose of not only recreation, but also the provision of services for this act. It might occupy local services such as entertainment, accommodation and catering for tourists. It may seem, that tourism brings only benefits, but further consideration shows that it also has disadvantages. Firstly, many countries depend heavily upon travel expenditures by foreigners as a source of taxation and as a source of income for the enterprises. Therefore, the development of tourism is often a strategy to promote a particular region for the purpose of increasing commerce through exporting goods and services.

Secondly, it provides direct employment for the people associated with occupations in bars and hotels. Thanks to it, the average standard of living of people increases well and at the same time unemployment is on the decrease. However, tourists cause environmental damage through forest fires, destruction of sand dunes and pollution. Consequently this serves negatively as increased pollution disturbs local residents and also it may discourage tourists from further entering the country.

After this, tourism undermines culture by commercializing it and this is often connected with increasing litter, graffiti, vandalism and noise - tourists do not always respect traditional cultures, which is sad but true. In general, tourism is an extremely profitable process in loads of countries, especially those in which the process of development continue to depend on this industry because this industry does not require a lot of literacy and also it yields maximum profits with less investment.

There are a number of benefits of tourism for both the tourist and the host destination. On a large scale it offers a good alternative to some more destructive industries for generating income both on nationally and privately. The tourism industry encompasses many different areas, so it also creates jobs in many different areas. With tourism comes hotels, resturants, car rental agencies, tour companies, service stations, souvenier shops, sports equipment rentals, and much more. All of this creates many different levels of employment for people in a given community.

In many places the introduction and development of tourism allows local people an opportunity for economic and educational growth that would not otherwise be available. In addition, it allows both the tourist and the local community a chance to experience other cultures, which broadens understanding. If properly used, tourism generated income can be tremendously beneficial to the host country and it's local communities. Tourism generated income can be used on a national and local level to better education, improve infrastructure, to fund conservation efforts, and to promote more responsible tourism.

INDIA IN THE PICTURE

Tourism in India has received a major boost in the past decade since the Indian Government realized the great potential of tourism of India during vacations. Tourism of India during vacations has grown by leaps and bounds with a great influx of tourists from throughout the world who have been irresistibly attractive to the travelers. India has the right tourism potential and attractions to captivate all types of tourists whether it is adventurous tour, cultural exploration, pilgrimages, visit to the beautiful beaches or to the scenic mountain resorts, Tourism of India has it all for you.

Travel through Indian states and cities bring to light, the cultural and the geographical richness of India. We provide you a glimpse to the richness of tourism in India with information on all the major tourist destinations of India and tourism services of India that will take care of all your problems while you are in India. India, located in Asia. Is bounded by the Himalayan ranges in the north, surrounded by the Arabian Sea, the Bay of Bengal, and the Indian Ocean. In 2006, about 4 million foreign tourists visited India and spent US$ 8.9 billion. In 2007, India's 5 million international arrivals - out of 903 million worldwide - were the world's 42nd highest.

India's tourism sector lags behind less endowed countries. Among India's shortcomings are "stringent visa requirements and airport density, which rank poor 106 and 121" out of 124 countries on the *Travel & Tourism Competitiveness Report 2007*.India's expensive hotel rooms stand at the rank 113. "People's openness to tourism" ranking is 97. At the same time, India has great advantages: price competitiveness ranking was a high 6th, while safety and security was a good 39th. The tourism sector is growing at double digits. India has a huge advertising campaign "Incredible India". Travel and tourism contributes 5.3% to India's GDP.

TOURISM BY STATE

Andhra Pradesh

Andhra Pradesh has a rich cultural heritage and a variety of tourist attractions. The state of Andhra Pradesh comprises scenic hills, forests, beaches and temples. Andhra Pradesh is the home of many religious pilgrimage centres, one of them being 'Tirupati,' the abode of Lord Venkateswara, which is the richest and most visited Hindu temple in India. Hyderabad is known for its rich history, culture and architecture representing its unique character as a meeting point for North and South India, and also its multilingual culture, both geographically and culturally.

Also known as The City of Nizams and The City of Pearls, Hyderabad is today one of the most developed cities in the country and a modern hub of information technology, ITES, and biotechnology. Hyderabad offers many attraction to the tourists. It is famous for its delicious *Hyderabadi Biryani.It is india's second largest metropolitan.* Andhra Pradesh is the home of many religious pilgrim centres.

Tirupati, the abode of Lord Venkateswara, is the richest and most visited religious centre (of any faith) in the world. Srisailam, the abode of Sri Mallikarjuna, is one of twelve Jyothirlingalu in India, Amaravati's Siva temple is one of the Pancharamams, and Yadagirigutta, the abode of an avatara of Vishnu, Sri Lakshmi Narasimha. The Ramappa temple and Thousand Pillars temple in Warangal are famous for some fine temple carvings.

The state has numerous Buddhist centres at Amaravati, Nagarjuna Konda, Bhattiprolu, Ghantasala, Nelakondapalli, Dhulikatta, Bavikonda, Thotlakonda, Shalihundam, Pavuralakonda, Sankaram, Phanigiri and Kolanpaka. The golden beaches at Visakhapatnam, the one-million-year old limestone caves at Borra, picturesque Araku Valley, hill resorts of Horsley Hills, river Godavari racing through a narrow gorge at Papi Kondalu, waterfalls at Ettipotala, Kuntala and rich bio-diversity at Talakona, are some of the natural attractions of the state.

Kailashagiri is situated adjacent to sea in Visakhapatnam, it is one of the beautiful sight which shows the entire beauty of Visakhapatnam having other side sea. A Beautiful park is developed on the hill top of Kailashagiri, the city boasts of having a Park on hill top that has a luxurious toy train, ropeway and beautiful view of beach front into which Eastern Ghats merge into the sea.

Further, Visakhapatnam is home to many tourist attractions like INS Karasura Submarine museum (The only one of its kind in India), the most beautiful and the longest Beach Road in India, Yarada Beach, Araku Valley (Known as poorman's Ooty, a lot of movies are shooted here), VUDA Park, Indira Gandhi Zoological Gardens, etc. The weather in Andhra Pradesh is mostly tropical and the best time to visit is in November through to January. The monsoon season commences in June and ends in September, so travel would not be advisable during this period.

Places to visit:

- *Hyderabad*: The capital of AP, it is a melting pot of various cultures, known for its historical monuments as well as modern marvels. The places to visit are-Charminar, Mecca Masjid, Salarjung Museum, Hussain Sagar, Lumbini Park, Snow world, Ramoji Film city, Water world, Hitech city, Golconda, Paigah tombs, Falaknuma palace.
- *Visakhapatnam*: Undoubtedly the most beautiful city on the east coast,

considered abode of *Devtas, Yakashyas, Kinners,* Fairies and Sages. They all are present here on glittering peaks, roaring rivers, beautiful hills slopes and valleys in one or another form. It boasts of some old hill-stations developed during British era like Mussoorie, Almora and Nainital.

Uttar Pradesh

Situated in the northern part of India, Uttar Pradesh is important with its wealth of monuments and religious fervour. Geographically, Uttar Pradesh is very diverse, with Himalayan foothills in the extreme north, the Gangetic Plain in the centre, and the Vindhya Mountain Range towards the South. It is also home of India's most visited site, the Taj Mahal, and Hinduism's holiest city, Varanasi. The most populous state of the Indian Union also has a rich cultural heritage, and at the heart of North India, Uttar Pradesh has much to offer. Places of interest include Varanasi, Agra, Mathura, Jhansi, Prayag, Sarnath, Ayodhya, Dudhwa National Park.

Rajasthan

Rajasthan, literally meaning *"Land of the Kings"*, is one of the most attractive tourist destinations in Northern India. The vast sand dunes of the Thar Desert attract millions of tourists from around the globe every year.

Attractions:

- *Jaipur*: The capital of Rajasthan, famous for its rich history and royal architecture.
- *Jodhpur*: Fortress-city at the edge of the Thar Desert, famous for its blue homes and architecture.
- *Udaipur*: Known as the "Venice" of India.
- *Jaisalmer*: Famous for its golden fortress.
- *Barmer*: Barmer and surrounding areas offer perfect picture of typical Rajasthani villages.
- *Bikaner*: Famous for its medieval history as a trade route outpost.
- *Mount Abu*: Is the highest peak in the Aravalli Range of Rajasthan.
- *Pushkar*: It has the first and one of the very Brahma temples in the world.
- *Nathdwara*: This town near Udaipur hosts the famous temple of Shrinathji.
- *Ranthambore*: Situated near Sawai Madhopur, this town has one of the largest and most famous national parks in India.

Index